JUST A SHOT AWAY

1969 REVISITED

KRIS NEEDS

NEW HAVEN PUBLISHING LTD

First Edition
Published 2019
NEW HAVEN PUBLISHING LTD
www.newhavenpublishingltd.com
newhavenpublishing@gmail.com

Cover design ©Andy Morten
andymorten@mac.com

For Helen, my soul mate

FOREWORD
By PETE FRAME

The sixties are a bit of a blur to me now. Good job I made a few notes. For me, they started with Duane Eddy at the Trocadero, Elephant and Castle, and ended with Mott The Hoople at the Roundhouse, Chalk Farm. The 500 or so weeks in between, every single one of them, were stuffed with unimaginably amazing records, fabulously intoxicating gigs, little shops that turned out to be treasure caves, and extraordinary adventures.

Mind-blowing bands, books, magazines, drugs, clothes, people; beatniks, folkies, mods, rockers, weirdos, beatsters, bluesers, hippies, movers, shakers, questers of every stripe.

Colours, changes, ideas, innovations, experimentation, positivity, optimism, inspiration, friendship, brotherhood, fun, peace, love and understanding.

Trends and movements merged and bubbled, bringing constant surprise. For years, it never let up, not for a moment, day or night. Too much excitement to hold anyone with a dream to the straight and narrow. Nothing was impossible. Turn on, tune in and drop out. Do your own thing. A lot of us got wonky and never recovered.

Hippie dreamer that I was, I dumped a secure and respectable city career and with a bunch of friends started the UK's first monthly rock magazine, *Zigzag*. To my surprise it was quickly embraced by the music business and during 1969, the first year of its existence, we met and interviewed Frank Zappa, Captain Beefheart, Jeff Beck and Ray Davies, among others.

Sometime during that summer, David Stopps invited me to Friars, the club he had recently started in Aylesbury – a town my mates and I had often visited for memorable gigs by acts like Georgie Fame & the Blue Flames, Manfred Mann and the Jimi Hendrix Experience.

I drove over to Friars and found myself in a wonderland. It was like landing in the middle of a stage musical with a huge cast of interesting, colourful characters, many of whom were to become lifelong friends. Immediately, I decided to leave my home town, Luton – whose exotic coffee bars had been demolished for redevelopment schemes and whose throbbing Majestic Ballroom, which had once hosted bands like the

5

Beatles and the Stones, had become a bingo hall – and move to the Aylesbury area. Stayed more than 30 years.

Among the eccentrics I met there was Kris Needs, with his bouncing walk and infectious grin. Perhaps he first impressed me when he played bongos in a duo with John Otway, his solo spot being a rambling monologue intoned in a voice borrowed from rugby commentator Eddie Waring.

I had been bonkers for years but for Kris the adventures were only just beginning.

INTRODUCTION
By KRIS NEEDS

Let's get one thing straight from the start. This is my 1969; as I remember it happening, fifty years ago before all the retrospective rehashes that tell you one thing when it meant something a lot different if you actually lived it; and, crucially, can remember it. The predictable route would have been to recycle the same old retro-cliches about how Manson and Altamont signalled the death of the 60s after Woodstock's glimmer of optimism but I was more concerned with getting my own life voyage off the launch-pad. I started '69 as a wide-eyed, somewhat nervous teenager staying in painting my psychedelic posters and wearing out my favourite records, and ended it entering the seismic coming decade as an idiot-dancing fifteen-year-old relishing a brave new world of regular gigs, astonishing music and untouchable heroes becoming in-the-flesh entities. The horizon now seemed as vast and exciting as it soon became. And I had seen the Rolling Stones and Jimi Hendrix. And met Mott The Hoople.

1969 might represent the death of the 60s dream to some hack scouring his Beatles and Stones tomes, but Altamont and Manson happening on the other side of the planet had little effect on what was happening in my Aylesbury home town, nearby London or my own teenage world at the time. Appallingly senseless as it obviously was, same went for Vietnam; at the time a flickering horror on the black-and-white TV while real life in post-war Britain was turning to full-blast technicolour, as the hoary saying goes. Perhaps because of Hendrix, I was more interested in Black Power, consolidated when the Last Poets invaded my radar the following year. John Peel, the newly-launched *Zigzag* magazine and our local club Friars Aylesbury were my lifelines.

It already felt like the truly great music was being made by untouchable gods and goddesses that I could only worship from afar as Jimi, the Stones, Tim Buckley, Captain Beefheart, John Fahey, Pearls Before Swine, the Doors, Moondog, Marianne Faithfull, Graham Bond, the Fugs and countless others swarmed around my overcrowded young brain. *Trout Mask Replica* can be dissected to death like it's always been there; it's almost inconceivable there was a time when it didn't exist. Obviously there could be no nostalgia market then; no retrospective boxsets, magazines retracing previous decades, internet making all the music you ever wanted to hear accessible at the click of a mouse or tap on a smartphone. In '69, there was no future beyond tomorrow or next week's gig. The weekly music papers dictated everything, although rarely in depth. If you wanted to hear a new album you bought it, borrowed it off a mate or hoped to hear it on Peel. You had to work to feed your obsession, whether traveling two hours to the imports shop or cajoling a blast in the local record emporium's listening booth. If the album was bought with hard-earned cash and turned out to be great, the feeling of joy and triumph could be overwhelming. As a music journalist for 45 years, it seems weird that, in the space of one day, I can be sent more music than I could afford to buy in the whole of '69.

When I started writing this book in February 2018, a monumental turning point came when I lost my beloved soul-mate Helen Donlon to cancer a few months later. An esteemed writer and respected figure in publishing, she loved this somewhat wild idea from the start, encouraging it and helping me write the proposal. As Helen's condition deteriorated and I struggled to care for her at the same time as writing, we became oblivious to the world outside. After she left us, gracefully and without fuss, life turned into a high-wire shoestring of grief, which made writing impossible and ended with total meltdown then hospital stretch after Helen's brother-in-law Andy found me collapsed in the front room of our cottage. Three months later, I returned to the book, still trying to cope with grief but with a different attitude. This should be even more of a precious memoir, drawn from a life only I have lived that can be cut short too easily.

From our coming together in 2013, I always wrote with Helen in mind anyway; would it pass her stringent literary requirements, does it make sense or interesting reading and, most importantly, will she like it? I still do that, even when it feels like I'm hanging by the thinnest of threads. Grief is the strangest trip I've ever been on; a roller coaster of devastating sadness and loss, vivid fever dreams and numbing through outside diversions (most recently replacing my entire wardrobe!). Through the love and support from my family and those who turned out to be real friends (see Acknowledgements), I got through the worst and can even appreciate some joy that I was so fortunate to spend just five years with this beautiful, remarkable woman and experience a rare love many may never even know. Life is still a high-wire to be plunged from at any time, triggered by the smallest thing. Thankfully, I have a relentless life support system in Jack, the extraordinary dog Helen raised from a tiny puppy when she lived on Ibiza. In fact, he saved my life, and has been a constant source of unconditional love and fun at my side during the endless hours writing this book. At times, it's like Helen's still here, especially that certain quizzical look he can shoot over.

The strangest twist has been moving back into the family home in Aylesbury, where I grew up and was living when I experienced everything recounted. My dear mum, now 93, is still downstairs and I'm sitting in my old bedroom playing the same records I loved 50 years ago. And she's still telling me to turn down my Stones records!

This book went through several incarnations after starting as an epic that could have filled a thousand pages had I tried to cover everything that went down musically, politically, culturally and socially in '69. Now it's coming as two volumes. Helen always stressed that, to bring anything new to the creaking table, I had to write from my own perspective, of how the year actually felt at the time, rather than go back over ground so well-trodden it's impossible not to slip on its smoothed-down surface. The death of Brian Jones on my 15th birthday or Altamont might have helped behead the original 60s jolly green giant but ultimately '69 heralded the start of the 70s, when all the groundwork bore fruit amidst its excesses, trends and troubles. If anything killed off the 60s, it was Ziggy Stardust, who I witnessed being born at our local Friars Aylesbury, whose own 50th I've recently helped celebrate.

Obviously there are perspectives and knowledge gained from 50 years reading, writing and investigating, often drawing from my own interviews, and even becoming friends with central characters. Mental snapshots and memories live forever in my brain on eternal rewind as a year when everything changed as I grew up fast. Happily, while bullying teachers, school meatheads and cold early girlfriends have long slipped into realms I rarely choose to rerun on my cerebral projector, emotions and passions nurtured in '69 can still be so strong and pivotal many remain in sharp focus: witnessing Hendrix for the first and only time, Mott The Hoople discovering their wild stage mojo and taking me into their corner, the tragic genius of Graham Bond, stellar gigs by the Third Ear Band, East Of Eden, Edgar Broughton and Van der Graaf Generator at our club. Meanwhile, whole tracts of memory from the more recent 70s and 80s have melted into a mix of snapshots, blurry vignettes and indelibly vivid scenes that can seem like surreal

9

dream sequences from someone else's film. Did I really sit in a hotel suite with Keith Richards for long nights when he picked up an acoustic guitar and played 'Wild Horses', blast his music hall comedian tapes and order shepherd's pie on room service? Or perch next to David Bowie in a dressing room after he'd unveiled Ziggy to the world, spend a riotously surreal afternoon with Captain Beefheart, get a blow-by-blow account of Woodstock from its MC Chip Monck or hang with the Last Poets and George Clinton? Or even spend last year sharing intimate phone calls and emails with Marianne Faithfull, my ultimate teenage crush, now one of my dearest friends?

Punk was already happening in my head so I'm not going to dwell on any act who didn't send a direct lightning bolt to my heart. These accounts and essays will spill all over the place, like my teenage brain at the time, falling backwards and forwards wherever the music and perpetrators take me. It's time to get these memories down of a time when everything felt just a kiss away before they fade forever. Nobody cared about any supposed loss of innocence; I was too busy trying to lose mine in every way imaginable, every molecule in my young, teeming brain tempered with bristling frustration that I'd been too young to join the party earlier. All that was soon to change, and not a minute too soon.

CHAPTER ONE

JANUARY

ANARCHY ON THE TV FROM JIMI; THE STONES RIDE OUT; THE BEATLES' ROOFTOP GOODBYE; UK JAZZ'S TRAGIC SYD BARRETT; DR JOHN & CCR'S BAYOU TAPESTRIES

Christmas '68 had been pivotal as my parents finally bought a record player; a little mono affair with built-in speaker. Showing remarkably astute taste, they also gave me my first three records: Pink Floyd's 'Point Me At The Sky', Jimi's 'All Along The Watchtower' and 'Nightmare' by the Crazy World Of Arthur Brown. The first album I buy in a record shop is Captain Beefheart's psychedelised delta opus *Strictly Personal*. Now in the land of the living, I hammer these to death.

Maybe it was because I couldn't afford to buy everything I saw in these glittering palaces called record shops, but one personality trait that started then and has remained ever since was an incessant desire to collect everything my latest obsession ever laid down, from stone classic to childhood fart on a 30-year-old bootleg. The fourth of January started like most Saturdays: wandering around Aylesbury town centre with my mates, visiting the Record Centre vinyl emporium and LP department upstairs at WH Smith's. Entering either, some supernatural force seems to grip my being as I leaf through the bins to find latest releases. Maybe stemming from making Stones-related lists at nine, if something interesting pops up, I frantically scribble down its track listing and timings, later to be laboriously copied into one of my dad's old teaching files in neat italic writing. These join the cuttings from that week's music papers that have their own files, according to artist (Tragically, I had to cut up music papers that now sell for a fortune 'cause they took up too much space in my bedroom).

Unsurprisingly, Peel has to be cited as the dogged evangelist behind much of the music in this book. I was resolutely glued to his Sunday afternoon Radio One show and those I could sneak at night. The all-time coolest taste guru with wryly self-deprecating humour and coolly passionate voice routinely played records that were so startlingly great they would stay with me for life. Before losing the pirate stations to government oppression in August '67, my Peel obsession started with snatching listens to his late-night Radio London show *The Perfumed Garden* in time-honoured under-the-bedclothes-with-transistor-radio fashion, opening up new worlds such as John Fahey's luminous blues excursions and new sounds from California by Captain Beefheart, Love and Country Joe And The Fish. Only by listening to Peel were you made aware there was a musical volcano erupting from the underground like an awakening giant's rectum.

Once Peel infiltrated Radio One, *Top Gear* initially went out between two and five on Sunday afternoons, co-presented with Tommy Vance and remaining vital listening in various forms for years. I still have exercise books in which I wrote down every interesting record Peel played, including many that shaped musical obsessions and attitudes I've carried ever since, such as hatred of boxes that amount to musical racism. I can still hear his tones announcing many tunes in this book and remember some of his lines. In late '76, Pete Frame took me to see Peel doing his late night show at Broadcasting House; one example of how god-like figures then became real presences in my life later. Sitting in the corner, all punked up, I watched in mute awe as the great man worked his magic. From 1977, when I was trawling the west end's record shops, I often bumped into Peel, finding myself recommending decent reggae at the Virgin Megastore or imparting the latest punk rock gem. His producer, the magnificent John Walters, was already doing a regular column in *Zigzag*, which led to the pair braving punk niterie the Vortex. I introduced them to The Slits - memorable after Ari Up banged Peel and Palmolive's heads together, but resulting in a legendary session. Now it was my turn.

My record collecting obsession was further motivated, even vindicated, by reading Canned Heat's Bob Hite possessed over twenty thousand rare blues records. Within 30 years I'll top The Bear by over ten thousand. Many are like my babies, each carrying its own story, conjuring a mood or event I can still taste.

As '69 dawned, evenings still found me usually staying in inking my psychedelic posters while subjecting the record player to my latest wax catch or rapidly-wearing-out fave. I'll only watch TV if there's anything good on so the Jimi Hendrix Experience making a rare appearance as special guests on *Happening For Lulu* is a Big Event;

especially as he'd spent much of the previous year cracking the US and recording *Electric Ladyland*. Now '69 would kick into life with Jimi igniting the most audacious display of spontaneous anarchy yet seen on British prime-time TV; unsurpassed until the Sex Pistols' four-letter retort against drunken Bill Grundy sparked TV-trashing outrage around the UK nearly eight years later.

Sitting at the dinner table glued to our vintage black-and-white TV set, I witness Jimi, in light satin shirt, shut his stoned eyes and tear off a pyrotechnic 'Voodoo Chile (Slight Return)' alongside a grinning Noel Redding and human paradiddle Mitch Mitchell. In just four minutes, Jimi shows why he's the world's number one guitarist; soaring through quicksilver salvos with his fingers on the guitar neck, finishing the song with one of those swan-diving feedback endings that could be as soul-clenchingly exciting as the number it was bringing to a close; sent from his groin to your solar plexus with a casual wrist-flick igniting screeching sexual cacophony. I always loved those two cliffhanger seconds as Jimi shut down his final shards of coruscating feedback with as much deft control as he used in launching them, finishing with one circuit-frying roar that ended like a question mark.

The camera pans back to Lulu, squashed between two mods in the front row. 'Whew, that was really hot!' she bubbles breathlessly. 'Yeah…well, ladies and gentlemen, in case you didn't know, Jimi and the boys won in a big American magazine called *Billboard* the group of the year.' Momentarily interrupted by a feedback belch from Jimi's direction, she continues, looking flustered. 'And they're gonna sing for you now the song that absolutely made them in this country, and I love to hear them sing it; 'Hey Joe'.'

Jimi's eyes flash with mischief as he shouts 'Block your ears, block your ears', kicking up another howling squall before signalling a crashing fanfare that subsides into their first hit's familiar opening chords. They nonchalantly dispense with the first verse, even derisively as Jimi chucks in the Beatles' 'Daytripper' riff then confesses 'I've forgotten the words.' After gliding through the guitar solo, he suddenly halts proceedings with a swing of his guitar and clanging chord before declaring, 'We'd like to stop playing this rubbish and dedicate a song to the Cream, regardless of what kind of group they may be in. We'd like to dedicate it to Eric Clapton, Ginger Baker and Jack Bruce.' The trio roar into 'Sunshine Of Your Love', Jimi soloing with the churning riff as Mitch nails Ginger's circular drum pattern. Barely a minute in,

13

Jimi announces 'We're being put off the air' and they slow the riff to a close. Brief shot of the audience, then panic-stricken Lulu, and that's it.

It seemed like harmless fun at the time but apparently the programme's tight script had called for Lulu to join Jimi on the final 'Hey Joe' verse that never came, before closing the show with her usual signature tune. What we didn't see was BBC producer Stanley Dorfman tearing out his hair, pointing at his watch and mouthing silent demands to stop all this right now. The switchboard was besieged with complaints, Experience banned by the BBC and Hendrix cemented his standing as foremost rebel icon (although afterwards he apologised to Lulu, who told him not to worry as it was 'fabulous television').

Watching it on Youtube, it's apparent that live TV had never been treated to guitar playing as incendiary as this and the Experience were rarely captured so relaxed; as Noel Redding recalled in his autobiography, maybe thanks to the lump of hash rescued from the sink by a BBC handyman. Little did we know this Lulu mutiny was the last mischievous jape undertaken by the trio that had formed just over two years earlier before it began irrevocably fracturing.

The following month, Hendrix will become my first gig of 1969. Fifty years on, he's still my ultimate hero and major obsession, along with Keith Richards. It all started with that humble first appearance on *Ready Steady Go!*, the Friday teatime super-mod hootenanny that became the essential outlet for cutting edge UK pop culture since launching in August '63; its motto 'The weekend starts here' as it kicked off with the Surfaris' 'Wipe Out'. It's almost impossible to convey *RSG!*'s importance, the mod-attired audience as much part of the show as the acts; cutting latest dance steps in hot Carnaby Street clobber, recreating what it must have been like on a typical night at the Flamingo. This was where traditional pop routines got roughed up and shown the future. My only problem at first was it going out the same time as when I had to go through the regimented ordeal of cub scouts. So I got myself thrown out for bad behaviour, things like jumping on Baloo's silly Mountie hat; just so I could watch *RSG!*.

Jimi's *RSG!* appearance on December 16 joined the systematic blowing to smithereens then reassembling of my attitudes to music and life ignited by the Stones in '64. It never entered my head that this UK TV debut of the unknown Hendrix would later be held as a historical moment in rock 'n' roll when, after slots from the Merseys, ex-Yardbird Keith Relf, Troggs and young mod Marc Bolan quavering through

'Hippy Gumbo', three dimly-lit figures appeared on some scaffolding and struck up the foreboding chords that exploded into seething murder ballad 'Hey Joe'. I was soon transfixed by the black guy with Blonde On Blonde hair, black satin shirt and white Fender Stratocaster singing about shooting down his lady. He thrust his hips against his guitar and, most shocking of all, seemed to play the solo with his teeth. By the end, my parents looked horrified at this new menace, or maybe it was the effect on the mesmerised gibbering heap that used to be their son.

It's impossible to convey the impact of Hendrix in a world where counterculture was still underground and racial taboos yet to be shattered. Jimi landed like an embodiment of everything forbidden, unfettered with impossible cool as this dazzling, drawling shaman flying the revolutionary flamboyance of primal rock 'n' roll and deep soul of the blues with chitlin' circuit showmanship and supernatural virtuosity radiating other-worldly, sexually-charged charisma. Within weeks, I was member 100 of the Jimi Hendrix Experience Fan Club, unable to understand why my parents wouldn't let me wear my 'I Am Experienced' badge or see Jimi on March 28 when he appeared at the local Borough Assembly Hall. Next came 'Purple Haze' - hammered by my Radio London pirate station lifeline and always striking like a mindblowing lightning bolt, consolidated by *Are You Experienced* confirming everything, its branches skyrocketing from Jimi's astral tree to outer space while minting a new psychedelic blues-rock. Jimi ended '67 with cerebral tour de force *Axis: Bold As Love* and taking first steps to *Electric Ladyland*, '68's magnum opus and greatest embodiment of his restlessly questing muse. Unbeknownst to Jimi, he was already igniting a black rock uprising.

By the Lulu show, Hendrix is the world's biggest rock star and highest-paid performer when sent out to do his expected incendiary thing to order at the world's arenas, festivals and stadiums by shark-like manager Mike Jeffery. '69 saw him feeling trapped by fame, endless tours and audience demands when he just wanted to explore his expanding musical visions, preferably in his own studio beyond the power trio format. At this point, Jimi and Jeffery's plans for the Generation night-club they'd acquired on Eighth Street in New York only revolve around turning it into their own private drinking lair equipped with small studio. It's an idea floated to increase the manager's hold, although both turn up at the local police precinct to (successfully) apply for a liquor licence, Jimi in full regalia.

Spending most of his time cracking the US after his June '67 Monterey festival breakthrough, Jimi had only played the Woburn Abbey festival in '68. Cracks had started showing in the Experience. Although Mitch's place was always secure thanks to his telepathic musical bond with Jimi as his perfect drummer, Redding objected to playing behind someone else's shining star and had formed Fat Mattress with old mate Neil Landon from the Flowerpot Men.

Then came the January fan club newsletter. After announcing, 'Jimi and the boys are now managed by Mike Jeffery solely, as Chas has decided to stay in this country and get ready to settle into family life, as his wife Lotta is infanticipating (sic),' secretary Jane Simmons addresses reports the Experience are breaking up with a statement: 'The Group itself will always be together as long as they are still breathing. I quote our own JH - they have an understanding between them that the group is as solid as any group can be, "it's just that we each like to do other things separately." Jimi has recorded an American group called Cat Mother. Mitch has taken part in the Rolling Stones' *Circus* film to be shown shortly on TV and Noel is recording a group called "Flat Mattress" (sic!). They will get together every month and do some gigs and record but I thought you'd like to know folks that it's definite - the Jimi Hendrix Experience are alive and well and living in London at the moment!'

After listing this month's European tour dates, Jane drops the big one - 'A Day For Us - At Last' at the Royal Albert Hall on February 18. Supporting will be Soft Machine and 'the new lineup of Traffic,' while Jimi is trying to get Spike Milligan and Marty Feldman to compere, 'as he is a big fan of both.'

Same place I'd seen Donovan. Unless Jimi is deemed so bad an influence I can't be allowed in the same room, I'll be able to go. But how? At this time it was an unimaginable fantasy.

The Devil Rides Out

Keith Richards' eyes flash black in the rear-view mirror of his blue Bentley as he hares along the Embankment at around a hundred miles an hour, sparking a smile as he waves regally to the Friday rush-hour traffic while swinging a sudden U-turn after realising he's overshot the road to the Stones' Chelsea HQ.

Those black eyes had seen it all by that 1980 afternoon when I first got to spend some time with my childhood hero; tumultuous success, teenage riots, Redlands drug busts, Anita Pallenberg, Altamont, the creation of *Exile On Main Street* (greatest album of all time), 1972's STP tour, life-threatening shooting galleries and, most recently, his torturous ascension out of heroin's death-grip. This September afternoon, Keith is a happy man, thanks largely to the beautiful laughing lady called Patti Hansen sitting beside him in the soft brown leather of the front passenger seat. Once we make it to the office, Keith and I will sit on a couch for over two hours emptying a bottle of Jack Daniel's and my Marlboro packet while he does his first smack-free interview for ten years.

This is the kind of surreal fantasy scenario I could once have only dreamed of. Sitting on a couch sharing memories and refreshments with Keith Richards? Naah! The Stones had been embedded in my soul for practically all my living memory and still are. Rather than having to consult countless retrospective works on their doings, I grew up with them as a driving force in my life and experienced them in real time. Whatever new obstacle befell the band I felt it with them and worried about it too. Whatever triumph they enjoyed made my week a good one.

It all started on the evening of Saturday 13 July '63, ten days past my ninth birthday, when the Stones appeared on top TV pop show *Thank Your Lucky Stars* playing first single 'Come On'. Despite marking their first and almost only stab at stage uniforms in dogtooth affairs from Carnaby Street, the band's tousled hair and raw, petulant energy cut a gritty swathe through the clean-cut cuties who had dominated the show since its first broadcast in 1961. These five shaggy unknowns immediately savaged the nation's blood pressure levels by not looking parent or army approved, immediately laying foundations for the upcoming generation gap. Sporting the longest hair, Brian Jones was up front, in the leader's spot, tossing his blond thatch while enthusiastically miming his harmonica part. He certainly flaunted most stage presence and charisma as Mick still looked like a nice economics student and Keith the shy, gawky rebel hiding behind his guitar.

My real Stones epiphany happens when the Stones make their debut on the third edition of *Ready Steady Go!* in August. From this edition, host Cathy McGowan, 'Queen of the Mods', joins old school host Keith Fordyce. Appearing on a show also featuring Jet Harris & Tony Meehan and Little Peggy March, the Stones had ditched the jackets for funkier leather waistcoats from Carnaby Street's super-hip John Stephen. I still remember Cathy approaching the band after 'Come On', Brian to the fore, introducing him as 'the guv'nor.' There seemed little doubt who the Stones' kingpin was. After Cathy inevitably asked, 'How do you cut your hair?', Brian replied he did it himself using two mirrors. I always pinpoint that appearance as when my lifelong Stones obsession ignited, like my young nervous system had been hot-wired into the mains and brain swivelled forever. From the age of nine, I was never the same again. My parents quaked and classmates spluttered into their footballs.

That hair was what first got the Stones noticed. This may be hard to understand when today's required 'average bloke' style is the army-friendly short back 'n' sides once so rigorously imposed by the establishment we opposed in the 60s, when long hair was a badge of honour among those who didn't want to look like everybody else. I mean, who would? It's hilarious or tragic that, after fighting the 'hair wars' that began for me in '63 and were positively raging in my life by '69, we've ended up with a nation of parentally-approved conformists. In '69, electric clippers were dentist-drill-level instruments of torture and army hair meant square, doing what the establishment tells you. Long hair was an act of hip, rebellious individuality, inspiring violent hostility anywhere from school or home to old-fashioned bigots feeling threatened because the ladies loved it. Thinking about it now, fighting to let my barnet sprout like the Stones is not even an underlying theme in this book; it was an obsession, born out of oppression, that stuck for life. When I take my dog Jack to the pet shop to load up, we have to walk past the barbers next door, where sad-looking robots sit being shorn like sheep. Ever-intuitive, likewise shaggy Jack rarely fails to squirt a protest or leave a loaf outside.

The Beatles-composed second single, 'I Wanna Be Your Man', is the clincher, the Stones' cool *RSG!* status compounded by their appearance on November 22 - the day Kennedy was assassinated (the shocking news coming after the show). The uniforms had vanished as they mimed their much better, scorching new single on which, in Oldham's absence, Brian boasted most blues-charged input. The rest of the bill, including Gerry and the Pacemakers, and Freddie and the Dreamers (and Kathy Kirby), seemed middle-of-the-road after Brian was captured at full-pelt; raking slide guitar riffs from his big, pale Gretsch. His blond hair and animated aggression still stood out from the others, his electrifying slide solo the most exciting bit of the song. I'm never the same again as the Stones become main motivation of my childhood. I watch every *Thank Your Lucky Stars*, *Top Of The Pops* and *Ready Steady Go!* appearance, monitor the radio as we don't yet have a record player, collect the magazines, join their fan club (number 10019!), subscribe to *Rolling Stones Monthly* and basically sow the seeds for my whole life. I start flouting rules, refuse to wear a school cap because I knew Brian wouldn't and laugh at how the band relentlessly defy convention. Under Andrew Oldham's skilled PR, the Stones are soon public enemies number one. Even at that age, I revel in the effect liking the Stones has on Beatles fans. I like the Beatles too but so do my parents and they'd played for the Royal Family wearing nice suits. It may be hard to understand now but this meant something then. The Stones are always getting into trouble and seem on a relentless course of audacious revolution on every front, from music to social behaviour. I become gripped by what Keith calls his 'passing it on' theory so embrace their influences: romantic-sounding figures like Bo Diddley, Chuck Berry, Jimmy Reed, Howlin' Wolf and Willie Dixon.

In January '64, the Stones hitch up with the Ronettes for a UK tour. I'm gutted when I'm not allowed to go when it hits Aylesbury's Granada cinema. Strangely, just the fact the Stones were in town turned on another new tap of excitement. Brian's domination lasted through the first album then ongoing hit cover versions of Buddy Holly's Crickets' 'Not Fade Away', the Valentinos' 'It's All Over Now' and Howlin' Wolf's 'Little Red Rooster'. No one who saw *Ready Steady Go!* on November 20 '64 could forget the startling image of Brian looking like the coolest pop star on the planet as he dispensed eerie quicksilver slide from his Vox teardrop guitar with deft, playful arrogance; they can diminish his role in the band, but they can never take away this. For Brian, taking the blues to number one for the first time was his most cherished achievement. Inspired by some kids being the Yardbirds for some event, I decide to form my own Stones for the school Christmas party; five little guys on toy instruments miming to 'Not Fade Away' (even if we'd rehearsed 'Little Red Rooster' in the classroom in front of the class). I was Mick, in black jeans and white shirt like his recent TV appearances (the effect slightly dampened when I slip over in the repugnant outdoor bogs before our set, although I got that dirty bluesman look).

Soon the Stones moved past the simple shock of sporting hair over the collar. '67's refusal to mount the Palladium roundabout and

Redlands bust turned them into martyrs for the exploding counterculture, turning the establishment further against them as their innocent rebel antics became a threat to society's very fibre. I even like the maligned *Their Satanic Majesties Request* and still do now, called to explain why at 2017's launch party for its 50th anniversary reissue. After defeating fumbled efforts to jail them, the Stones return from the psychedelic abyss to reclaim their blues roots with *Beggars Banquet*, but first came the modern reinvention of their punky adolescence with 'Jumpin' Jack Flash'.

First time I heard that was at the first time I saw the Stones; at the NME Pollwinners Concert in May '68. Weirdly, that came about through my school. Not from lessons - I only liked English and Art, and for a budding young counterculture revolutionary, Aylesbury Grammar School seemed old and oppressive, its teaching staff a mixture of veteran begowned old-timers with Cambridge in their eyes, eager university spewings or closet psychos who would now be hauled over the coals for their abusive antics. Sadly, the music department was represented by two inadequate losers who took their frustrations out on those who dared to be different (like a book crashing on my head courtesy of disgraced midget Mr Eardley). Sadistic gym teachers propagating shorts-clutching rugby antics and their savage sub-homosexual persecution putdown rituals that put me off sport for life. Anyway, I'd already been put off sport for life by the power-mad masochistic wannabes who passed for PE teachers and tactics. I credit the school for my lifelong hatred of uniforms, short hair, traditions, 'teams' and conforming confinement. My classmates were either university-bound swots or ignorant jock lunkheads who put me down as 'weird' or 'bent'. You could already see how they'd turn out - hideous wife, squawking kids, boring life-wasting job with TV in the evening and pub at weekends. But their bullying abuse fired me further not to be like anybody else. There was a more exciting world out there than the tiny little one they aspired to.

The strange thing was, much of my education about the new revolution came from one of the teachers, who also was certainly not like everybody else. Through '67, our chemistry teacher Mr Robin Pike delighted in pinning up the latest psychedelic posters, newspaper features or memorabilia on the walls of the lab as evidence of that weekend's activities. It turned out Mr Pike led a brilliant life, starting with going to school with Brian Jones. By day he'd be teaching the finer

20

points of chemistry; by night catching major club gigs in London. It was inevitable we'd strike up a conversation. School was only made bearable by reading the four music papers I got every week under the desk. Noticing them one day in early January '68, he asked if I was interested in an outing he was organising to see Donovan at the Royal Albert Hall on the 31st. My first concert.

Now, Robin is my oldest friend. His other major contributions to this story will emerge but, in '68, he shone like a cool oasis in a staid grey cloud. Sitting in the quiet front room in his house near Tring, Robin quietly recounts a remarkable story that starts with going to the grammar school in his Cheltenham home town with Brian Jones. The fact Robin went against the contemporary grain by steering clear of drugs and alcohol makes him an unimpeachable source, his memories only dimmed by time itself.

'At one point in the sixth form, I had to repeat a year after I had an illness, and came into the same year as Brian Jones,' he begins. 'We were both doing A level chemistry. I used to work in the post office at Christmas and, by the sixth form, was on a round delivering Christmas mail, which included Hatherley Road, where Brian lived. Because Christmas mail was very busy, I shared a post-round with Brian. He had half the round and I had the other half. He had the half with his house on it so he would nip in to his house and hang out at home then cycle back into town and sign off. At times we would cycle out of Cheltenham where the sorting office was together.

'What I remember particularly is, back then mail was delivered on Christmas Day, which was quite special then. Anybody who was out was all smiley and friendly and it was all Christmassy. So I cycled out on Christmas Day with Brian. He wanted a drink so he asked a milkman, because milk was delivered on Christmas Day too, and the milkman gave him a bottle of milk. At that point we were very friendly. As a person he was a different kid in school; very moody and difficult as a pupil in relation to the teachers. He was particularly charming that Christmas though.

'He was very into jazz and went to all-night jazz clubs. In the downtime of a chemistry set he would be talking of his activities. He used to regularly hitch to London to stay with Alexis Korner, who he was friendly with. There were a few stories relayed about how he was staying in a room in Alexis's flat in one of these multiple occupation things. In the next door room was a prostitute. He used to make out -

21

with there not being a very thick wall between the two rooms - that he was having sex with Alexis, and the lady next door was shouting "Stop it, leave him alone". There was quite a colourful side to Brian's time at school.

'He was a very strong and very keen swimmer. I worked all over Cheltenham, including the swimming pool, now the lido. I was in the basket store, where you changed and put your clothes into the basket and got a ring for around your wrist. He came through and had his basket and went swimming.'

Brian fled Cheltenham's insular music scene in March '62, hoping London would appreciate his vision of blues as commercially-viable mainstream breakthrough. Having honed his dazzling guitar skills at over a hundred gigs, he was able to enter Korner's orbit as a fellow blues musician, appearing at his seminal Ealing Club as Elmo Lewis, his molten distillations of Jimmy Reed and Elmore James as the UK's first electric slide guitar exponent transfixing Mick Jagger, Keith Richards and Dick Taylor in the audience. By May, Brian was advertising for like-minded musicians in *Jazz News*, auditions at the Bricklayers Arms off Broadwick Street in Soho first attracting boogie-woogie pianist Ian Stewart, then Keith Richards - nervous because he'd incurred scorn, including from Korner, for unleashing Chuck Berry licks at his recent Ealing Club appearance with Mick. Keith told me how he'd sneaked into the rehearsal room a few minutes before Stu knew he was there. 'He was just sitting there playing, wearing little black leather shorts. Oblivious. I was already nervous because I was the Chuck Berry guy. He was just sitting there playing but every now and again he'd stand up and look out of the window. Then he'd go (Keith stands up, looks out the window and cocks his forearm) "PHWOAAR!! Look at that!" Ha ha ha! It was the strippers down in the street going from job to job.'

Rehearsals with Brian and Stu followed, attended by Mick when he wasn't singing with Korner's Blues Incorporated. The guitar-driven root of the Stones sound hatched after Brian, Keith, Mick and others, including the legendary Phelge, moved into two squalid, stinky rooms on the second floor of 102 Edith Grove, Chelsea. 'You wouldn't have liked to live there,' said Keith. 'It was disgusting.'

With Mick often attending LSE classes, Brian and Keith studied Muddy Waters, Little Walter and Jimmy Reed records, igniting the 'ancient art of weaving' and 'Rolling Stones are a two guitar band' ethos as they bounced and sparked off each other. Forget Ry Cooder, it was through Brian that Keith was first exposed to the open tuning that shaped his guitar sound later that decade. He also heard Robert Johnson for the first time. Of course, Brian already knew Johnson's devilish legend, and did a solid job carrying it on. Brian renamed the nascent Brian Jones Blues Band the Rollin' Stones from Muddy Waters' 'Mannish Boy' for that famous July '62 Marquee stand-in spot regarded as their first gig. By late '62, the new band had solidified as Jones, Jagger, Richards, Stu and rhythm section Bill Wyman and Charlie Watts.

After that freezing winter, things started hotting up in early '63 with demos and the Crawdaddy residency at Richmond's Station Hotel (which drew their mates the Beatles in April), going ballistic after 19-year-old PR hotshot Andrew Loog Oldham came in as manager with business brain Eric Easton. Master-hustler Oldham created his 'anti-Beatles' bad boy hype from what was already there; he just made sure the world knew about it after bringing in his new broom - adding a 'g' to Rollin', slashing the 's' off Richards, relegating Stu to road manager, seizing their Decca deal and cementing the image Brian had already minted for public consumption.

First single 'Come On' is where we came in. I wondered if Robin Pike was surprised when his old classmate popped up in the Stones.

'I don't remember being surprised, just thinking "Ah, there's Brian". He was the sort of person you wouldn't be at all surprised where he popped up. Later, when I was living in Exeter in a house with a lot of people, there were quite a few girls there too. One was talking about how she'd got to see Brian after a Stones concert and got backstage through some window. She even had a letter from Brian, I think. She was telling this story and I said, "well, I went to school with him." She found it difficult to believe as I was a teacher. The first time I saw him in the Stones was in Exeter about 1965.'

The first band Robin saw was the Animals at Exeter University in '65, followed by the Stones at a local cinema. A trip to London saw him witness the NME Pollwinners' Concert headlined by the Beatles over the Stones and Who, along with his first club outing to the Flamingo, where he saw the Mike Cotton Sound. At this point, Robin started the school dances he would take to Aylesbury the following year, booking Cotton for Exeter school.

Along with the dances, Robin started running coach trips, starting with the fabled Sunday nights at the Saville Theatre in London's west end in '67.

'I'd always been very interested in theatre. Since I was a teenager living in Cheltenham I'd been to London to the theatre. Having seen the Animals and the Rolling Stones I began to get interested in modern music. It coincided with 1967, which I regard as the pivotal year for everything. I got really interested in the exploding music scene, particularly the Saville on a Sunday night. I was there on the first one with the Four Tops in November 1966, went to virtually every one and was there for the last one. It was part of a whole picture really, like a tapestry.

'The Saville was absolutely stunning. It was amazing really. The Four Tops hadn't played in this country before. I don't think we'd seen any Tamla Motown artists. They came on in fluorescent suits and danced, in time. There was a huge band, chick singers and it was spectacular. I don't think anybody in this country had seen anything like it. It was a small world then. Everyone was there. Jagger was dancing in the aisles, the Beatles, everybody. You looked at it and I've said this before, there was black and white television and suddenly there was colour television. There was no ambling onstage and tuning up. The timing was fabulous. That was the first Saville show and it went on from there.

'I took coach trips there; a small coach which left Aylesbury around six o'clock from outside the grammar school. It was nothing to do with the grammar school at all. People turned up and got on. I got the tickets and we went. It was all done by post but I always got probably about thirty tickets.'

Unfortunately, I missed those Saville trips so Donovan at the Albert Hall was my first gig. Supporting were Tyrannosaurus Rex, who I loved from Peel's shows. Marc Bolan sat cross-legged on the floor, warbling through 'Deborah' and other songs that would appear on their first album, while beshaded Steve Peregrine Took pattered his bongos. During 'Frowning Atahualpa' they were joined by Peel himself, who read a children's story from a bed of flowers. Donovan was good, backed by an orchestra after getting into jazz, but the night belonged to Bolan and seeing my DJ hero in the flesh.

Then came Robin's trip to the NME Pollwinners' Concert on May 12; coachload of school kids, nobody in uniform, going to a gig. Best education you could wish for!

It was truly surreal finding myself surrounded by several thousand screaming teenyboppers, watching bands I'd seen on *Top Of The Pops* and immediately fascinated by the onstage rigmarole of scuttling roadies fixing stage lights and amplifiers. It was like a crash course in '68 pop as acts came and went doing two or three songs; Status Quo in psychedelic finery pushing 'Pictures Of Matchstick Men', Love Affair with 'Everlasting Love', fantastically-exciting Showstoppers with 'Ain't Nothin' But A House Party', The Association doing 'Windy' in brown suits, the Paper Dolls winning my teenage heart in their string bikini ensembles cooing 'Something Here In My Heart', the Herd fronted by 'Face of '68' Peter Frampton, Amen Corner, the Tremeloes, Lulu singing 'Morning Dew', the great Dusty Springfield, Cliff and The Shadows, the Move howling covers of Moby Grape's 'Hey Grandma' and Spooky Tooth's 'Sunshine Help Me', Roy Wood exercising his new wah-wah pedal and Scott Walker facing down the screamers with Jacques Brel's 'Amsterdam'.

The Stones were a surprise addition to the bill and I swear I started vibrating with delight when two local mini-skirted saucepots in our party returned from a backstage raid bearing the shock news. The Stones hadn't appeared live for nearly two years and their last album was treated with disdain, making their appearance a perfectly-timed masterstroke to announce 'We're Back!' When they came on and got presented their Best R&B Group award by Roger Moore, there was unbridled pandemonium unlike anything I've experienced before or since. The screams drowned out everything, although I was too busy basking in this special moment and checking out their clobber as Keith lunged into the world's first airing of 'Jumpin' Jack Flash'. Raising a finger at the kaftans of '67, he sported black leather jacket and white drainpipes as the event's punkiest-looking rock 'n' roll apparition.

Sporting pale blue shirt and dark blue velvet strides, Jagger was all over the place inciting the crowd as Marianne Faithfull, wearing his razor blade-patterned shirt, and Anita Pallenberg threw roses from the front row. Mick might have long got his stage act down to a fine art but 50 years ago was like a sex-crazed mongrel let off the leash, throwing his ballet shoes and tambourine into the throng.

This would be the only time I saw Brian Jones in the flesh, resplendent in fringed green buckskin jacket, white frilly shirt, red keks and scarf. Last year Marianne told me 'I was there with Anita, trying to be nice to Brian. We felt sorry for Brian.' After a practically-inaudible 'Satisfaction' they were gone. The way ancient memories pan out, I still have images of Brian smiling and strumming like a blond-crowned god and the Stones trooping back to the dressing room past the side of the stage, Keith twirling his scarf over his head in triumph.

Unbeknown to anyone, including Brian, this was the last gig he'd play with the band he'd formed six years earlier, unless you count that December's ill-fated Rock 'N' Roll Circus. Robin went to that too; 'the early evening session where they did the introductions. Jagger was the ringmaster, of course... It was very interesting, quite informal and just a small group of extras, which is what I was; I had a poncho and we sat round the outside of the ring. John Lennon and Yoko were there with Julian, just sitting. I went up to John and asked for his autograph, which he and Yoko signed. That gives you a flavour of how informal it was. The Who were walking around. There were a lot of pauses where the director held up everything, because the lighting was quite primitive and had to be manually adjusted to light the circus ring.'

That same month, the Stones unleashed the return-to-basics uproar of *Beggars Banquet*, striking like a cobra now cracks were showing in the Beatles' united front. 'Sympathy For The Devil' was premiered on David Frost's Saturday night TV show. They looked satanic, Jagger with his longest hair yet dyed black for *Performance*, Keith continuing his ongoing hard drug rocker transformation and Brian smiling in his inner world at the grand piano in a floppy hat. I've always considered this public unveiling, climaxing with Mick on his knees taking off his shirt to reveal Satan painted on his chest, as the flag going up on the Stones moving into the towering late 60s-early 70s peak where they earned the title of the greatest rock 'n' roll band in the world and became figureheads for the post-hippy climate of sex, drugs and decadence. It suited them better than beads and kaftans. And Keith was back in the black clutch of the blues.

Back to 1980 and, after 17 years of Stones worship, I was stepping through the gate with Keith himself literally in the driving seat. He must have sensed there was a wide-eyed lifelong fan sitting behind him in the Bentley rather than another hack, visibly loosening up as he started talking about the Stones' '69 renaissance. 'That was the most important time 'cos it showed we could cut it live now,' he reflected. 'But we were only doing what we always did; playing our blues and hoping the people would like it.'

1969 might have been the year the Stones returned to live performing and released *Let It Bleed*, but it was also peppered with tragic death and start of the Jagger and Richards friction that would ebb or flare for decades. The touch-paper to the Stones demolition of the hippie dream had been ignited when Jagger started filming *Performance* in September '68. Directed by Donald Cammell with cinematographer Nic Roeg, the film's mind-twisting orgy of sex, drugs and violence remains one of the most brutally-surreal products of the whole era. Jagger played a reclusive pop star called Turner, who then-partner Marianne Faithfull told him to characterise by combining Brian's exotic stoned torment and Keith's outlaw cool. James Fox shone as cold-eyed East End gangster Chas, forced into exile when he crosses the boss by murdering one of their own. He ends up at the Powis Square flat Turner shares with Anita's Pherber and Michelle Breton's Lucy, plunged into their heady world of hallucinogenic chaos and decadence. As the unstable Cammell, who only made three more films before shooting himself in the head in '97, said, 'The movie was finished before Altamont and Altamont actualised it.' At the time, it brought the hottest date of my life - with a California blonde who'd started at Aylesbury College - to a premature end after she stormed out of the cinema and hooked up with a local skinhead who decked me when I went looking for her.

The filming with his lady left Keith at a loose end. A new song had been brewing since he looked out of the window of friend Robert Fraser's flat the previous autumn and saw people scurrying for cover as a sudden monsoon battered the street. As the song took shape it grew to perfectly capture all the war, killing and social collapse of that tumultuous year, along with the dread and anger seething inside Keith as he killed time while Anita cavorted with Jagger on the film set. He started throwing on a blanket of heroin to numb the pain and anxiety, planting seeds for the addiction that would almost poleaxe the band next decade. Soon he will take the song then called 'Give Me Some Shelter' into recording sessions for the next Stones album and it will become their all-time apocalyptic classic, oozing ominous dread and warning after his deathly guitar shimmer intro. Even now, it's the first encore on the No Filter Tour.

This was the moment when the Stones told the world it was fucking up and things would only get worse, with the ongoing inner city riots, rape and murder of Vietnam and appalling Manson murders in August. When recording it Keith broke the neck of the guitar he was using, possibly imagining it was Mick's neck. Rather than copy the blues, the Stones were reinventing them into a black new form.

Brian started his last year on the planet on holiday in Sri Lanka (Ceylon), where he visited an astrologer who told him to take care around water. While he was away, the court refused an appeal on his second drug conviction, making a work permit to tour the US out of the question. Keith, Anita, Mick and Marianne saw in 1969 at Rio de Janeiro, holed up in an isolated ranch. In her autobiography, *Faithfull*, Marianne says the vibes were 'weird' as one of many repercussions from Mick and Anita's on set affair while filming *Performance*. 'Keith and I were still feeling very jangled,' she writes. 'The shadow of *Performance* cast a pall over the whole trip.' Describing the situation boiling into 'a lethal brew', Marianne left early, inadvertently placing Anita in the 'sixth Rolling Stone' role she readily acknowledged. In a couple of years, Marianne would be freed from the Stones' claustrophobic orbit altogether, telling me recently, 'Anita was much more wrapped up in that world than I was. I got out very quickly, really, I was the first to go and thank god; not that I don't love and admire them and think they're wonderful but I couldn't handle it. I know I couldn't.'

As an early 2017 Christmas present I felt she may appreciate, I sent Marianne the deluxe reissue of *Their Satanic Majesties Request*. After all, you were there, I told her. 'Was I? Yes, I suppose I was. Over the years Allen Klein gave me endless Rolling Stones records and I've lost them all, moving around. I was in New York, then I was in Ireland; all gone. Also I went through a long period where I can't say I particularly cherished those memories. I've got over that now but he would give me all these records and of course they were really valuable and I would think to myself "Uh-huh, what do I care?" I'm completely different now. I don't feel like that.'

Mick and Keith earn their Glimmer Twins nickname on the boat to Rio, Keith recalling being surrounded by all these 'upper English people' while dressed in a diaphanous djellaba, Mexican shoes and tropical army hat. After a while, the toffs realised who the tight-lipped Stones foursome were so started asking probing questions like, 'What are you really trying to do?' When a woman stepped forward from the group and declared, 'We've been asking you for days and you just won't say. Can you give us a glimmer?', Jagger turned to Keith and announced 'We're the Glimmer Twins.'

Down in Brazil, guzzling cough mixture and smoking potent local weed, Keith continued honing ideas that had been marinating since the previous year, then worked on at their rehearsal space in an old warehouse in Bermondsey before they entered Olympic Studios in early February. (Ten years later I had the pleasure of recording at the mythical studio myself with my punk band the Vice Creems, which was actually The Clash for that day. As I struggled to overdub my lame vocals over the towering music cooked up by producer Mick Jones, the sense of who else had stood in that same vocal booth only contributed to my nerves. I could feel old ghosts watching from every corner.)

'You Can't Always Get What You Want' had been the first song to take shape for the Stones album after Jagger brought it into the studio in November '68. His words seem to celebrate the end of the decade the Stones helped shape by lacerating it after all those lofty ambitions and counterculture ideals seemed to plummet in flames along with any innocence that might be left. 'I went down to the demonstration to get my fair share of abuse' referred to the Grosvenor Square demo he had briefly observed the previous March and referenced in 'Street Fighting Man'. The woman at the Chelsea Drugstore hoping to meet her connection was Marianne.

If Mick had the lyrics and melody, 'You Can't Always Get What You Want' was still what he described as a folk song before producer Jimmy Miller gave it a shake and brought the funk. With wonderful pianist Nicky Hopkins on board, they booked Al Kooper for the session, which he felt compelled to fulfil after bumping into Brian on King's Road. When Charlie couldn't master the groove, Miller got behind the kit and supplied the drum-track that survived until the finished cut, bolstered by Rocky Dijon's congas. Charlie gallantly stepped aside, later saying Jimmy made him rethink recording his drums in future. Meanwhile, Kooper based his piano on Etta James' cover of 'I Got You Babe' (recorded in Memphis with the Muscle Shoals rhythm section), then later added electric Dylan organ and French horn intro. Kooper remembers Brian lying on the floor reading a magazine article on botany during the session.

At some point around then Mick records 'Memo From Turner' for *Performance* but Keith refuses to participate in the promised soundtrack so Jagger sings it with Kooper, Ry Cooder, Traffic's Jim Capaldi and Chris Wood.

So began the Stones' '69, possibly the most traumatic year of the career that had started seven years earlier and, miraculously, continues in robust shape half a century later.

Up on the Roof

While the Stones were catching flak for scoffing at traditions and uniforms, the Beatles could proceed in revolutionising pop, until '66 when their ongoing evolution started forging next steps in music and for a short time they teetered between counterculture royalty and family favourites. It might seem hard to believe now but, to the world outside the underground, the most controversial aspect of this progression was the Fab Four's sprouting hair length and, as revealed on '67's 'Strawberry Fields Forever' video on, the facial sproutings that went with it. Lennon's NHS specs and 'tache combination had been hard to swallow but when he became a full-blown hairy hippie with Yoko Ono beside him he even felt compelled to record 'The Ballad Of John and Yoko' to lament the ongoing lambasting that reached its peak in '69. George looked like a mystic and Paul had a full beard. Never mind *Sgt. Pepper*'s breakthroughs, follicular expansion was held as the Beatles' most brazen defacing of the lovable moptops they'd evolved beyond.

After that first sighting in 1962 when the Beatles performed 'Love Me Do' on Saturday evening TV pop show *Thank Your Lucky Stars*, I'd got caught up in the mania that erupted after 'Please Please Me' and 'From Me To You', swapping bubble-gum cards in the school playground. Reading endless retrospective dissections of the Beatles from a reign that lasted barely seven years is often nothing like it was growing up with them as their story unfolded. In '62 they were another group in suits, with something bright and different.

When the Stones came along I abandoned them for a few years as I pledged allegiance to the former's more rebellious movement (later discovering the two bands were close mates who plotted their careers in cahoots so their releases didn't clash). After the Beatles crashed through the acid barrier with 'Tomorrow Never Knows', I realised it was cool to like both.

30

At the end of this month, reports come in the Beatles had played a lunch-time set on the roof of their Apple Corps HQ on Savile Row. Now it's known as the band's last ever public performance but, coming after late '68's panoramic-if-patchy *'White Album'*, the Beatles still seemed for life, bolstered by the recently-released *Yellow Submarine* soundtrack, featuring 'It's All Too Much', their magnificent, sky-peeling psychedelic anthem. Macca felt a return to the basic rock 'n' roll ethos that first inspired them might ignite a communal spark and defuse frictions that had rubbed up the previous album. Breaking from recent multi-tiered studio surgery, the original plan was to film a show with new songs and release an album that could be played live. Many believed the rooftop show was a sign the Beatles were planning to gig in the post-scream-age era, not the final swan-song before they unofficially dissolved around September (the final crunch coming when, on Jagger's advice, three Beatles out-voted Macca to hire Allen Klein as manager).

Directed by Michael Lindsay-Hogg, the Beatles had agreed to let their recording sessions and rehearsals be filmed as they tried to rise above simmering tensions and play like a normal four-piece. With Yoko always at Lennon's side, this proved impossible. The sessions were later described by Harrison, who walked out at one point, as 'the low of all-time.' When he returned five days later it was with fiercely ambitious US gospel-soul singer-keyboardist Billy Preston in tow to melt the ice (himself enjoying a star-studded Apple hit this year with 'That's The Way God Planned It').

With action moved to Apple HQ, the rooftop sequence was intended as the grand finale as the Beatles managed nine takes of five new songs before police arrived to stop the fun. They sure did look different from even three years earlier with Macca's beard and Lennon's tresses, complementing his stoned granny look with Yoko's brown fur coat. The last time they'd appeared on a stage had been San Francisco's Candlestick Park on August 29, '66. Whatever came next, we knew it made a great *TOTP* video when 'Get Back' was released as a single in April.

Meanwhile, US police confiscated 30,000 copies of John and Yoko's *Two Virgins*, declaring the full frontal cover 'pornographic'.

Death of a Mysterious Jazz Legend

Nobody could have any idea that, within the next 18 months, Brian and Jimi would be taken away in circumstances so avoidable they still make me weep. As '69 dawned, I'd only mourned one music-related death - Otis Redding in December '67. Everyone else was still here. Of course, now rarely a week seems to go by without being called to write an obituary for another sad loss, including many I'd interviewed, become friends with or those admired from afar who will soon be appearing in these pages. One fatality occurred early in '69 that I wouldn't learn about until 2016 after discovering the unearthly genius of a jazz pianist called Mike Taylor. His body was found washed up on the beach at Leigh-on-Sea, Essex in the first week of January, but avoided the music papers I devoured each week and took decades to be acknowledged beyond his small circle of friends and fans. Taylor had been British jazz's bright young hope, studious in his spectacles and smart in his suit, who'd transformed into the bedraggled barefoot acid casualty sleeping rough who showed up at London's hipper clubs banging a clay hand-drum. He was just 30 when he died and it was that time again before Taylor started his ascension from little-known foot-note to enigmatic lost genius, doomed to be cited British jazz's acid-buckled answer to Syd Barrett.

Taylor was brought to my attention while interviewing veteran poet Pete Brown for a feature about pioneering R&B colossus Graham Bond, another criminally-overlooked key figure in 60s music, who also fell victim to drugs (in his case heroin) before dying mysteriously under a tube train in '73. The abrasively eloquent Pete Brown is one of those resilient 60s survivors who kept health and marbles by binning drugs during make-or-break '67 and survived to become the fierce creative force who continues wreaking smaller-scale havoc today while former comrades and fellow musicians have crumbled around him.

'Mike Taylor was friends with various friends of mine,' he recalled. 'There was a flute player called Mike Burke who played on some stuff that (fellow pioneering poet) Michael Horovitz and I did, and John Mumford. They worked with Mike Taylor, who was semi-pro for a long time. He had a brief thing of being professional, then fell to pieces and disappeared. He was a peripheral figure but Graham liked him and they were friends. Ginger also liked him and collaborated with him on a couple of Cream things. There was a plan to do a record with me, but

Graham wasn't in great shape and Mike wasn't either so that never came off.'

Those few words were enough to fire up the kind of quest that's kept my soul alive for the last 50 years, usually involving gleaning scraps of info and tracking down relevant records. Taylor's story opened into one those rabbit hole flows that traversed similar ground to his friend Bond's rise and fall, both being orphans who rose brightly through precocious talent before darkness descended; prodigious geniuses left hanging on to reality by the flimsiest of threads after drugs moved in.

'Mike Taylor's life and work were so enigmatic that his very existence seems almost to have been a hoax,' says a 2007 liner note, yet he pops up in the intertwining stories of Bond, Brown, Jack Bruce, Ginger Baker, saxophonist-squatting legend Dave Tomlin, percussionist Glen Sweeney's Third Ear Band, Jon Hiseman's Colosseum and others. Never filmed and interviewed once, Taylor bequeathed only 1965's *Pendulum* and '67's *Trio*, along with three tracks he co-wrote with Baker for Cream's *Wheels Of Fire* and two compositions on the New Jazz Orchestra's second album.

Italian writer Luca Ferrari's excellent *Out Of Nowhere: The Uniquely Elusive Jazz of Mike Taylor* then arrived as a work of major research that told the pianist's story for the first time. It reveals Taylor born in Ealing in June 1938, brought up by his grandparents after both his parents had died by the time he was six. He embraced jazz piano while serving in the RAF between 1956-58. By the early 60s, he was living in Twickenham with wife Ann, enraptured by Bill Evans' *Explorations* album, Soho's underground jazz scene, European art movies and marijuana. He soon collided with livewire Dave Tomlin, who had come into jazz the New Orleans route, and trombonist John Mumford, leading to all-night jam sessions in the Nucleus coffee bar basement in Covent Garden.

Speaking in Luca's book, most mention Taylor's officer's politeness and introvert personality, Tomlin recalling 'He looked like a bank clerk and acted like a mystic.' Everyone remembers an intensely-driven man of few words. 'You could hardly have found a more immaculate and polite chap than Mike,' says bassist Ron Rubin in the notes of *Pendulum*'s 2007 reissue. 'He was almost in the Ivy League mold, highly intelligent, well-read and thoughtful, as well as being a totally uncompromising musician.'

Taylor asked Tomlin to join the band he was forming, recruiting double-bassist Goudie Charles and, after Ginger was rejected due to the loudness of his playing, 17-year-old drummer Randy Jones. Although fixated with Horace Silver, Art Blakey's Jazz Messengers and Thelonious Monk, Taylor avoided copying anyone, obsessively creating his own manuscript paper using a five-point pen and a quiet, meticulous presence when playing his compositions and deconstructing standards like 'Night In Tunisia' to fit his self-devised techniques of merging jazz with modern European music. Surviving by driving a van for his grandfather's wallpaper business, Taylor saw his quartet solidify into its classic lineup when 19-year-old drummer Jon Hiseman (introduced by Graham Bond) and bassist Tony Reeves joined Tomlin. In August '65, the group opened for Ornette Coleman's trio at Croydon's Fairfield Hall. That October saw the quartet record *Pendulum* at Lansdowne Studios in Holland Park, its tireless boss Denis Preston producing a translucent mix of reinvented standards ('A Night In Tunisia', 'But Not For Me' and 'Exactly Like You') and Taylor's 'Leeway', 'To Segovia' and title track. Released the following May on Columbia, project instigator Ian Carr called it 'a landmark in British jazz.' While the album enjoyed positive reviews, Taylor preferred to let 'the music speak for itself' rather than do interviews. Now a collectors item, I managed to track down *Pendulum*'s scarce CD reissue, which sounds both timeless and ahead of its time as it merges spacey free expression over solid rhythmic anchor and Taylor's virtuoso blues grounding, Tomlin a luminescent firefly dancing over his oblique piano flurries.

Soon after, Taylor's mind started unravelling as he showed worrying signs of depression and tried to gas himself. He discovered LSD, split with his wife and moved into a flat in Kew Gardens. Hiseman, who recalled him becoming 'progressively stranger in 1965', moved in, joined by Tomlin. The quartet, with Reeves replaced by Ron Rubin, Jack Bruce or both, played several gigs while waiting for *Pendulum* to be released, including a December ICA show also including Tomlin's Sextet, Graham Bond's Organisation and John Stevens' Trio. When the heroin-addicted figure of Graham Bond turned up on Taylor's doorstep in '66, it had a profound effect on the pianist's encroaching mental derailment; maybe the fatal catalyst. Some say Bond moved in, others they jammed and smoked together at flats around London. Taylor's escalating drug use and fraying mind were reflected by his smart-suited appearance changing as his hair and beard grew into what was described as a 'hippie-come-tramp.'

Graham Bond's own story marked another startling transformation from bright-eyed musical prodigy leading one of the UK's most potentially world-shaking bands into drug-sodden desperation. The parallels between the two musicians started early with Bond forever haunted by being abandoned after his October 1937 birth in Romford, Essex. He never knew who his parents were (although when he found out Aleister Crowley had fathered a child with a Basildon servant girl on his birth-date became convinced he was the Great Beast's son). After spending his first months in a Dr Barnardo's home, he was adopted by civil servant Edwin Bond and wife Edith, who called him Graham John Clifton Bond.

A lonely asthmatic kid bullied for being overweight, Bond started learning classical piano at six, taking up alto sax and yoga breathing at fourteen to defeat his asthma. On leaving school he became a refrigerator salesman and by the late 50s was infiltrating London's happening jazz scene; sporting a tight-fitting suit, using his salesman's patter and alienating purists with his avant-hurricane sax style. In 1960, he got noticed by Pete Brown, who contributed poems to Michael Horovitz's *New Departures* proto-fanzine, which had introduced beat poets, jazz and avant-garde artists to the UK after starting in '59. Horovitz was one of the organisers of 1965's Wholly Communion gathering of the tribes for London's nascent counterculture, headlined by Allen Ginsberg at the Royal Albert Hall. It's strangely reassuring to find him still out there in his 80s, gamely performing poems punctuated by enthusiastic kazoo. Introduced by my Helen, a close friend of his, we met in 2016 at the London Book Fair, where he cut a dash in purple hat as he recalled the Soho jazz scene through which Mike Taylor moved like a ghost and Graham Bond commanded with a bang.

'In 1960 I was quite a jazz fan and started putting my poetry to music with Live New Departures. I would go to all the night clubs, often from what I heard on the jazz grapevine. Pete Brown and Victor Schonfield were talking about a great new sax player who reminded them of Cannonball Adderley. So I went to the Troubadour in Brompton Road and there was Graham playing bebop classics. He was improvising wildly so Pete Brown and I started scatting with him. He was very good, very fluent. Dick Heckstall-Smith was part of our troupe and suggested adding Graham to some of the pickup groups who played with mine and Brown's poetry. Graham and Dick became good friends.

'The great thing about Graham was, when I first met him, even in the Troubadour where everybody else was in their underwear, he would be in a businessman's suit and talking like a salesman! He would harangue audiences, "I want you all to hear this, this is really great jazz music." But when he stuck his alto in his mouth, all that selling was coming out of his horn. There's a famous quote in the front of *The Horn* by John Clellon Holmes, where Charlie Parker is quoted saying, "If you haven't lived it, it won't come out of your horn." The way Graham played, all that experience, probably having knocked on doors over and over having to go through these routines, was coming out of his horn.'

While Taylor sculpted luminescent spatial textures coated in twinkling intricate subtlety, Bond was an elemental polar opposite after joining tenor stalwart Don Rendell in May '61 and appearing on the landmark *Roarin'*. 'It was one of those classic horn duos, like Ornette Coleman and Don Cherry,' says Horovitz. 'Don Rendell and Graham were every bit as wonderful when they were wailing. Graham was very good at turning on audiences and fellow musicians. He used every ounce of energy he could muster to make the best communication.'

As blues became the hip new sound, Heckstall-Smith joined Alexis Korner's Blues Incorporated in '62, followed by Baker (after Charlie Watts threw in his lot with the interval act at their Marquee residency). The members played spinoff gigs, including the Cambridge University Spring Ball where Heckstall-Smith and Baker were floored after a young double-bass player, just down from Scotland, asked to sit in. Jack Bruce soon joined Blues Incorporated.

As Horovotz points out, Live New Departures had already grabbed the Marquee. 'As usual, we poets are the unacknowledged forerunners who saw the talent. We had a residency at the Marquee in '62-63, before it became the home of Alexis Korner and British R&B. We featured all these great jazzers and, after we introduced Jack Bruce and Ginger Baker to Graham, we had the premiere of that quartet that also included Heckstall-Smith. I thought they would be brilliant and they were. They would become the Organisation but we presented that quartet long before Alexis.'

By October '62, harmonica tornado Cyril Davies had become unhappy with Blues Incorporated's jazzy direction and left to form his own R&B band. Stating he needed another 'genius' to replace Cyril,

Korner asked Bond, who had acquired a Hammond organ. In January '63, after Blues Incorporated moved their residency to the all-night Flamingo on Wardour Street, Korner gave Bond the interval spot with Bruce and Baker as an outlet for his uproarious Hammond incantations; British R&B's first experience of the organ's power, hotwired with an enormous Leslie speaker. Future prog gods such as Jon Lord, Keith Emerson and Rick Wakeman gaped at the audacious Bach quotations that electrified 'Wade In The Water', Bond's signature song.

'Everybody went to see what Graham was doing and picked up ideas from him,' says Brown. 'I always say the Graham Bond Organisation were to musicians what the Beatles were to the public at the time. He had all sorts of ideas for showmanship with bits of technology. At the end of that, you really felt like you had seen something major and beyond just Britain. It was a big thing that always felt very important.'

In February 1963, Bond told a disbelieving Korner he was leaving, taking Bruce and Baker with him. 21-year-old guitarist John McLaughlin joined from Georgie Fame's band. When early recordings from Klook's Kleek appeared on the *Solid Bond* double album in 1970, it positively sparked with the infernal alchemy crackling between the players, Cream's live electricity forged in Bruce and Baker's supercharged dog-fights. In August, Baker fired McLaughlin for being 'a miserable moaner' and Heckstall-Smith joined. Bruce switched to electric bass and the Graham Bond Organisation took their volcanic jazz-driven R&B around the country to ecstatic receptions. They recorded their first album for EMI-affiliated Columbia between gigs, *The Sound of '65* featuring blues standards, Bond originals and spiritual-derived 'Wade in the Water' and 'Early In The Morning'. Two songs were written by Jack Bruce (with fiancé Janet) at Bond's insistence. 'He allowed Jack to record his first proper vocals; that was the beginning of Jack as one of the greatest singers of all time,' says Brown. It was one of that year's best albums, even if I didn't see a copy until a '69 school trip allowed me to trawl bins at Oxford Street's HMV store and experience its brilliance in the listening booth. So my lifelong Bond fixation began.

Friction between Bruce and Baker erupted into the drummer sacking the bassist and threatening to stab him if he returned. 'Very weird,' says Brown. 'They were symbiotic, so they loved each other but also hated each other and did bad things to each other.' October '65's

There's A Bond Between Us featured tracks recorded when Bruce was still a member, including Bond's classic 'Walkin' In The Park' (destined to be a '69 45 debut for Jon Hiseman's Colosseum).

1966 saw darkness invade Bond's life, starting with the death of his adopted father and divorce papers from the wife he'd left four years earlier. He cloaked his troubles in heroin and magick, ballooning in size and pursued by police after failing to pay maintenance. He started wearing billowing robes and poring over Tarot cards; too much for Ginger, who left in June to form Cream with Eric Clapton from John Mayal's Bluesbreakers. An incredulous Jack Bruce quit Manfred Mann to accept Ginger's invitation (manager Robert Stigwood refused to entertain Bond as keyboardist). While Cream rose to superstardom, Bond felt abandoned again and plunged further into his downward spiral, replacing Baker with Hiseman but struggling to fit into rapidly-evolving times.

Anti-drugs and no-nonsense, Hiseman insisted Bond kick smack, which he did, going cold turkey on a boat up the River Shannon. After Hiseman coaxed £500 out of Polydor to record an album, Bond, Heckstall-Smith and the drummer went into Olympic after a show and recorded their scorching set until dawn. The deal collapsed when Bond spent the advance and couldn't pay the studio, leaving it unreleased until the afore-mentioned *Solid Bond*. Bond and Baker, along with Mike Taylor's group, played the seminal weekly Spontaneous Underground multi-media events held between January-June '66 at the Marquee; a UFO precursor organised by fearless trailblazer John 'Hoppy' Hopkins and Steve Stollman, brother of Bernard, who founded my beloved ESP-Disk label in New York. The early Pink Floyd were almost residents, cutting their teeth as they evolved from primitive R&B to interstellar space flights. Taylor also appeared at Spontaneous Music Ensemble dynamo John Stevens' newly-opened Little Theatre Club in Garrick Yard, which started to showcase jazz warriors who were too far out for Ronnie Scott's.

Taylor washed dishes at a Lyons tea-shop to make ends meet but, after *Pendulum* got great reviews, was asked for a follow-up. Tomlin had gone and Jack Bruce alternated or doubled with Rubin on bass on its mixture of standards ('All The Things You Are', 'While My Lady Sleeps', Billie Holiday's 'The End Of A Love Affair' and Victor Young's 1941 'Stella By Starlight') and ominously haunted Taylor originals like the evocative 'Two Autumns'. *Trio* was Taylor's last relatively sane act before acid tightened its hold on his fragile mind. As Hiseman puts it, 'Something shifted in him…and no one ever knew quite what. He created a world, pulled himself in it and shut the door…His mind was in another place completely, divorced from reality.' Taylor tried to obliterate his past by throwing away his self-scribed scores (including a suite derived from the mathematics that built the Pyramids for three drummers, probably Hiseman, Baker and Phil Seaman, called 'Horn, Gut and Skin'), which Hiseman retrieved from the trash.

Hiseman taped a jam session between Taylor, Bond on alto sax, Tony Reeves and Barbara Thompson on reeds which he described conjuring 'an intense slow-burning feeling', Taylor on scintillating form. Of these drugged-up jam sessions, Bond later said, 'It was extremely avant-garde for the period, but also very melodic. With Taylor, it was another Bach coming into existence.'

After splitting from Live New Departures in '65, Pete Brown was fronting his Poetry Group and, through his friendships with Baker and Bruce, started attending Cream rehearsals. As he told *Rolling Stone*, 'They asked me to come down to the studios to see if I could put words to these tunes they had. I tried a few things out and they said it seemed alright so we took it from there. (After trying writing with Ginger and Eric), Jack and I seemed to have large areas where we think alike.' After collaborating on 'I Feel Free', Brown and Bruce created 'Sunshine Of Your Love', 'SWALBR' and 'Dance The Night Away' for '67's *Disraeli Gears*.

This left Bond feeling old hat. 'Times change and Graham had not established himself enough,' says Brown. 'By the time you got to 1966, psychedelia crept in and, although Graham tried, his material didn't move with it yet. He got trapped in what was left of the R&B-jazz circuit with not much support. Dick and Jon stayed with him as long as they could but Graham was increasingly unreliable.'

Horovitz would see Bond hanging around Notting Hill, where the poet had lived since 1963. 'Graham seemed to have become very lost to various drugs. His body changed, his music changed, his clothes changed and his drug habits changed. He came to Notting Hill every now and again. He'd be wearing these hippy togas, beads and stuff that kind of covered up this almost grotesque obesity, resembling some kind of Buddha-like abbot. He was always perspiring, dripping with sweat. He was sort of happy sad. He'd say "Oh, give us a song Mike," so I'd sing one of the songs which I'd known him like a lot and he was almost weeping with delight. I was sorry Graham was so lost to drugs because he had been such an original, energetic jazz musician.'

Bond tried to interest Brown in making an album of sound poetry with Taylor, but both were too far gone. Another motivating cog in Bond's brain could have been his old pal Pete writing lyrics so successfully with Bruce. Bond asked if he could do the same for him. The pair sang songs Brown brought along that went so well Bond suggested recording them. 'Of course, I was delighted because Graham was an important figure in my life,' says Brown. 'So I wrote some songs, sang them through with him and he asked me to join the band, though I turned him down. That's what made me start singing because, although it was partly bullshit because he wanted me to write successful songs for him, he liked what I did. So I started doing it.'

Brown formed the Huge Local Sun to demo Bond-intended songs such as 'The Week Looked Good On Paper' and 'Late Night Tyre Service' for Polydor, lineup including Heckstall-Smith and John Mumford on horns, John McLaughlin, Danny Thompson and Laurie Allen. 'If someone I won't mention hadn't put a block on it, it would have been the best band of all time,' he told *Rolling Stone*. He formed the First Real Poetry Band after his one-off supergroup Neon Blacklist (guitarist Davey Graham, Bond, Heckstall-Smith, Mumford and Laurie Allan) got as far as one gig at Sheffield University before buckling under its weight. Brown greeted '69 with his Battered Ornaments, who included guitarist Chris Spedding, saxophonist George Khan and future Ronnie Lane collaborator Charlie Hart on organ. By '69, they had signed to Harvest and released coarsely-energised *A Meal You Can Shake Hands With In The Dark*.

By now, Taylor had left Kew Gardens and become a vagrant, sleeping on floors after shuffling around the west end with his hand drum. As his mental blizzard intensified, he slept rough in Richmond Park, conversing with the deer (sounding eerily close to the fate currently befalling Syd Barrett, now out of the band he formed by '69). Unable to cope with Taylor's disintegrating mentality, Dave Tomlin had left in early '66 and was teaching music at the London Free School, nexus of Notting Hill's embryonic counterculture that spawned the carnival and *International Times*. His next musical venture helped unleash the Third Ear Band on the world. After opening in December '66, UFO was in full swing as the counterculture's weekly scrambled hootenanny at an old hall in Tottenham Court Road. Opening night with Pink Floyd featured Tomlin's Giant Sun Trolley, started after he clicked with hand-drum maestro Glen Sweeney at the Free School. Sweeney was another veteran of the early '60s Soho jazz scene, who'd played R&B in bands and free jazz with trombonist Dick Dadem in Sounds Nova. Sometimes Taylor would join the duo with his hand drum but is most remembered for lying in the middle of the dancefloor for nearly a whole night.

On August 23 1967, Taylor was booked to play Ronnie Scott's Old Place but turned up barefoot and played his hand drum and pipe while Ron Rubin soloed. Now a shambolic figure aggressively declaring 'I'm a man of God!' if approached, he still appeared sporadically at the Old Place, chanting, banging and maybe touching piano. He returned several times, including the occasion captured by a photographer that showed him, long-haired and bearded, communicating deeply with the piano. Compared to the bespectacled young man poring over scores just five years earlier, it's tragic. As his unravelling accelerated, friends refused to open their front doors.

Intriguingly, Taylor is credited with co-writing Ginger Baker's tracks on Cream's '68 magnum opus *Wheels Of Fire,* 'Passing The Time', 'Pressed Rat and Warthog' and 'Those Were The Days'; largely dismissed as throwaway indulgences (but would have ensured royalties for Mike if he'd lived long enough). Taylor's last showing was two compositions (sublime Bill Evans-style 'Ballad', melancholic Segovia arrangement 'Study') on New Jazz Orchestra's *Le Dejeuner sur L'Herbe*, joining 16 musicians roped together by Hiseman, including Bruce, Ian Carr, Barbara Thompson and Trevor Watts. Taylor turned up out of it at an NJO gig at Conway Hall, Red Lion Square in November '68, supposed to play the middle spot with Hiseman. Barefoot and ragged, he didn't speak, preferring to communicate with hand gestures.

A few days later Taylor walked, fully-clothed, into the waves at Leigh-On-Sea. He was rescued by police and dried out but, on release, walked a mile along the coast towards Southend then repeated the exercise successfully. It took a week to identify him. His death seems like a final act to defeat dark forces he believed out to get him from the outside world he rejected. Dave Tomlin is probably closest to the truth when he says, 'The acid he had taken caused him to the see the world as a nightmare. Everywhere he looked he saw hell…That's why he walked into the sea. He was in terrible despair.' Awarded an open verdict at the inquest, Mike Taylor is buried at Southend-On-Sea cemetery.

Taylor's former drug buddy Graham Bond still had four years left on his doomed clock. Over fifty years later it's proved how childhood trauma, abusive or vanishing parents, bullying at school or other factors can later manifest in addiction or ill health; an issue rarely acknowledged when tabloid media glorifies someone's excesses as 'rock 'n' roll' or covers their death. Traumatic childhoods obviously contributed to Taylor and Bond's fragile mental conditions; not built for potent LSD or harder drugs.

'Yes, Graham was in certain amounts of pain,' concurs Brown. 'When we were sitting on a tube train going to a jazz-poetry gig, he said he had decided quite early on that he wanted to die, although he wanted to do it slowly just in case he changed his mind! That might have come from his experiences as an orphan. He didn't want to be a junkie, but there was also an element of romanticism, which I always called the Curse of Charlie Parker. Many mistakenly thought that because he was a junkie he played like that; completely wrong because he played like that anyway. People think in all forms of art that to be the great artist you have to be fucked up. And of course people attracted to various kinds of art are sometimes fucked up people! Graham was incredibly fucked up and didn't survive.

'When I started, I was self-destructive a la Dylan Thomas because I thought that's how you had to behave, but then I realised it was fucking killing me so I stopped! That was probably the best decision I ever made. I look at other people and think "Why did they abuse themselves so much and think they had to do that to produce what they were producing?" It had a totally negative effect. Graham, Dick, Jack and Ginger were supermen. They had this extraordinary constitution. I've never met people like that, who could do nine gigs a week and still drink like crazy and take fucking smack and Christ knows what. They were amazing musicians but happened to be around at a time when you worked nine days a week so got even better and better. Their constitutions also became unbelievably strong.'

By the time Hiseman and Heckstall-Smith formed Colosseum in October '68, Bond had been declared bankrupt, mainly owing maintenance payments, while singer-dancer Diane Stewart had become his second wife and musical collaborator. Mercury Records' London A&R chief Lou Reizner was a fan who brought him to the label; first to

42

write for Welsh proto-proggers Eyes Of Blue, contributing their LP *Crossroads Of Time*'s title track and 'Love Is The Law', which reflected his increasing Crowley obsession. Reizner also hired Bond as musical director for opportunistic London-based Dutch design duo Marijke Koger and Simon Posthuma who, while finagling themselves into the Beatles' inner circle with psychedelic paint-jobs, formed The Fool and would be recording in New York. Bond leapt at the chance but had to kick smack again before he could go. This time his River Shannon boat sprang a leak, leaving a maniacal Bond committed to a Dublin mental institution, says Pete Brown. He escaped after discovering it was 'an asylum for priests, who all thought they were Napoleon or Jesus. He said it was the worst place he'd ever been in, and he'd been in a few.'

After going cold turkey on the boat to the US, Bond joined The Fool's recording sessions. The Fool's album looked better than it sounded, its cover like their mural on the beleaguered Apple shop on Baker Street. '(Reizner) was a terrific guy,' recalls Brown. 'He was a big fan of Graham's, helped get him to America and arranged recordings. The Fool was a disaster because they were musically-useless psychedelic exploitation fodder who were impossible to work with. But that was his way in. He must've been there for over a year. He played on one of the great Screamin' Jay Hawkins albums; they got on really well and did gigs together. He also recorded with Hendrix at the Record Plant. He worked with all these great people who clearly respected him as a musician. It had a good effect and gave him new self-respect.'

Bond was still in the US when Mike Taylor washed up on the beach, recording two albums released later in '69. For now, he was an incendiary legend in my rapidly-evolving mental filing cabinet as I fantasised about at those steamy niteries where he'd held court. If only I could go to such a club...

Babylon and the Bayou

As Fugs-Holy Modal Rounders member Peter Stampfel started his monthly column in *Zigzag 4*, 'New Orleans! What magical visions that name conjures up! Jazz and the blues, swamps and voodoo queens...and never more so than recently, what with the music of Dr John and Creedence Clearwater Revival. These two groups have created a mythical place unrivalled for sheer magic. Creedence Clearwater recalls the days of the riverboats as they never were, but should have been.'

Dr John's *Babylon* is the year's most far out masterpiece, and sounds even weirder 50 years later. Mac Rebennack had materialised in early '68 as a mythical Sun Ra-like witchdoctor figure called Dr John the Night Tripper, spewed from a Louisiana swamp rather than outer space. Growing up in New Orleans' scabrous underworld of pimps, prostitutes and drugs, and doing jail time, Rebennack was steeped in the Crescent City's second line traditions and bar survival tactics when he hit LA's '65 Wrecking Crew studio scene. He developed the Dr John persona from a distant relative potentate who specialised in selling protective amulets, unveiling it on *Gris Gris* as a shimmering other-worldly ghost ritual conjuring psychedelic blues out of murky pulses, chants and narratives; the era's headiest psychedelic statement. *Babylon* remains his strangest, its dense fever dream cauldron, the Vietnam war and King-Kennedy assassinations provoking his stab at commenting on darkening times.

In his surreal liner notes, Dr John describes the title track's hallucinogenic swirl of jazz horns, exploding bombs and gongs as 'my own sick view of the world then – namely, that I felt our number was up. We were trying to get into something…with visions of the end of the world; as if Hieronymous Bosch had cut an album.' The theme continues on abrasive hoodoo vamp 'Black Widow Spider' and desolately adrift 'Twilight Zone', while the trippy 'Glowin' ends with the Doctor's pleading croak to 'keep on keeping on.' After relatively bright female incantation 'Barefoot Lady', closing pair 'The Patriotic Flag-Waiver' - a redneck-baiting acid cowboy anthem - and 'The Lonesome Guitar Strangler' scramble into rampant weirdness. *Rolling Stone* was non-plussed when they reviewed it months later: 'Try to imagine Mose Allison stoned and trapped in a swamp with a chorus of mistaken Baptist harmonies.' Irresistible. So sad to hear the world just lost its unique witch-doctor.

Creedence had appeared the previous year with their self-titled debut chiming with roots-homaging reactions against psychedelia's excesses ignited by Dylan's *John Wesley Harding*. The Band's *Music From The Big Pink* persuaded Eric Clapton to split Cream. Rock was getting simple again and CCR led the rustic charge looking to earth rather than spangled skies. *Bayou Country* appeared in the first week of

'69 as their clincher, led by 'Proud Mary' hitting the top ten. Around this time I was getting into this thing of trying to dig beneath the weird noises I'd loved in psychedelia and plug into a song's essence and finer points. Playing my Liberty 45 of 'Proud Mary' on turntable repeat, it was those guitars that got me, that churning riverboat momentum and beautifully-constructed solo inspired by Steve Cropper of Booker T. and the M.G.'s. Apparently, John Fogerty wrote the song after being discharged from the National Guard. 'Born On The Bayou' was inspired by an old movie called *Swamp Fever* and everything Fogerty could translate into a mythical childhood through Howlin' Wolf's gothic incantations; a creative virus that spread through 'Keep On Chooglin'' and 'Graveyard Train'.

The album boasted two eight-minute tracks, bringing me to another teenage quirk related to that obsession with copying down track listings. For some reason, I always experienced a curious buzz if an album boasted tracks over four minutes, holding the belief that anything below locked down the creative spirit. Tracks that strayed beyond the length of a normal pop song might capture those moments when genius struck, needing those extra minutes to provide room for maximum exploration. On their longer songs, Fogerty's concisely-constructed solos stretched like Cropper on juke-joint grooves. (Of course, a few years hence I realised the value of a two-minute killer). *Bayou Country* showed a band finding its feet then busting out. Creedence will release two more albums this year that consolidate the promise.

RECORDS

Peel's playing 'People You Were Going To', first single by Van der Graaf Generator. I've already been primed for their evocative kinetic magic and their singer's coarse-throated dramatics by last November's Peel session, when they performed the single 'Afterwards' and sinister 'Necromancer'. Buying the 45 is another matter. Released on Polydor, it's sitting in the Record Centre's singles bin one week then frustratingly gone by the following Saturday when I'd scraped up seven shillings and six pence to buy it. Later I find it's been withdrawn, but hopefully there'll be an album soon.

On the LP front, over at Stax, the earliest example of the blaxploitation soundtrack arrives with *Uptight*, created by Booker T with his M.G.'s. The movie was a '68 remake of John Ford's treatment of Liam O'Flaherty's novel *The Informer* with the IRA replaced by black activists in the Cleveland ghetto, 1921 troubles relocated there four days after Martin Luther King's assassination. With sizzling score, it's a taste of things to come.

Later described by the artist as 'overdubbed rather than played,' Neil Young's self-titled first solo album boasts future set stalwart 'The Loner' and 'The Old Laughing Lady', all bathed in Jack Nitsche's orchestral arrangements. Young's already on to the next, which will be released in May as *Everybody Knows This Is Nowhere*, recording with guitarist Danny Whitten, bassist Billy Talbot and drummer Ralph Molina, who call themselves Crazy Horse. Its future classics will include 'Cinnamon Girl', 'Cowgirl In The Sand' and epic 'Down By The River'.

We bought Led Zeppelin's self-titled first album (Atlantic) and loved its cheeky blues classic hijacks, like weighty screaming epic 'How Many More Times' amping up Howlin' Wolf's 'How Many More Years' and Page's cataclysmic bowed-string freakout on 'Dazed And Confused' (highlight of the New Yardbirds' transformative Peel session the previous year). Zep are said to have signed to Atlantic on Dusty Springfield's recommendation. Who knew how predatory they'd get, whether it was blues men finding their songs snaffled and retitled or under-age girls who fell at their feet?

Folk-rock is crystallised on Fairport Convention's often-magical second LP *What We Did On Our Holidays* (their first for Island). Hello to the ethereal purity of Sandy Denny, goodbye Ian Mathews, who leaves to form country-rock band Mathews Southern Comfort. Produced by Joe Boyd. ...*Holidays* is studded with FC classics, including 'Fotheringay', Dylan's 'I'll Keep It With Mine', guitarist Richard Thompson's 'No Man's Land', traditional 'Nottamun Town', Sandy's riveting 'She Moves Through The Fair' and rousing singalong 'Meet On The Ledge'. Loved the Judy Dyble lineup; this is something else.

The Beach Boys' wave seemed to have peaked with *Pet Sounds* three years earlier, largely lowered by the failure of Brian Wilson's smiley *Smile* to make it past his drug-fuelled traumas and patchy *Smile* finally emerging instead. *2020* (Capitol) is the one with the Charlie Manson rework. Iron Butterfly had fluttered out of San Diego in early '68 with *Heavy*'s uncertain psychedelic rock and baroque flavours before *In-A-Gadda-Da-Vida*, with side two's epic title jam sticking solos around its gigantic monster riff, struck a seismic chord when edited into a hit single, turning the album into one of the first mega-sellers, shifting over 30 million. Now it sounds oddly tame, but several barriers had been broken, including track lengths, laying a hard rock template. Ball attempted to do it with songs, melodic horror-rock, organ-woven prog and ethereal psycho ballads but lacked the weight to stop Iron Butterfly crash landing.

CHAPTER 2

FEBRUARY

JIMI TAKES OVER; OSCILLATIONS IN NEW YORK CITY WITH THE FUGS, ESP-DISK & SILVER APPLES; MOTOR CITY MADNESS WITH THE MC5; MARIANNE FAITHFULL'S BREAKTHROUGH MOMENT

The three most significant events of my teenage years happened between May '68 and the month we now enter. I've mentioned popping my Stones cherry and acquiring the record player I'd craved. The third is seeing Hendrix play the Royal Albert Hall on Tuesday the eighteenth at what will be his penultimate UK indoor concert. Everything that now happens can somehow be traced to these three seismic events (along with Mott The Hoople at Friars laying out my life's path later in the year).

My seat in the seventeenth row of Upper Orchestra East cost seven and six (same as a 45rpm single). It's close enough to see facial expressions from a downwards trajectory behind the action. This is my first big, high-volume rock gig, with Marshall amp lights glowing red and buzzing audience of freaks and fans waiting for the biggest star on the planet. I'm so excited to be seeing my ultimate hero in the living flesh I can barely sleep the night before and am a nervous coiled spring on the coach trip organised from my school with tickets miraculously acquired by Robin Pike.

Just one revelation from retracing my life here is that I heard about the Jimi outing from an announcement made in school assembly one morning by the deputy head master; the same Mr Lloyd-Jones who gave me a hard time about the length of my hair and is therefore responsible for me not having visited a barber since 1970. He even made me remove my jumper in full view of the school at one assembly because it had a round neck (and was emerald green). But, as Robin likes to point out, L.J. and headmaster K.D. Smith were actually quite liberal and tolerant, allowing him to run coach trips from the school and stage annual school dances (as we shall see). How Robin pulled off acquiring a coach-worth of Jimi tickets when the event was sold out is a story in itself, especially in this age of easy-click online booking. Back then you had to work to get desirable tickets. I'll let him tell it.

'The first time I saw Hendrix was in a Golders Green pub basement (the Refectory, Jan '67). I queued up outside with other people. There was no stage and only seats around the outside of the bar area. Hendrix came down and it was amazing really. The song I particularly remember was 'Like A Rolling Stone', a favourite of mine. I also saw Hendrix at the Saville when he played 'Sgt Pepper's Lonely Hearts Club Band', which had barely been released, then subsequently as well.

'I was known in the school as the person who could get tickets and ran my coach trips. A pupil in the sixth form came to see me and said he would like to run a coach trip to Hendrix at the Albert Hall and could I get the tickets? I said, "I'll see what I can do." I was training in child psychotherapy at the Tavistock Institute in Belsize Lane at that time and, because I was attending an evening session, was allowed Thursday afternoon off school. In 1969, I would generally drive up to London and do various things, so I drove up and parked outside the Albert Hall, which you could do then, and went to the box office. They said, "Completely sold out, no tickets at all." Then he said, "I think there's a phone number on the bottom of the big poster outside." So I went outside to the display and there was the phone number. Opposite at Queens Gate was a phone box. I put the money in the slot, rang the number and it was MAM, the agency and management company. I said, "I want to buy 30 tickets for the Jimi Hendrix concert at the Albert Hall; I have the cash." They said "Come to the office" and gave me its number in Regent Street. So I drove to Regent Street, found this side door and upstairs I went. There was a little window, you rang the bell and this guy appeared. I said "I'm the guy who rang about Jimi Hendrix tickets." I had a big envelope with the money all in small change because everyone had given seven and six. I gave him the cash and he gave the tickets. I didn't go on the coach trip for various reasons. I went to the next week's one that was filmed. I was right at the front and it was just amazing because he did a lot of theatrical stuff for the film.'

This was six days later, when the Experience returned to the Albert Hall for a second show added after the first one sold out. Some was released on the *Experience* albums and filmed for a movie that's still never happened. On 'Room Full Of Mirrors' he was joined by percussionist Rocky Dzidzournou, Chris Wood and Dave Mason, the encores of 'Purple Haze' and 'Wild Thing' seeing Jimi smashing his amps and '67 sunburst Strat as pandemonium takes over. There's chaos in Jimi's brain, despite then living in relative domestic bliss with Kathy Etchingham at Handel's old building on Brooke Street. Hendrix lore has always dictated that second show was fantastic and the first only average but, back in Upper Orchestra East, I've bought the programme for half a crown and, between support bands Mason, Capaldi, Wood and Frog and Soft Machine, read Jimi declaring, 'I am what I feel. I play as I feel and I act as I feel....You can say my music is erotic and whatever you like, I don't care. What others say or think just doesn't worry me. People still mourn when other people die. That's self-pity. The person who is dead isn't crying. When I die I just want people to play my music, go wild, freak out, do anything they want to do. Enjoy themselves. The mechanical life – where cities and hotel rooms all merge into one – has killed that enjoyment for me. So I've just got to get out. Maybe to Venus or somewhere. Some place you won't be able to find me.'

This is already much different from seeing Donovan here a year earlier. Then the support band was Tyrannosaurus Rex, whose magical moon incantations eclipsed the headliner's big band jazz delusions. Tonight, it's Mason, Capaldi, Wood and Frog, the Winwood-less Traffic playing loose jams, followed by Soft Machine, now down to the three-piece lineup of singer-drummer Robert Wyatt, keyboardist Mike Ratledge and bassist Hugh Hopper. They play complex excursions from their just-released *Volume Two* and Wyatt does his 'Moon In June' vocal outing that will appear on the breakthrough *Third*. I'm too in a state of high anticipation for Jimi to take as much notice as I should.

After Soft Machine, the Marshall mountain grows and another drum-kit moves up. Those red lights glow as simmering excitement swells until erupting into a roar. There's Jimi, a smiling psychedelic space peacock in his feather-festooned black hat, afghan waistcoat, flowing turquoise shirt and black strides with patterns down the sides. He plugs in his white Stratocaster and steps up to the microphone.

For nearly 50 years I've strained to recall every nuance of that pivotal night. Although avidly collecting Hendrix bootlegs since Richard Branson sold me my first one at his original Virgin shop (on Oxford Street above a shoe shop) in 1970, this show has always been overshadowed by the following week's performance released legally. No tapes were known to exist but, just as I started this book, an item appeared on E-bay containing a soundboard mix of the whole show! It confirms that, far from being the morose shambles painted in press and biographies, backed by Mitchell and Chas Chandler, Jimi was on blazing form, leaving an uptight Redding and unusually slothful Mitch in the dust as he soared, scorched and shivered the rafters of the venerable old hall.

At the time, many simply couldn't get past an almost immobile Jimi playing his ass off instead of dry-humping his guitar and setting it ablaze. Instead, he stood majestically static as he scaled monolithic blues mountains with a barely detectable sense of anger and frustration. He seemed bathed in a supernatural charisma that wasn't the stage lights, moving in shimmering slow motion like a lightning rod conducting sounds from other planets, bringing the house down with every flick of a bejewelled wrist or screaming eagle star-wail.

The bootleg means I can report his first words to us audience: 'It'll take a minute and a half to…tune our instruments here and there and all the gang watching us do it, you know…You don't mind me talking to you tonight? We was playing for, oh let's see, we was playing in, er in America, right…Then we played Germany. We're very tired and so we haven't practised at all, but (what) we're gonna do is jam, okay?' He then leads the band into work-in-progress instrumental 'Tax Free'. After its mid tempo limbering up, he thanks the audience for 'staying this long' and announces 'Fire' ('a blast from the past…since we don't know anything else; let me stand next to your little old lady and pass the j…let me stand next to your fire!'). After that scorcher, he eases into the slow blues safety zone with 'Getting My Heart Back Together Again' (soon to be retitled 'Hear My Train A-Comin'). The tape confirms my feeling on the night that, far from getting muddied up by the RAH's infamously dreadful acoustics, the natural reverb gave Jimi's guitar an extra echo chamber as he roared out of the abyss with sky-scraping power and resonance, striving to hit his equivalent of Sun Ra's space chord; that one note that will crack the universe and unleash waiting swarms of liberated ecstasy and spiritual catharsis. This was one great solo that, after Jimi's customary live marination process, will manifest in the peak version at Santa Monica Civic in spring '70. So brightly did Jimi flame on, you just didn't notice the sluggish rhythm section floundering below. Phwoar.

Later, Jimi's stationary stance throughout the concert was blamed on too much pre-show cocaine, but from where I'm sitting his whole set comes across as the most potent demonstration yet of his frustration at being expected to showboat through hits for crowds expecting the wild man of rock. He seems happier stretching out on these epic blues lifelines, dispensing the 'Fire's almost dismissively. After those long scuffling years honing chops, showmanship and patter on America's gruelling 'chitlin' circuit', delivering a show for his paying audience is still ingrained in his DNA, as with any fellow performers on that little-highlighted scene, from James Brown and George Clinton to countless others who struggled but never broke out of the backwoods dives and funky ghetto bars. Jimi introduces another requisite 'blast from the past' with 'We'd like to dedicate it to somebody's girlfriend; we don't know who she is yet, but let's see now, we'll find out later on after the show...a thing called 'Foxy Lady'.' As that instantly-recognisable feedback note swells like a rhino's boner, Jimi adds, 'You wouldn't understand, not right now, anyway.' 50 years later, 'Foxy Lady' remains the ultimate lust anthem; no tight-trousered shrieker will ever come close. Tonight's version is a stone killer with one of those deadly closing salvos where Jimi can't stop coaxing libidinous screams from his guitar.

The next song is introduced as a 'slow blues...recorded in 1778 in the Benjamin Franklin studios, a thing that was called "Red House".' One of the only songs to remain in Jimi's set for his whole performing career, this is one killer version; his guitar swooning, crying, shouting and gliding through a midway swinging jazz tempo stretch for twelve blistering minutes. Nobody else ever played with such untamed emotional blood-letting. After a stream-of-consciousness explanation that affirms 'Sunshine Of Your Love' as a current set staple in tribute to recently-spilt Cream, Jimi invokes a squalling 'Spanish Castle Magic' that, after his first starburst solo drops into the riff that will underpin 'Message To Love', becomes a vehicle for an astral jazz solo that seems to be looking for the gate into that other dimension that always seems to bother him, dropping to a drizzling blizzard aboard a malfunctioning flying saucer that lands back in the song eleven minutes later. Jimi sounds bursting to break free of his lumpen rhythm section, perhaps longing for the guitar concerto he's planning with New York violinist-arranger Al Brown or the 'sky church music' he's been talking about in the press. By this point, he had still hardly moved but, as this epic wonder attests, had higher things on his mind than shagging his amp for the masses.

Jimi fields requests for 'Purple Haze' and other faves from the baying crowd. 'Hold on, hold on, I'm gonna try one that's silly,' he says, striking up roaring static that becomes 'The Star Spangled Banner', delivered like a US jet in Vietnam napalming an innocent village. While the Woodstock version will be forever branded as the defining moment of the 60s, this is the first the UK knew he was doing it; a mind-blowing shock. Although faster than Woodstock, even without the towering early dawn majesty, Jimi shows he's already got the machine guns and rocket's red glare in place set to stun. This becomes the intro to 'Purple Haze', which seems to flick a switch in Jimi's psyche to provide another memorable moment I can still picture as he drops into a squat-thrust, humps a rumbling snake growl from his groin and rubs his guitar neck to ignite the dazzling sonic fusillade that brings the crowd to its feet. Still the greatest riff in rock; the one that started everything, given a savage kicking tonight.

That's it. Mouth hanging open, I watch Jimi swing his guitar over his head into the air and into a roadie's waiting hands before sauntering down the tunnel to the dressing rooms. There's enough noise from the crowd to bring the trio back. 'We're up here to sing for you. Thanks for staying with us this long; it's really outta sight,' declares Jimi before unbuckling a searing 'Voodoo Chile (Slight Return)', flaunting new riffs and molten lava runs (only song played from *Electric Ladyland*, released five months earlier). A final guitar rogering is Jimi's way of saying goodbye and seems to send him through several galaxies in minutes. Heard now, I can't believe that last solo, almost howling for its life before shattering into one final metallic roar.

Hendrix cherry popped to smithereens, I had no idea I'd witnessed the beginning of the end for the Experience and it was the last time I'd ever see Jimi. In 1986, *Creem* asked me to do Jimi for a special they were doing called *Guitar Heroes*. I wrote, 'Much of the showmanship had been dropped in favour of long, bluesy jams, delivered with bowed concentration. It was the best show I'll ever see. At times it seemed that the roof of the old building would roar off into the starry night. Hendrix's blues were awesome, his high keening screams wrenched the heart from its socket. The growling violence of 'Voodoo Chile (Slight Return)' was like being in the electric chair. His feedback created sounds which have never been repeated.'

A few days after the show, Jimi discovered he couldn't open his club on New York's Eighth Street because he's black and there's already four Mob-run Italian joints on that strip. His engineer Eddie Kramer convinces Mike Jeffery the studio Jimi initially envisioned should occupy the whole space. Work will now start on Electric Lady and will take over a year to complete, cost around a million dollars (much coming from mega-festivals he'll be forced to play to finance it). Tragically, he will only get to use it for a few days.

Welcome to New York City

In 1969, the Big Apple is an untouchable forbidden metropolis; dirty, dangerous, crime-ridden, and unspeakably glamorous. I'd first become aware of it watching King Kong get blasted off the Empire State Building and as Gotham City in *Batman* comics, before discovering the great music that had come from its corners, clubs and studios. New York had already given us the Ronettes and Hendrix when the Velvet Underground manifested singing about the gutter-level action on its streets, mentored by the fascinating Andy Warhol, who appeared on UK teatime TV like a pale trembling ghost. The city's dark allure further crystallised in my teenage beehive mind when reading about the impossibly exotic creatures who resided there, including Sun Ra, the jazz pianist who claimed to come from Saturn; Moondog the blind Viking statue who recited his poems on the streets over self-invented instruments; Nico, the beautiful model, actress and singer who fleetingly elevated the Velvet Underground and stepped out with Brian Jones at Monterey; the Greenwich Village folk scene that gave the world Bob Dylan, Fred Neil and Phil Ochs, before Tim Rose and Tim Hardin carved their names in its gnarled trunk; a record label called Douglas that got Hendrix on the same LP as Timothy Leary and would soon change musical history with Harlem's revolutionary Last Poets, who Jimi recorded with.

That was just the tip of a sky-scraping iceberg. On a broader level, a mysterious underground record label called ESP-Disk seemed to epitomise the city. 'You never heard such sounds in your life' shouted the sleeves on albums by Sun Ra, marauding Lower East Side activist poets The Fugs, mysterious acid-folkies Pearls Before Swine, speed-crazed oddities the Holy Modal Rounders, shambolic proto-punks the Godz and totemic jazz greats including my beloved Albert Ayler. If the Velvets soundtracked New York's night-stalking streets, ESP-Disk bottled its restless soul and jazz impulses, its primitively-packaged LPs shimmering like sirens on a Greek rock when I started exploring the exotic grottos of Kensington Market. For months too I would gaze at the shrink-wrapped sleeves in the windows of One Stop Records (whose mailing list I subscribed to when I didn't have a record player) before daring to venture inside and hear them. ESP-Disk occupied a luminous dug-out in my brain that has burned ever since and still glows quietly in the corner, ready to reignite whenever called.

The label was started in 1964 by lawyer Bernard Stollman, who vowed to record jazz's 'new thing' after being lightning struck by an Albert Ayler performance. This most underground of labels flew a defiantly countercultural stance with its DIY presentation and fearless representation of New York's jazz uprising, giving first airings to Ayler and Pharaoh Sanders before developing its rock roster. Stollman had little regard for trivialities like accounting, keeping cash flow going by fronting sessions and production. Most ESP sessions took place at RLA Studios, run by producer-engineer Richard Alderson in a condemned block on West 65th Street that would make way for Lincoln Center. During his seven-year tenure, Alderson partnered with Harry Belafonte, who invested in state-of-the-art studio machinery, renaming it Impact. With promotion centred on college radio, jazz and underground publications, most albums sold a few hundred, although epochal releases were repressed as new markets opened in Europe. The barely-existent royalties may have clouded the label's reputation but, more recently, it's been recognised how many crucial artists or eccentrics would have remained undocumented without ESP. As Stollman explains in Jason Weiss's *Always In Trouble: An Oral History Of ESP-Disk: The Most Outrageous Record Label In America*, 'they gained something priceless. They had an album…It was a galvanic thing that launched them. Our aim was to document the work of the community of newly emerging composer-performers of the generation who were identified as free improvisational, who had followed bebop and its immediate successors, such as Coltrane. ESP filled that need.'

If New York City still seemed like Conan Doyle's Lost World in '69, the following years saw me falling deeper under its spell through escalating media coverage before witnessing and meeting leading figures from its next generation of artists, rockers and iconoclasts, including the New York Dolls, Ramones, Blondie and Suicide, at the same time discovering the city's disco alter ego that flourished on the

55

same streets as a crucial parallel underground. New York's subliminal pull grew even stronger when the 80s brought hiphop, electro and pioneering radio station tapes. The itch became a mad, inflamed rash, exacerbated by those visiting the city returning with epiphanies that inevitably started with that first senses-blasting glimpse of the Manhattan skyline in the yellow cab drive from the airport and unique energy sizzling under the sidewalks, along with an overwhelming selection of gigs, clubs and events; every night of the week around the clock.

My desire could only be quenched by experiencing this ultra-cool cultural hotbed myself and, in 1983, I finally made it over there. I was beyond excited that memorable morning waking up for the first time in Manhattan at my good friend Marc Mikulich's 11th Street apartment (who I'd met a few years earlier when he was in the UK and gave me a single by his Band Of Outsiders, one of the city's great lost groups). As he showed me around the East Village with another friend called Steve Mirkin, I was like an excited puppy running around, almost humping the downtown landmarks. First stop was St Mark's Place and Sounds, heaven's own record store, where I met NY scene veteran Binky Phillips and got a banana copy of the first Velvets album for 30 bucks. The shop was over the road from the blue-painted Polish National Dom Navadowy, aka the Dom, where Warhol had hosted his Exploding Plastic Inevitable shows.

My soul felt like a massive door had been flung open as I stood on the sidewalk outside Max's Kansas City (even if it was now a corporate-friendly gym or something), gazed at the Five Spot jazz epicentre and stood in the same St Mark's Bar where the Stones shot the 'Waiting On A Friend' video, basking in the knowledge these were the same cracked streets many of my heroes had roared or staggered along in previous decades. Within a few weeks I got bold enough to venture deeper into Alphabet City, finding that Ed Sanders' old Peace Eye bookshop, infamous jazz club Slug's Saloon and Sun Ra's former Sun Palace were now death-stalked ruins overrun by psychotic drug dealers and desperate junkies. It was an electrifying buzz experiencing the around-the-clock black radio stations and even walking along Fourteenth Street past the old Academy Of Music (now the Palladium) to Union Square subway station, Lou Reed's 'If you go down to Union Square, you never know what you might find there' ringing around my cranium. I became obsessed with New York's past history and still am now it's a

56

different city. Be warned that at any given opportunity I'm liable to fly off on historical flights about a particular neighbourhood or building.

In '86, I made New York my home for the next five years, at one point residing at 437 Twelfth Street - the famous Poets Building where neighbours included Allen Ginsberg, Richard Hell and avant-disco pioneer Arthur Russell. It was still the most exciting city on the planet; dark, bad, dangerous and a lot more. I explored every corner of Manhattan by foot, from Spanish Harlem to the Lower East Side, experiencing its spectrum of highest highs and lowest lows while living out the first Velvet Underground album. I witnessed everything from countless immortal sights, treasure-packed record shops and epoch-making gigs to hospital wards, methadone clinics, police cells and the most dangerous spots in Alphabet City.

Returning to Aylesbury in 1990 after a savage subway mugging, New York remained my home-from-home as I returned to visit my son Daniel Lee, before it started transforming into today's giant mobile phone as dollars and artifice started dulling the subterranean artistic currents that once drove it like an engine, along with sky-high rents, Mayor Giuliani's 'zero tolerance' anti-crime blitz and long-running establishments replaced by a plague of juice bars. Having long stopped exploring New York from the inside, I now look retrospectively at the broader picture from the outside, first-hand experience replaced by finding out what was actually going on around whatever burnt-out block, dive bar or scuzzy club I'd visited. All this knowledge achieved some fulfilment in projects like my sadly-aborted *Watch The Closing Doors* compilation or writing books on the New York Dolls, Blondie and Suicide.

This '69 February in New York, San Francisco firebrand Bill Graham attempts to showcase the city's more out there artists who don't fit his normal Fillmore East rock bills with an event featuring Silver Apples, Allen Ginsberg, Norman Mailer and The Fugs. After readings from the authors, The Fugs' profane brand of lacerating street punk poetry disintegrates when their acid-fried bassist, deciding he's transformed into Paul McCartney, insists on playing the Beatles songbook and is dragged off to Bellevue hospital. Silver Apples take the stage at one in the morning.

Within months, both Fugs and Apples will have imploded, leaving their disparate legacies as two of New York's most innovative bands after their final first phase albums go up like farewell flares; Silver

Apples' second album *Contact* predicting music's electronic future and The Fugs' *The Belle Of Avenue A* wheezing death throes of the era they'd enlivened and broken ground for.

New York's counterculture revolution was always diametrically opposed to the west coast's peace and love idealism. Like it did with all movements, the city injected its own street realism, cynical humour and fearless trailblazing, sending shockwaves that often ranked highest on the long-term seismograph. Before Warhol and the Velvet Underground set the city on course for the next decade, New York's counterculture had wriggled in the Dylan-ignited West Village folk boom while the Fugs' ramshackle gaggle of degenerate beat poets rose from the east, celebrating unfettered sexual liberation and recreational drug use as they lobbed lyrical Molotov cocktails at a government plunging its country into war. Led by Ed Sanders and Tuli Kupferberg, the Fugs had been releasing LP broadsides - on Folkways, ESP-Disk and now Warner Brothers – since 1965 but were throwing in the towel after that relatively subdued swansong.

'(The Fugs) invented the Underground,' wrote Miles in *International Times*. Lester Bangs called them 'the first truly underground band in America.' Ten years before CBGB's Bowery uprising, they pioneered punk-style disruption under their Zap! Zap! Total Assault On The Culture banner; unable to play instruments, swearing live and on record, getting thrown off record labels, banned from venues and boasting a fat FBI file. The Fugs caused deeper-rooted moral panic than the Sex Pistols ever would and, by planting graphic urban narratives over primitive beats, pioneered hiphop too.

Born in Kansas City in 1939, Sanders got his literary epiphany reading Ginsberg's *Howl* at seventeen. He dropped out of Missouri University and enrolled at NYU, graduating with a degree in classics in 1964. Ed was drawn to the artist community in the Lower East Side, writing his first poem in jail in '61 after trying to board a Polaris submarine during an anti-nuclear war demonstration. Flying the motto 'I'll print anything,' he started mimeographing *Fuck You: A Magazine Of The Arts*, like a New York gutter version of Michael Horovitz's *New Departures*, that ran for thirteen issues with contributions from William Burroughs, Gregory Corso, Artonin Artaud and Andy Warhol.

Before the lower Manhattan neighbourhoods between Houston and 14th Streets and Avenues A to D became the East Village - one of New York's most devastated, dangerous no-go dope areas in the 70s and 80s

- it was just a slum with cheap rents. Ed moved into the former kosher meat shop at 383 East Tenth Street and Avenue C where he opened the Peace Eye bookshop. With Allen Ginsberg living over the street, it became a focal point for writers, artists and musicians. Struck by Dylan, Ed imagined setting his words to music. After clicking with radical poet next-door neighbour Tuli Kupferberg, he asked him to write for his magazine. Born in 1923, Tuli had graduated from Brooklyn College in 1944, starting his own magazines *Birth* and *Yeah* along with writing books including *1001 Ways To Beat The Draft*. Ed and Tuli went on Civil Rights marches, wondering how protest songs would sound mated with pop music they danced to at the Dom then setting their lyrical barrages of hedonism and anti-war railing against folk, proto-psych and traditional Yiddish melodies. They recruited poet Ken Weaver, a former Cold War Air Force spy who'd moved to New York in '64 who became third leg of the group's 'crazy tripod'. Initial musical accompaniment was provided by warped speed-folk duo the Holy Modal Rounders, whose fiddler Pete Stampfel was impressed when he turned up at Peace Eye to find the pair had written around 60 songs they couldn't play. 'It predated the punk thing by ten years,' he said later. Hailing from Milwaukee, Stampfel arrived in New York in '59, hooking up with guitarist Steve Weber from Philadelphia in '63 through partner Antonia. Discovering a mutual love of amphetamine, Stampfel and Weber formed the Rounders, releasing a 1964 album on Prestige (on which 'Hesitation Blues' 'I got the psychedelic blues' was first use of the p-word on an LP).

After Tuli christened The Fugs from a shagging euphemism in Norman Mailer's *The Naked And The Dead*, they played their first gig at Peace Eye in February '65, Warhol contributing floral cloth wall hangings, crowd including Burroughs, Ginsberg and other luminaries. The Fugs then built a following invading local galleries, poetry readings and the Bridge Theatre on St Mark's Place. 'We were sort of a punk band,' said Tuli. 'Our idea was that anybody could do this.' The band's gleefully-depraved onslaught mixed fierce opposition to the Vietnam war with a fun-packed menu of sex, drugs and primal rock that made the East Village a hipper alternative to the campfire gentility of Greenwich Village folk. It was anti-folk before the term existed. 'I would love to say that this was a deliberate plot and we had a vast scheme to change American civilisation but part of it was just to have fun,' said Sanders. 'I was a poet and I thought (The Fugs) was a joke and a game that would be over in a few months. But then it went on and on.'

The Fugs' first career boost came from legendary Harry Smith, who'd given the folk boom its raw materials with '52's *Harry Smith's Anthology Of American Folk Music* drawn from his extensive 78s collection. 'I knew him first as a filmmaker, artist, anthropologist and scholar of string figures,' Ed told me in 2009 (here begging the question how the 15-year-old me would've reacted if told he'd be chatting with a Fug 40 years later). 'He would hang out at my bookstore beginning in early 1965. From things he said when I formed The Fugs I became aware of his connection with Folkways Records. He pitched us to (label boss) Moe Asch as a jug band and the rest, as they say, is history.'

Usually, I'm allergic to the 'rest is history' get-out cliche but make an exception in Ed's case. *The Village Fugs Sing Ballads and Songs of Contemporary Protest, Points of View and General Dissatisfaction* was recorded in two afternoon sessions at Cue Studios on 46th Street in April and September '65, hoisting the Fugs' scabrous manifesto over basic percussion and primitive psych-folk. 'Slum Goddess' and 'Supergirl' were crudely-profane street vignettes, Tuli's 'Nothing' predated Richard Hell's 'The Blank Generation' as downtown nihilist anthem, 'I Couldn't Get High' contained the first mention of LSD in a song and William Blake was set to music on 'Ah, Sunflower Weary Of Time' and 'How Sweet I Roamed From Field to Field'.

After the album made 142 on the *Billboard* charts, The Fugs signed to ESP, who reissued it and asked for a second (then released the unreleased bulk of the very first session as *Virgin Fugs* in '67 without asking permission). After leaving the Fugs, Peter Stampfel had formed an electric band in '67 called the Swamp Lillies with struggling writer Sam Shepard on drums, guitarist Bill Barth and Boston-born singer Nancy Jeffries. When it disintegrated, Barth and Jeffries formed the intoxicating Insect Trust while Shepard, Rounder Steve Weber and pianist Richard Tyler created the Moray Eels, playing songs such as 'Black Leather Swamp Nazi'. In the meantime, ESP released the magnificently-deranged *Indian War Whoop* after the Rounders reformed, going on to record *The Moray Eels Eat The Holy Modal Rounders* for Elektra.

Even if The Fugs left ESP under a cloud of acrimony by '67, they were grateful to be introduced to Richard Alderson, expanding their sound at his studio through January-February '66 (just after Sun Ra had recorded his *Heliocentric Worlds* LPs for the label). The studio band included pianist Lee Crabtree (who later played on Pearls Before Swine's *Balaklava*), and guitarists Vinny Leary and Pete Kearney. *The Fugs* (reissued as *The Fugs Second Album*) straddled garage-psych on 'Group Grope', rollicking folk-rock on 'Dirty Old Man' and the abrasive jollity of Tuli's anti-war 'Kill For Peace' will always be relevant. As Ed told me, '"Kill For Peace" is as old as the *Iliad*, the Roman raids on the Parthians of ancient Iraq and as new as CIA drone planes firing missiles in valleys in Afghanistan.' The album shocked everybody by reaching 89; first underground LP to make the top 100. The Chicago branch of the FBI contacted its Washington HQ asking if The Fugs could be prosecuted for un-American activities. The FBI ruled they were not obscene but kept them under surveillance and on file with the likes of Ginsberg.

After a stretch at the Astor Place Playhouse on Lafayette Street closed after The Fugs burned a Lower East Side flag to show how innocuous flag-burning could be, they secured a June '66 residency at the Players Theatre on MacDougal Street, where they staged riotous shows over the next 18 months, their lewd disorder attracting backstage visitors including Richard Burton, Peter O'Toole, Tennessee Williams and Leonard Bernstein. Dylan and Paul McCartney became fans along with a young guitarist playing downstairs in Café Wha? called Jimmy James, then working up the stage act that would seduce Chas Chandler and find him fame in the UK as Jimi Hendrix. The Fugs gave him his first fuzz-box.

After Atlantic Records' Jerry Wexler requested demos, with licence to be controversial, he agreed to an album, recorded under the working title *The Fugs Eat It* with a band including drummer Bernard Purdie, bassist Chuck Rainey and guitarist Eric Gale. Wexler unexpectedly threw them off the label as Warner Brothers had been negotiating to buy Atlantic, who feared The Fugs would harm its selling potential. Reprise Records boss Mo Austin liked the band enough to sign them (after gaining approval from label owner Frank Sinatra). Ironically, Reprise was owned by Warners.

The Fugs played TV shows, festivals, gigs and Ed let go of Peace Eye. Asking him about this insane time, he replied, 'Ever been picketed by right wing nurses, as we were in California in 1967? We had to have a civil liberties attorney ready to be called when we toured. And while most fans were very friendly, now and then there was hostility. Plus the

FBI tried to get the Justice Department to indict us. The era was wonderful, but had its whiffs of teargas and danger.'

The Fugs' most infamous antic was exorcising the Pentagon in October '67; Ed read an exorcism composed with Harry Smith before leading a mass chanting of 'Out demons out!' with hippies sticking daisies in army rifle barrels. Some of it was captured on *Tenderness Junction*, which displayed a lusher high-tech sound with Warren Smith arranging strings. 'Turn On Tune In Drop Out' featured lyrics by Timothy Leary and Ed's graphic 'War Song' replaced 'Kill For Peace' frivolity. The Fugs toured Europe, playing the Roundhouse and charging through a frenetic 'Turn On Tune In Drop Out' on Friday tea-time BBC culture show *How It Is*, which featured John Peel and Oz's Richard Neville expounding as regular columnists and was essential viewing every week.

The Fugs started recording their next album with a $25,000 budget. Ambitious and extravagant, *It Crawled Into My Hand Honest* honed collages with clips of exorcisms, chants and prayers, introduced Ed's redneck persona Johnny Pissoff in his growing fixation with 'Beatnik country' and serenaded a 'river of shit'.

The Belle of Avenue A was The Fugs' last spurt for 15 years, stripping down the sound on Tuli's 'Bum's Song' as a return to howling radical modern folk from the street. Ed continued his country fixation on 'Yodelling Yippie', while Weaver's ferocious 'Four Minutes To Twelve' was a nerve-shredding indictment of the President; '...there's a madman at the wheel.' (See, they're still relevant). But the end was nigh. After a last show on February 22 in Austin, Texas, the Fugs stepped down after years of police harassment and hostile threats; the worst Ed being mailed Dostoevsky's *The Idiot* housing a fake bomb, followed by a telephoned death threat. 'It took bites out of our spirit,' he told me, burnt-out and tired of being a 24-hour Fug, now suffering 'rock zone fatigue.' Tuli opposed the split, feeling the group had more to do, but continued as a solo performer, publishing books and poetry. Before moving to Woodstock in '74, Sanders released two beatnik country solo albums, *Sanders' Truckstop* and *Beercans On The Moon*, then continued writing books and poetry, including definitive Manson tome *The Family* and '75's autobiographical *Tales Of Beatnik Glory*.

What did he think of 21st century New York? 'The main difference, is no more rent control! Without genuine rent control, or cheap rents, then the kind of Culture of Spontaneity and the building of what I call

Goof City is impossible. So, "back then", say 1960-1969, the food was cheap; the pot and peyote were cheap; the beer and tequila were cheap. Cheap but exquisite. The living was as the song says, easy. Things were exploding in performance and in combining various art forms: Civil Rights marches; the birth of folk/rock; happenings, the rise in recording technology: two track to four track to eight and sixteen track in just a couple of years. The invention of the glorious wah wah pedal in late 1966! Good sound systems so that you could star the vocals!'

Moon Tunes

While the Fugs were predicting punk, a few blocks over, between the Albert Hotel near Broadway and Max's Kansas City on Park Avenue South, Silver Apples were laying templates for a future more distant. The psychedelic musical ectoplasm wrangled from a nest of old oscillators by Simeon Coxe as he exhaled disembodied vocals over octopus-like super-drummer Danny Wilson's heartbeat pummelling on Silver Apples' '68 self-titled debut album sounded like nothing else on Earth. Refining the process in a better studio, *Contact* is the duo's masterpiece, although Simeon huffed away my enthusiasm in 2012. 'I find it hard to get my head around that. To me, we were just limping along doing the best we could with our limitations in terms of the equipment and the abilities we had. I never thought of us as being ground-breaking.'

To grasp the colossal significance of the ground Silver Apples were harvesting then, it should be pointed out that Kraftwerk were still tootling flutes at arts labs, Alan Vega had not yet met Martin Rev to form Suicide and the Velvet Underground were pulling back on their frenzied experimentation after John Cale's departure. By '69, most psychedelic bands had binned visionary new strata in favour of more earthy hard or progressive rock. Silver Apples had always been out on their own, with only the lone wolves that New York still had in packs for company, their pulsing rhythms lashed with avant-garde dissonance predating German motorik, electronic dance music, hiphop and indeed Suicide, one of the few outfits they influenced immediately instead of decades later. 'Watch out for Silver Apples; they are the next thing,' declared a besotted John Lennon on TV.

Born in New Orleans and growing up a promising artist, Simeon hit New York City after turning 21 in 1959, finding the city on the cusp of its most shape-shifting decade, but littered with human relics of past revolutions. He joined those still gravitating to the Cedar Street Tavern on University Place, a fixture that opened in 1866 on Cedar Street before relocating to Eighth Street in 1933. In 1955, when the bar was purchased by local butcher Sam Diliberto and window washer brother-in-law Joe Provenzano, it became a favourite artists' watering hole as a cheap, low-lit spot away from squares and tourists. Described on Lori Zimmer's Art Nerd New York site as 'a booze-fuelled Abstract Expressionist think tank,' peering through the dense smoke it would have been possible, on any given night, to make out Jackson Pollock (before he got banned for tearing a bathroom door off its hinges), Willem de Kooning, Mark Rothko, Franz Kline and beat writers Ginsberg, Gregory Corso, Frank O'Hara and Jack Kerouac (before he was banned for allegedly pissing in an ashtray), their volatile voices amplified by liquor.

'I was there every night,' recalls Simeon. 'You'd go in there and see people like Bill De Kooning and Jackson Pollock sitting there drunk and proselytising about this and that. The visual arts scene was exploding in New York. It was like, anything goes. These artists were hanging out in places where they would exchange ideas. One time, Leroy Jones came in with Eddie Fisher and Elizabeth Taylor on either arm, went to a back table and was telling them all about black power. New York was an open-ended cauldron of creativity. You were not only encouraged to do something completely different, it was almost necessary to get anybody's attention. If you did the ordinary, everyday kind of thing, you were just another band, but if you wanted to be taken seriously as someone doing something experimental it had to be pretty blatant. We felt that way, so that's the atmosphere we were creating in.'

Simeon resided at the infamous Albert Hotel on University Place and 11th Street, a key location in New York's cultural history last century. Named for painter Albert Pinkham Ryder, whose brother opened it in 1887, the early decades of the 20th century saw the register signed by Robert Louis Stevenson, Mark Twain, Thomas Wolfe and Anais Nin. By Simeon's time, it had become a rundown downtown folk and rock flophouse, guests including Dylan, Tim Buckley, Mothers Of Invention, Doors, Canned Heat, Butterfield Blues Band, The Mamas & The Papas (who wrote 'California Dreaming' there), Tim Hardin, Moby

Grape and Lovin' Spoonful (who rehearsed in the basement). Moby Grape's damaged drummer Skip Spence was committed to Bellevue for six months after taking super-strong acid and chasing around the hotel with a fire axe, eventually motorbiking to Nashville and recording the harrowing confessionals of May '69's *Oar* (which, like many, I wouldn't get to hear for decades).

Simeon became good friends with a 'very intense' composer called Harold Clayton who liked inviting drinkers to his Bowery loft to hear his creations. Harold and his jazz pianist wife Sylvia took Simeon to Slug's Saloon, 'an absolute junkie trash bar' on Third and Avenue B where Sun Ra and his Arkestra held down their residency between 1965 and 1972, when the club closed after jazz musician Lee Morgan was shot dead outside by a lady. Situated deep in the increasingly drug-infested East Village, the long dark room with bare brick walls played host to Ra and his crew every Monday, playing non-stop for seven hours until four in the morning. 'Sun Ra stayed on the little stage behind his keyboards but the Arkestra would be everywhere,' remembered Simeon. 'Standing on the tables, even the men's room. One time I was standing in there and Marshall Allen continued his sax solo while standing astride one of the urinals. They would play for hours.'

While Ra's freeform space anarchy inevitably impacted on Simeon, Clayton introduced him to composer Hal Rogers, who'd attended a Bronx school for exceptional kids and had dozens of symphony scores committed to memory, following the twelve tone and atonal concepts based on mathematical processes. Rogers introduced Simeon to Stockhausen and Simeon credited the mathematics for Silver Apples' rolling bass lines and repeated phrasing. Hal had a World War Two oscillator he'd found in a junk shop hooked up to his stereo, which Simeon played around with. 'I loved the thing,' he sighs. Simeon also remembers Hal drunk on vodka playing his oscillator along to Beethoven. One time after he passed out cold, Simeon played with the device and a new sound started gestating in his head. 'I played it with an old rock 'n' roll record and was absolutely hooked. That's where my fascination with electronics came in. Without that I don't know where I would have been.' He borrowed it, buying it off him for ten dollars. It now became the 'Grandfather Oscillator' in his set-up.

After the group dissolved, Simeon remained at the Albert, joining an outfit called the Overland Stage Electric Band playing Doors songs around coffee shops and Café Wha?. The Doors band balked when

Simeon brought his oscillator, except for drummer Danny Taylor. Simeon's new gadget (later called The Simeon but always The Thing for its owner) became a draw, leading to the band departing, except for Taylor. Simeon commenced soldering frenzy, wiring in more oscillators and electronic detritus found on the streets and in shops, getting shocks in the process. Simeon and Danny decided to play self-written material, calling themselves Silver Apples after an 1897 William Yeats' poem *The Song Of The Wandering Aengus*. Simeon explained the silver represented the moon which watched their night-time activities (also the solder that held together his set-up). The Apples was the New York connection. Using a self-built tower of old oscillators, Simeon devised a system of telegraph keys and pedals to control the sounds with his hands, feet and elbows using 86 different manual controls. 'At the same time as I'm moving the dials with my right hand on the lead oscillator,' he told *Ptolemaic Terrascope*, 'I'm working my elbow up and down across a bank of telegraph keys so that my forearm is keying in two or three of the other oscillators that have been pre-tuned to different notes. So that way I'm creating a little rhythm section. At the same time I have some on/off switches underneath and so I'm playing a sort of repeating, rolling bass line with my feet. On top of that, I had to sing. In the meantime, Danny's wheeling away on the drums. That was basically our act. It was almost like a one-man band with a drummer.'

Silver Apples became first house band at Max's Kansas City, opened at 213 Park Avenue South in December '65 by Mickey Ruskin to provide a watering hole for New York's modern art movements. Max's liberal manifesto and intellectual atmosphere welcomed gay customers and turned a blind eye to pill-popping and shagging going on in the infamous, red-bathed back room and telephone kiosks. Warhol's menagerie made Max's their own and its name known to the world.

'That's where we played a lot. The audience was all artists and poets and actors and other musicians. Not just regular type audiences: it was a very art-within-art kind of thing. It was relatively easy to cruise through that environment. You didn't get much off of it but you could have a gig once a week at different venues around to keep yourself going.'

Warhol was a fan and (vainly) tried to stick the duo behind his superstar Ultra Violet like he'd mated Nico with the Velvet Underground, painting a portrait of Simeon and presenting it to him as part of the wooing process. The duo's first major gig was in front of

30,000 punters in Central Park, crowd bemused by Simeon's mound of oscillators, effects boxes, guitar pedals and old radios perched on a table. Insurance business dropout Barry Bryant became their manager and tried to secure a record deal. One of the few interested parties, Kapp Records' John Walsh, was interested in adding Silver Apples to the small independent's roster as its first band. Their self-titled first album saw the duo squeeze the mountainous Thing and Danny's enormous drum kit into the label's tiny four-track studio. With the designated producer claiming illness, studio virgins Simeon and Danny ended up producing the album themselves through trial, error and advice from a bemused engineer. 'We just put in some microphones and started playing "Oscillations". The result was a total mess. When I think how good we might have sounded if we could only have had some help from that producer I get angry; because those records are all that survive.'

After the album reached 193, Silver Apples toured the US, staying with the Grateful Dead in San Francisco and, with characteristic invention, recording *Contact* knowing Kapp was on the way down because their manager astutely included a second album guarantee in their deal.

'I feel *Contact* is our best work from that period,' affirms Simeon. 'By then, we were on the road and most of the stuff that we were doing would be worked up during sound checks. Then when we went cross country to Decca, which was the parent company of Kapp Records. We'd go in their LA recording studio and be there for a week putting stuff together using their four-track board, then carry the tapes on the trip back so when we got back to New York we could just embellish the songs we'd worked up, so it had more of a cohesive feel to it. It's more like what we were doing live, how we sounded independent of a record label trying to get us sounding more conventional or commercial. (Kapp) were really desperate to have something more conventional come out of us but we never gave it to them. *Contact* was an extension of the first, all electronic and drums and me doing the vocals. By then we were into a rawer, less polished sound. This was because so many of our contemporaries were adding violins and choirs to what used to be rock! We were pissed so we went the other way. We talked about getting a sound like as if the wires were sending razor blades into the speakers and mincing them.'

When I licensed 'Confusion' for my *Dirty Water* punk compilation, I said it, 'stripped their sound to basic elements of Danny's drums and

Simeon's duelling vocals letting off slogans, joined by odd scrabbling noises like an old Japanese ukelele as the tempo speeds up and down.' The track was B-side of 1969 single 'You & I' with its lo-fi drone, moody organ and tearful love ditty vocal, the heart-struck desolation continuing on the oddly-poignant 'I Have Known Love', with lyrics by Eileen. 'Ruby' was a prime example of the duo's simple brilliance, Simeon harking back to bluegrass roots with raucous banjo and coarse vocal recalling Peter Stampfel's old timey amphetamine shriek. 'You're Not Fooling Me' is possibly the quintessential S.A. anarcho-romp, Danny's subtly-propulsive beats topped by relatively normal vocal, along with keyboards like a fairground mirror in a car crash, disintegrating into distorted chaos before jerking back into focus. Danny's drumming is imbued with a funkier swing, uncannily presaging Can's Jaki Liebezeit, and the distended snakes of the sinister 'A Pox On You' are possibly the most irritated a machine has sounded on record. Final track 'Fantasies' wasn't even finished, its luminous hurdy-gurdy topped by Simeon's chord change instructions to Danny, along with his WC Fields impersonation, none of which were intended for the finished version.

The LP's cover essentially poleaxed Silver Apples. Simeon was struck by the yell of 'Contact!' when an airplane's propeller was cranked by hand, applying it to communicating with people. Kapp's advertising agency had connections with Pan Am, which allowed the pair to be photographed inside assorted cockpits - after incoming flights to JFK airport were directed to a section of tarmac to face the sunset depicted on the cover, the pair cockpit-hopping to catch rays. Simeon and Danny giggled at drug paraphernalia they'd snuck in 'for a giggle' next to the airline's logo. Barry Bryant took the joke further by adding a shot of a fatal Swedish air crash, the pair superimposed in the wreckage playing banjos. As Simeon said in the mid-1990s interview with *Ptolemaic Terrascope*, 'So the photo message of the album became: here these two freaks somehow manage to pilot one of these passenger jets with all their dope and they end up crashing the thing, somehow surviving intact, killing all the passengers, and could care less about the whole thing. When Pan Am saw the finished album they sued us for $100,000. We didn't want to do anything that would harm the record label; after all they were our bread and butter. Their advertising agencies produced the imagery and got everything signed off and everyone agreed to everything, including Pan Am. It wasn't until much,

much later when it was already out on all the record shelves for sale that some executive at Pan Am decided that this was not good publicity and got the legal department to go to work on it and got it banned. They can't take a joke.'

Hysteria followed with albums withdrawn, lawsuits, judges putting restraining orders on songs being performed, and US Marshals trying to confiscate their equipment at shows. Many stores never received the album, scuppering regional promotional activities and the band, although they limped on for a few more months.

Panic in Detroit

Detroit meant Tamla Motown and cars until that day in early '69 when Peel played 'Kick Out The Jams', the unbelievably exciting title track of The MC5's same-titled debut album. With Brother J.C. Crawford's testifying introduction, sheet metal guitars on big riff overdrive and Rob Tyner's frenetic call-to-arms vocal, it sounded like an electric revolution that was gonna change everything and I had to have it.

It didn't disappoint. *Kick Out The Jams* was rock 'n' roll's first exciting live album, its *James Brown Live At The Apollo* recorded over two hot and steamy nights at Detroit's Grande Ballroom the previous October. Even then, kids wanted the loudest, hardest, fastest and most powerful extreme rock 'n' roll imaginable. Heavy metal would never fit the bill - too postured, squeaky and self-obsessed. This was unfettered and didn't mind admitting a debt to similar spirits uncaged by jazz in recent years. Next to this Black Sabbath, who I saw play to 50 punters the following year, sounded dull and lumpen. We wanted flash, and the MC5 had it.

Rolling Stone's first front cover story of '69 is the MC5. For this suburban 14-year-old looking for rock 'n' roll nirvana but still not quite sure what it would be like unless it sounded like Hendrix or the Stones, the piece gouged so many boxes with thermonuclear ink they threatened to explode. Reading it again 50 years later I can still see why, but with the hindsight of age and experience at the forefront of the punk movement the MC5 are credited with igniting know this was sadly another flash in the pan. Even by the end of the year they'd be acrimoniously splitting from guru-mentor John Sinclair and make only two, more traditional albums before imploding in the usual torrent of drugs and fall-outs.

The Five had started in '64 as a blues band, playing covers and their topical blues songs as their lineup solidified at Tyner, Davis, drummer Dennis 'Machinegun' Thompson and guitarists Wayne Kramer and Fred 'Sonic' Smith. Their breakout from the bars happened when local radio entrepreneur Russ Gibb opened the Grande Ballroom in 1966 and used the Five as house band at the venue credited with nurturing Detroit's counterculture and rock 'n' roll scene; the ultimate in wild, never-to-be-repeated one-offs, run by freaks for the Motor City's freakiest. Practically every great band of the time played the 1800 capacity venue that was like a final defiant death-gasp from the beleaguered Motor City and hedonistic playpen, dancing in the ruins of a city heading towards decades of decline, depression and oblivion. Detroit had been a haven for outlaws, outsiders, activists, subversives and lunatics for centuries. By the mid-60s, it was a magnet for hippies and draft dodgers and hardline rock bands. The Grande was built in the 1920s during a healthy time for Detroit's entertainment industry. The Moorish/Art Deco building at 8952 Grand River Avenue was designed in 1928 by local engineer and architect Charles N. Agree, after he was approached by its local businessman owner Harry Weitzmann. The building originally had retail stores on the ground level and an elegant sprung ballroom. After the ballroom scene was poleaxed by the Depression and Second World War, the last big bands played there in the early 50s before the Grande became a shuttered hulk used for storing mattresses.

In 1966, Dearborn high school teacher and local radio DJ Russ Gibb visited a friend in California and got taken to see the Byrds at the Fillmore, where he was stunned by the light show and struck by Bill Graham's advice to start such a club in Detroit. After scouting vacant ballrooms, he settled on the Grande, cut a deal with the owners and asked local writer, activist and jazz critic John Sinclair for help, along with local underground paper *The Fifth Estate*. Their mission was to give Detroit its own Fillmore-style club and turn the old dancehall into a psychedelic pleasure palace. Detroit was then a tough, industrial city with declining employment but passionate love of rock 'n' roll, which had to be as tough as the crowds it attracted. 'There was a whole bunch of problems in Detroit which gave birth to industrial strength rock 'n' roll,' says former Grande manager Tom Wright. With eye-blasting posters designed by Gary Grimshaw, Gibb's opening nights featured the Chosen Few (who included future Stooges axeman Ron Asheton) and 'Detroit's only avant rock minded manifesting MC5' in October. Audiences increased every week into happening '67, going crazy on frequent Five nights, many on acid as they craved the ultimate in high-energy no-nonsense rock 'n' roll. *Louder Than Love: The Grande Ballroom Story* by filmmaker-Detroit home boy Tony D'Annunzio positions it as one of the 60s' most vital rock 'n' roll venues, a hotbed of excess where, according to Kramer, 'the whole audience was on one wavelength.'

As I would soon be able to vouch, nothing compared to having a regular club run by likeminded individuals rather than faceless money men; separate from the music biz mainstream and, most importantly, all yours. That long-lost form of unity also marked the Cavern, Ealing Club, Roxy and CBGB - proper local scenes where respect had to be earned by those that played there. If bands didn't cut it at the Grande, they were told so in no uncertain terms, an attitude likened by Kramer to the Colosseum in ancient Rome.

The MC5 was a reaction to what Kramer described as being 'very frustrated with the slow pace of change, and what we viewed as an intolerable situation, between racism, police oppression, the war in Vietnam, outmoded drug laws. We took the lead from the Black Panther Party in that they were the vanguard and voice for their community. We felt we could be the vanguard and voice for our community.'

America's ghettos had been feeling anything but peace and love during that long, hot '67 summer. Detroit was even regarded as taking a progressive lead in race relations with a large black middle class that worked its way up over the decades in different professions. Lower down the totem pole, unemployment was rising and black workers treated badly if they did manage to land a job at the auto plants. There was widespread disaffection with social conditions, underfunded schools, unfulfilled promises and, particularly, the predominantly white, racist police force. Detroit went off like a powder keg for six days in July, its riots considered one of the largest in US history in terms of destruction and body count. After an estimated 10,000 rioters had smashed, pillaged and fought for four days, the carnage ended when Governor Romney sent in the Michigan National Guard, and President Johnson deployed the army. 'My home town is burning down to the ground, worster than Vietnam,' rumbled John Lee Hooker in 'The

Motor City Is Burning', written two months later and released in '69, (along with that year's 'I Don't Wanna Go To Vietnam' on his *Simply The Truth* album, which reasoned, 'We got so much trouble at home, we don't need to go to Vietnam.')

The riot's aftermath saw 43 dead (33 black), 1,189 injured, over 7,000 arrests and 2,000 buildings destroyed. Many black businesses were burned out, affected areas staying ruined for decades, while white flight to the suburbs intensified and drove Motown and the auto industry out of the city. The Grande was left untouched, being a funky key artery in the city's cultural bloodstream whose incineration would have benefitted nobody more than the establishment they were rebelling against. The riots were still a recent open wound when John Sinclair hooked up with the Five in late '67. Then writing for *Downbeat*, Sinclair hit it off with Rob Tyner, who shared his love of outer limits jazz by Sun Ra, John Coltrane and Pharoah Sanders and saw its high energy parallels with the Five's wildly freewheeling rock 'n' roll.

'High energy is a total and environmental involvement of the musician and the audience,' explains Sinclair in the *Rolling Stone* piece. 'It happens when your senses and emotions spew themselves completely onto a medium. Sure, it's a political thing, just dig the energy…not just white power or black power but everybody's power. We were the only group to play up at the Battle of Chicago ('68's Democratic Conference where the Five opened the park concert before the riot started).' Sinclair published a typical MC5 setlist, which included their debut single 'Borderline', Pharoah Sanders-inspired 'Upper Egypt', 'Ice Pick Slim', 'Five For Shepp', 'Kick Out The Jams', 'Motherfucker', Dylan's 'Ballad Of A Thin Man', Coltrane's 'Tungi', 'Looking At You', 'Come Together', Ray Charles' 'I Believe It In My Soul' and mass freak-out 'Black To Comm': 'At this point, we try to create the highest sound/energy levels we are capable of, using volume, muscle power, gallons of sweat & total intensity…if everyone in the audience joined in we could erupt into the universe,' declared Sinclair.

Wayne Kramer burned to make music of the spheres, like free jazz players who 'opened the door for me and showed me how to start breaking the boundaries in the world of rock. If I took my best Chuck Berry solo, you know the highest velocity I could play it, and moved it to the next level, I would be going into the kinds of things that Albert (Ayler) was trying to do with his saxophone or that Pharoah Sanders was trying to do - to move into a more pure, sonic dimension…start to incorporate polyrhythms and subdivisions and move out of the western concepts of rhythm and outside the concepts of western harmony. Those were the things we were trying to do in the MC5.'

Sun Ra took his Arkestra to Detroit in June '67 at Sinclair's behest, playing the Community Arts Auditorium on Wayne State University with the Five. Ra made his Grande debut blowing off Led Zeppelin on March 16th before two nights with the MC5. He returned that May to play the Detroit Rock and Roll Revival with Chuck Berry, MC5 and Stooges. As writer Ben Edmonds said, 'MC5 and Sun Ra were visionary brothers-in-musical-arms, fearless explorers charting unknown territory the rest of us might one day occupy.'

These ideals fed into the Stooges, the Five's 'little brother band' and Detroit's other most notorious live onslaught. Initially blasting a wall of feedback-sodden noise enhanced by mutated Hawaiian guitar, vacuum cleaner and miked-up toilet, the Psychedelic Stooges evolved into the fearsome Stooges before the audiences' eyes. Charismatic, crowd-diving Iggy Pop, guitarist Ron Asheton, his drummer brother Scott and bassist Dave Alexander whipped up a racket of stunning brutality, nihilist anthems such as 'No Fun' looming out of demonic freeform pileups, like all the Motor City car plant conveyor belts were seizing up at once. Beyond punk rock, free jazz or what's now known as noise, the Stooges' elemental extreme carnage came across like a primal howl from the depths of the most ravaged souls. That '69 feature describes them as a 'a totally bizarre experience' and their singer having 'the potential to make Jim Morrison look like a tame puppy.'

In mid-'68, Sinclair answered Black Panthers honcho Huey Newton's declaration that white people who want to help the struggle should form their own party by setting up the White Panthers. His manifesto was based on the creation of 'a cultural revolution through a total assault on the culture by any means necessary, including rock 'n' roll, dope and fucking in the streets.' The police stepped up persecution of the MC5, putting them under surveillance and under constant threat of arrest. After all, their reputation as drug-crazed harbingers of free love and black power-style revolution boiled down every element of the establishment's hatred of the counterculture into one brazen entity. 'The most important thing was our solidarity and unity; that we were together in mind, body and spirit,' writes Kramer in his autobiography, *The Hard Stuff*. 'It was us against them.'

The MC5 were signed to Elektra by A&R field man Danny Fields. In an idea revolutionary for the time, they decided to record their first album live. 'Our strength was our live performance,' recounts Kramer. 'This was where we'd focused our energy, and if we could be captured on tape, it would be a radical and fitting introduction for the group on the world stage.' *Kick Out The Jams* was recorded at the Grande on Wally Heider's new eight-track mobile studio, Elektra production stalwart Bruce Botnick engineering. Stoked by 'Brother' JC Crawford's hellfire announcement, the Five stampeded through their incendiary repertoire, a crazed gaggle of rock 'n' roll assassins preaching revolution and channeling free jazz fury through hot-wired guitars on 'Rocket Reducer Number Nine' and 'The Motor City Is Burning'. Kramer points out the band could be erratic live; 'brilliant' or 'a train-wreck.' He never recovered from his E-string going wildly out of tune as he struck the opening chord of 'Ramblin' Rose' and felt the band 'front-loaded' their set with too many killers, so it tapered off rather than building to a climax.

The album made 30 in the charts, despite Lester Bangs' derogatory review in *Rolling Stone* that likened them to '16 year old punks on a methedrine power trip.' The shine started fading at the Grande and in the MC5's revolutionary idealism after the album's release; not helped when Sinclair received a hefty prison sentence for possessing two joints (resulting in John Lennon campaigning for his release, ultimately successful). They left Elektra after taking an ad aimed at top store Hudson's emblazoned 'Fuck Hudson's' blended with their tangles with the music business and FBI. Signing to Atlantic in May, the Five dropped politicising for retro-rock 'n' roll on *Back In The USA*.

Eight years later, I found myself sitting in Warner Brothers' Soho offices with Rob Tyner; now a plump, bespectacled but pleasant figure compared to the be-afro'd rock 'n' roll animal on the front of *Rolling Stone*. That night I took him to the Vortex on Wardour Street to witness London's own punk revolution, obviously a much tamer affair than the groundbreaking excess at the Grande, but still a volatile show of rebel energy. He recalled the Five's initial peak; 'Now we would be looked on as middle-of-the-road but in those days we were the maniac fringe. We were faced with the situation where we were, stylistically speaking...I hate to say this it sounds so dumb...ahead of our time. We tried to change people's musical and social beliefs too quickly and too radically. Then there's this vast social backlash that happens. The cops don't wanna know about it because they have to change their attitudes about everything. They like everything pretty much as they've got it, pretty much because they've got control over it, and the government don't want you to do it because it changes everything. You're talking about a new social order, and I know new order sounds a little ominous. There's always been this resistance to change, especially when it comes to rock 'n' roll for some reason. I wanted us to be totally original. I thought what we were doing was totally unprecedented, at least in rock 'n' roll. There was plenty of jazz music, like Sun Ra, where people improvised and played for free. When we started doing it with electric instruments, the energy levels that we achieved were so profound that audiences either absolutely hated it or went crazy. I thought that it would be a long term effect.'

The only time I ever saw The MC5 live was when then-surviving members Kramer, Davis and Thompson, augmented by Alice In Chains singer William DuVall, appeared at Massive Attack's Meltdown at London's Royal Festival in June 2008. They came on after Primal Scream, who I spent a lot of time touring with in the 90s as their DJ (a book in itself!), then both came together for a communal blow-out finale on 'Black To Comm' after both bands played the Five's 'Rocket Reducer' and Scream's 'Movin' On Up'. They were even joined by Sinclair reading his writings. For a moment, I could imagine what it must have been like at the Grande. So could Bobby Gillespie, who told me, 'I used to take magic mushrooms or acid and listen to the MC5 and imagine I was in the Grande Ballroom, then imagine I was up onstage playing with them. We did 'Black To Comm' with the Five and that was just insane, the energy. That was one of the high points of my life! I mean, I was stood beside Wayne Kramer, who was just to the right of me. It was such a fucking thrill. The greatest, aren't they? Just proper rock 'n' roll. We're absolute MC5 freaks, so to actually be up there with Kramer, Davis and Thompson was too much for us. It was just amazing.'

Three years later, Sinclair was recording his *Beatnik Youth* album at my friend Alan Clayton's studio. Over insidious soul choruses and free jazz backdrops, Sinclair growled, railed and guffawed with animated passion undimmed by his 70 plus years. I wondered if his time had   come.

'I hope so!' he roared. 'I've never stopped. People knew about me from 40-45 years ago because of the MC5 and John Lennon, but everything I've done since then is totally underground. I write for a magazine. I've got my own radio station online. I just continue to be productive. I keep praying they'll say 'Oh I heard your last record', but they never say that or buy any, but I keep doing it anyway. My motto is, They can't stop me!'

Angel of Death

The first Stones-related record of '69 is by Marianne Faithfull, who had previewed A-side 'Something Better' at the Stones' ill-fated Rock and Roll Circus the previous December. Gone was the angel-voiced popstrel of 60s hits like 'As Tears Go By' and 'This Little Bird'. The B-side was her original version of 'Sister Morphine', her transformative reflection of a life increasingly wracked by hard experience. It was the first flare from a lyrical talent that would blossom in coming years. The song commenced its ghostly whisper with chords familiar from the Stones' version on *Sticky Fingers*, recorded after hers. Then the voice; a wracked bloodless monotone exuding agonised narcotic despair; 'Here I lie in my hospital bed/Tell me Sister Morphine when are you coming round again?' She doesn't know where she is or why she's there, just needs Sister Morphine to 'turn my nightmares into dreams'. Enhanced by the slide guitar's lacerating night spiders, the song's deathly hopelessness and tangible craving for sweet release mesmerises for five pleading minutes until reaching its terrifying punch-line; 'Cause you know and I know in the morning I'll be dead…and you can sit around and you can watch all the clean white sheets turn red.' Harrowingly claustrophobic but starkly direct, no song had gouged so deeply into the drug addict's tormented psyche (even if it was from the angle of a dying man in hospital after a car-crash). What could have happened to the angelic-sounding popstrel whose exquisite sequence of singles after 1964's 'As Tears Go By' embodied the ephemeral era in which they were produced? Or the folk-fixated musical wanderer on the four albums that came out until Marianne's career abruptly ceased in '67 as her relentlessly-scrutinised romance with Jagger became a national obsession?

As a starry-eyed fan from the age of ten, I'd witnessed Marianne sing her first hit at David Bowie's 1980 Floorshow filmed at the Marquee in '73, been gripped by Andrew Tyler's astonishing *NME* interview the following year and grabbed '76's 'country Marlene Deitrich' comeback album *Dreamin' My Dreams*. Then *Broken English* appeared that November. Forgotten 60s casualty no longer, Marianne had returned to rekindle her solo career on her own terms, the creative, self-ignited spark that first manifested in '69 on 'Sister Morphine' now a raging forest fire.

I was still that star-struck fan when Island Records' late and much-loved press officer Rob Partridge took me to a Jermyn Street restaurant to conduct Marianne's first interview about *Broken English*. Burying herself in an ancient black leather jacket and fighting a cold with vodka and orange juice, the lady was warmly engaging company and obviously relished being grilled by such a blatant long-time fan. Although that unmistakably beautiful face betrayed the experiences of recent years, Marianne carried a luminous charisma of her own making; a still bewitching fallen angel as tough as that old leather jacket, with a wicked sense of humour. At this particular time, flush with personal triumph against many odds, she practically disowned her earlier self when she confided, 'I've never had to try very hard. I've never really been expected to try at all. I've always been treated as somebody who not only can't even sing but doesn't really write or anything, just something you can make into something. This is the first time anything's been asked of me in the music world. I've got quite a good brain and all that, which I've never had to use in singing at all. I was just cheesecake really, terribly depressing. It wasn't depressing when I was 18, but it got depressing when I got older because you're a person just like anyone else, even if you are a woman.'

Through fabulous period gems such as 'Come And Stay With Me', 'This Little Bird', 'Summer Nights' and 'Counting' she can be be heard fighting to assert herself as a woman cast into a rusty old music business greased by men, bent on cutting the puppet strings that had dangled her onto gruelling package tours and confounding the pop conveyor belt she'd been dumped on with early glimmers of rebellion and self-assertion. It all started here but, in her flurry of triumph and achievement that evening in '79, she predictably dismissed her pop star period because she was in control for the first time.

'Yes, I'm there,' exhaled the lady in a cloud of cigarette smoke. 'I exist. I'm not thinking about something else. (*Broken English*) was recorded as an album. It's a new thing for me, I've never done that before. If I'd have carried on after I did 'Sister Morphine' I would have come up with something interesting, but I didn't. I lost heart. I couldn't stand it and broke away until three years ago. I could have (gone on to great things) but I didn't see that, because I can only see that far, I really have got no imagination at all. When I found that the music business was so vile and ghastly I wanted nothing to do with it. I thought the best thing would be to do something else completely. If I'd have stayed, I'd be dead.'

When were talking 40 years later, Marianne put an extra slant on her survival of the Stones' circus. 'I was brought up on my father's commune. That was about the group mind and that's what I still kind of believe in. It's really why I was able to do that in the 60s with the Stones.'

Born in December 1946, Marianne's father had spied for the British Army and her mother Eva was the daughter of Austro-Hungarian nobleman Artur Ritter Von Sacher-Masoch, a former ballerina then a dancer in Brecht-Weill productions. Marianne's maternal great great uncle was Leopold von Sacher-Masoch, whose erotic novel *Venus In Furs* spawned the word 'masochism'. After her earliest years on the commune, Marianne's parents divorced when she was six. Her mother took her to live in Reading, where she attended the local convent school. By her early teens, Marianne was singing popular folk songs of the day a capella at Reading's coffee bars. At sixteen, Marianne discovered Soho's night-life and Miles Davis's revelatory *Sketches Of Spain*. Within a year, Marianne had met artist John Dunbar, whose cool contacts brought her onto London's hip party circuit. It was at a launch bash for Adrienne Posta that she first met hotshot dynamo Andrew Loog Oldham, manager of the Rolling Stones but looking to establish himself as the British Phil Spector with a stable of pop stars. Oldham noticed the quietly beautiful girl in shirt and jeans and wondered to her boyfriend if she could sing. Marianne herself quotes Oldham's much-repeated line, 'I saw an angel with big tits and signed her.' The manager's first direct overture was a telegram to the Faithfull family home in Reading a week later instructing Marianne to be at Olympic Studios at 2pm. She got the train to Paddington and found the studio, recalling Oldham directing the session like a manic Spectoresque maestro in shades. Mick Jagger and Keith Richards sat there silently, not speaking to anyone.

'As Tears Go By' was one of the first songs ever written by the nascent Jagger-Richards partnership. Legend long has it that Oldham forced the two Stones into songwriting by locking them in his kitchen until they came up with something. For 'As Tears Go By', Mick wrote the words while Keith came up with the melody, the former demoing the song at De Lane Lea studios in March with session guitarist Big Jim Sullivan. In 1980, Keith told me, 'I can thank Andrew Oldham for many things, but more than anything for forcing me to sit down and write these horrendous songs, 'cos when you start it's always the worst. We'd farm them off to somebody else cos we didn't wanna know. Gene Pitney, Marianne Faithfull? Sure, have this one. You've gotta get all that shit outta your system before you can really start writing. At the time you write 'em you're even amazed you can write that. 'I'm just the guitar-player.' Hats off to Andrew just for making me find out I could do it.'

Marianne says Oldham told the two Stones, 'I want a song with brick walls all around it, and high windows and no sex.' They brought him back the mournful reflection of what they called 'As Time Goes By', which Oldham altered so it didn't clash with Dooley Wilson's ballad in 1942 movie *Casablanca*. Marianne has long been second to nobody when it comes to reinterpreting other people's songs, supernaturally gifted in making them her own as she digs into the words to grip the composition's heart then provides her own unique spin by injecting every syllable with clearly-enunciated but gut level emotional response. Even if she wasn't yet aware of it, it started with 'As Tears Go By' as she plugged into its character looking back at her life and taking stock, first revisiting the song with the wisdom of 23 years' experience on '87's post-heroin *Strange Weather*. Sitting in a New York lounge, she told me then that 'As Tears Go By' was more suited to being sung by a 40-year-old woman than a 17-year-old girl; 'It was then that I experienced the lyrical melody of the song for the first time.' When I reminded her of this comment in our 2011 interview at London's May Fair Hotel, she reasoned with some ebullience, 'This happens a lot in pop music. Older people couldn't get a look in during the 50s or 60s and were rarely able to emphasise childhood. That's exactly what it's about; a girl looking back on her childhood, bless her. She's obviously been hurt for the first time, but that's not the case with me. I feel wonderful!' And seven years later, reaffirming that point, she recorded it again for spellbinding late-life classic *Negative Capability*. 'It is the third time I've done it and it will be the last time,' she said after the session. 'I wanted it to be better than both other versions and it is. I am

71. My voice is not what it was the first time I did it and it's not anything like as sad and tragic as it was the second time when I did it with Hal Willner. This is wonderful because it's in full possession of all my understanding and faculties. I really understand the song now and that's good.'

Back in '64, when it came time for an album, Decca assumed it could release the usual hit-plus-filler pop album but, exercising single-minded defiance, Marianne declared she wanted to put out a folk set, refusing even to compromise by mixing both genres on the same record. The result was two albums released the same day that April; *Marianne Faithfull* featured hits plus covers and *Come My Way* roped together folk club standards and re-recorded 'House Of The Rising Sun'. As if proving her point, *Come My Way* made number 12 while the hits-led 'pop' album reached 15.

Held against her later work, the ensuing Decca singles seem like they were made in the distant past by another singer but carried their own period magic when I revisited them to write notes for Ace Records' compilation of every A and B side. The hit momentum launched by 'As Tears Go By' was maintained by Marianne's haunting version of John D Loudermilk's 'This Little Bird'. 'Summer Nights' made number ten as July's next single. April 1966's third album, *North Country Maid* is once again more of a folk record than hit-plus-filler pop album despite half of it being released months earlier on the US-only *Go Away From My World* LP.

Marianne's personal aspirations were overtaking those exquisite little singles, and she began finding her pop music career dwarfed by the enormous changes roaring through British pop culture and impacting on her personal life. Referring to the summer of '66 as 'Year One' in her memoir *Faithfull*, her shotgun marriage to John Dunbar was floundering but she loved getting stoned with Anita Pallenberg and Brian Jones at their Courtfield Road pleasure palace, along with other exotic characters she was getting to know in Stones circles, including antiques-dealer-to-the-stars Christopher Gibbs, photographer Michael Cooper and most significantly Mick Jagger who, according to her memoir, became her boyfriend after a show at Bristol's Colston Hall that October. Almost overnight, Marianne became the crown princess of hip swinging London. But all the optimism and escapism swiftly soured as the established declared war on the counterculture by trying to use the Stones as scapegoats, starting with the infamous Redlands bust that cast Marianne at the centre of a stage never asked for. Maybe symbolically this life-changing event occurred the same month that last 'pop' single was released. By the time *Love In A Mist* came in March Marianne was on the way to becoming the most famous 'Miss X' in Britain. She returned to Olympic that November with Oldham back as producer, resulting in February '67's sublime version of the Ronettes' 1965 minor hit 'Is This What I Get For Loving You'. The single kicked off *Love In A Mist*, Marianne's fifth album in three years. Yet the track listing is still a haphazard collection hurled together by the record company to uphold her profile and satisfy her contract. Much of the album still navigated the wispy baroque-pop and folk-rock Marianne of the previous two years, including several cover versions; three from Donovan, two by New York folkie Tim Hardin and two from Jackie DeShannon.

Although the next two years saw Marianne routinely regarded as Jagger's girlfriend, it was Marianne changing Mick as she accompanied him through the ongoing rapid evolution of the Rolling Stones from pop conveyor belt teen idols through '67's psychedelic dalliance then reinvention the following year as omnipotent blues-rock carnivores. As the Stones entered the purple patch that would establish them as the world's greatest rock 'n' roll band, Marianne became Mick's muse, expanding his reading list by giving him books (most famously, Mikhail Bulgakov's *The Master and Margarita* that inspired 'Sympathy For The Devil'), strengthened his social climbing fixation and helped work out his next moves, like developing his Turner persona around Brian's stoned isolation and Keith's outlaw cool for *Performance* (which she would have appeared in had she not fallen pregnant).

Marianne's own speedy growing up in public, conducted while wrestling a music biz straitjacket, resulted in the sort of classic first phase even the Stones had to go through, if at much higher speed, profile and pressure levels. If Marianne had been allowed to follow the instinctual personal growth that could see her making the unprecedented move of releasing two debut albums on the same day before going on to create a minor Brit-folk classic when she was one of the country's favourite pop stars, her career might have continued to progress alongside the Stones, instead of becoming stifled by her boyfriend's transformation between 1968 and '69 into kingpin rock 'n' roll godhead. She had never been comfortable with commercial pop and being Jagger's girlfriend gave her the perfect excuse to abandon what she called this 'dead end' and venture into films, including '68's soft-core *Girl On A Motorcycle* and stage acting in Chekhov's *Three Sisters*.

Then came that pivotal moment when she started writing her own songs – starting with 'Sister Morphine'. As she writes in *Faithfull*, 'As soon as I fell in love with Mick Jagger I began to see pop music on an entirely other level. Since I no longer had to work, I could let the whole damn thing go. Until 'Sister Morphine', I didn't have the slightest interest in writing songs. 'Sister Morphine' was in my head, my feelings about what it might be like to be an addict.'

Mick's relentless strumming of a haunting guitar motif around the house through '67 ignited a creative outlet that had never attracted Marianne before, although it was initially to give his riff a home as a song with the lyrics it was crying out for. 'Mick would always be strumming chords around the house and then forget about them, but these I remembered,' she told me in '79. She wrote the words in Rome after being struck by a bolt of inspiration. Although she had barely tried heroin then, Marianne somehow came up with the most graphic depiction of an addict's hopeless plight and despair since the Velvet Underground's 'Heroin', although much heavier as the song gets into the death-bed mindset of a car crash victim in agony.

'Yeah, I was very pleased with those,' she said with a proud smile. 'A lot of it's imaginary, some of it's experience, and some of it's what you are imagining, in your highly paranoid state, that you would like to happen. You just take it out to the furthest limit. I was very paranoid at that time.' In her autobiography, she elaborates, 'People tend to assume that 'Sister Morphine' comes from an incident in my life, that it's a parable of a junkie's last hours…'Sister Morphine' was in my head – a story of what it might be like to be an addict…A vivid series of pictures began forming in my head, and I wrote a story about a morphine addict. It had something to do with Keith and Anita, though they were no more addicts than I at this time. They were just beginning to dabble in smack. But I think one of the reasons I wrote those lyrics was I knew Keith would like them. I might have cast Anita in one of the roles. Say Keith was the man in the car and Anita was the nurse, what would happen?' She also revealed the line about 'the clean white sheets stained red' was inspired by the pregnant Anita haemorrhaging on the boat trip to Brazil. A doctor gave her morphine, much to the envy of Keith and Marianne.

The song was recorded at LA's Elektra Studios in July '68 while the Stones were working on the album that would become *Let It Bleed*.

Jagger produced and played acoustic guitar, accompanied by Jack Nitzsche on piano, Ry Cooder on slide and Charlie Watts on drums. The same squad also played on Marianne's swooning rendition of Barry Mann and Gerry Goffin's 'Something Better', the optimistic ying to 'Sister Morphine's darkly claustrophobic yang that she performed at the Rolling Stones Rock And Roll Circus in December, her flowing black dress arranged around her like giant flower petals as the camera panned in circular motion.

'Something Better/Sister Morphine' would have been Marianne's final Decca single the following February, but once the same company big-wigs who'd already stalled *Beggars Banquet* for months over its toilet wall sleeve got wind of the graphic drug song, the single was pulled after two days. But as Marianne reveals in her memoir, the song was of vital importance to her low self-esteem and new need to write her own songs. '"Sister Morphine" was my Frankenstein, my self-portrait in a dark mirror...my miniature gothic masterpiece, my celebration of death.'

You sound like the angel of death, I ventured.

'I was,' she replied, with chilling ice cold honesty.

I had to ask her what had happened to her voice, which Tom Waits later described as, 'like spooky oil on a squeaky gate.' 'It sounds exactly as if it's broken like a boy's voice, it's really weird,' she explained. 'I suppose it's years and years of life, drinking and smoking, time...'

Marianne added that, when the single, her precious new baby, was pulled, her relationship with Jagger started its inexorable disintegration. By the time the Stones' version appeared in '71, 'I was the character in the song. You have to be very careful what you write because a song is a gateway, and whatever it is you've summoned up may come through. It happened to Mick and Keith with that whole satanic business. I then became a victim of my own song.'

Of course, when 'Sister Morphine' loomed again on *Sticky Fingers*, press or powers-that-be never batted an eyelid. Marianne had to wait until *Broken English* ten years later before she could blossom and be acclaimed as a vital artist in her own right (and to emphasise her point included her new version of 'Sister Morphine' on the B-side when its title track was released as a single). Marianne told me how she finally fixed the absence of her songwriting credit from *Sticky Fingers* with help from Keith Richards. 'Mick is mean. He'll always be a student of the London School of Economics! Keith wrote to Allen Klein and told him that I'd written them. Jagger and I had split up, very bad blood and all that. This story I heard from Allen Klein – Keith Richard told him that I did write the words and needed the money. So now and again, I get a royalty cheque for 'Sister Morphine'. I've been living off 'Sister Morphine' for years. I just got one today; £485!'

As I've already said, through 2018 I talked to Marianne frequently during the creation of *Negative Capability* which, driven by her supernatural re-interpretative skills, florid lyricism and stellar group of musicians she loves like a family, emphasises her unique place as a force of nature in the beating heart of modern music. Recording in her adopted home city of Paris, Marianne has long since made peace with her earlier past in the 40 years since *Broken English*, the new album inexorably overshadowed by grief at losing close friends such as Anita Pallenberg and Martin Sharp. It is a very brave record; fearlessly wrought from iron courage and struggle, like the best ones. Fifty years after 'Sister Morphine', she made her masterpiece.

When Helen passed away *Negative Capability* had just been finished. I'd literally just received the finished work. Although it predictably seemed to prove too real and raw-nerved for even the 'hip' media she has every reason to be proud. Now I find it impossible to hear without being cast back to that traumatic period of surreal grief, the opening piano chords of 'No Moon In Paris' enough to send me into deep melancholy but, in 2018, the album served a greater purpose than any record before or since. Our almost daily phone calls carried on for months, my lifeline through an impossibly difficult time; full of love, laughter, sadness and our respective pain. Again, this is for another book, and one day it will be.

RECORDS

Single of the month is Jane Birkin & Serge Gainsbourg's 'Je T'aime...moi non plus' (Fontana). Incredibly it's one of the year's most controversial singles, created after Brigitte Bardot asked Gainsbourg to produce a passionate love song then balked at the steamy outcome. Having risen to the challenge, resourceful Serge cast around for a heavy breathing substitute, even asking Marianne, before corralling his girlfriend, English actress Jane Birkin, after the two became an item working on a film. It had a profound effect on a teenage boy and still sounds unique.

Flying Burrito Brothers: *The Gilded Palace Of Sin* **(A&M)**
Music's roots-referencing sea-change that got under way after *John Wesley Harding, Music From Big Pink* and the Byrds' *Sweetheart Of The Rodeo* continued with the album that really introduces Gram Parsons into the world. As adopted by the Beatles and the Stones, rock had been divested of its technicolour dream-coats, stripped back to the bone and often shacked up in the country. The Flying Burrito Brothers take this ethos to extremes on their debut album. Recorded at A&M Studios in Hollywood, Gram, Chris Hillman and band including Sneaky Pete Kleinow's hot-wired pedal steel broke through musical barriers by invoking Everly Brothers harmonies and Otis Redding soul over amped-up country rock, including 'Sin City' ('This old town filled with sin, it'll swallow you in'), 'Hot Burrito One and Two', 'Hippie Boy', about '68's Chicago riots, and 'My Uncle', about the draft. The album also featured their version of James Carr's 'The Dark End Of The Street' and 'Do Right Woman' as country-soul flagbearers of Gram's 'cosmic American music'. Dylan named it his favourite country-rock album but it didn't sell. 'I'm almost certain the whole thing is a parody,' Pete Frame will write in *Zigzag*, citing Gram's white suit, 'which seems to have been cut from patterns discarded by Tom Jones' tailor.' He adds, 'It must be a big put-on. It's as if they sat in a room and ruminated and discussed the whole country music sphere, collating a long list of the most typical aspects.'

Cream: *Goodbye* **(Polydor)**
Cream called it a day after the previous November's Royal Albert Hall farewell shows captured in Tony Palmer's BBC film, leaving a hole when they disbanded that was only partially filled by *Goodbye*, culled from live recordings ('I'm So Glad', 'Politician', 'Sitting On Top Of The World') and one each from the trio (Clapton's sublime 'Badge', Bruce-Brown's 'Doing That Scrapyard Thing' and Baker's 'What A Bringdown'). Baker and Clapton had already formed the short-lived Blind Faith with Steve Winwood, while Bruce, who had recorded *Things We Like* with McLaughlin, Heckstall-Smith and Hiseman in August '68 (not released until 1970), started planning his first solo album with Pete Brown.

Meanwhile, Ten Years After release *Stonedhenge* (Deram). After arriving in '67 then busting out in '68 with their Undead set live at Klook's Kleek (including 'I'm Going Home' earning Alvin Lee his pesky 'fastest guitar in the west' soubriquet), the new album saw the band expand into progressive rock and deploy Canned Heat-style dynamics on future Slade set staple 'Hear Me Calling', although overall impact is diluted by individual solo indulgences... The Isley Brothers *It's Your Thing* (T-Neck) furthers their transformation from Motown-manufactured second stringers (boasting one hit with 'Behind The Painted Smile') to conscious funk band, led by its title track's contagious declaration of independence ('It's your thing/Do what you wanna do/I can't tell you/Who to sock it to.')... Jefferson Airplane have the live *Bless Its Pointed Little Head* (RCA), culled from three nights at San Fransisco's Fillmore West the previous October. This one I borrowed and, like the MC5, tried to imagine being in that crowd grooving to the sound of the acid ballroom at full throttle. Somehow, that was the nearest I got to booking a full flight with the Airplane after 'White Rabbit'. For an idea of how the drugs crept in, compare it with the recently released *Sweeping Up The Spotlight, Live At The Fillmore East, 1969*, recorded that November (although guitarist Jorma Kaukonen is never less than on stinging form).

CHAPTER THREE

MARCH

RIGHT ON FOR THE DARKNESS: JAMES BROWN, BLACK PANTHERS, TEMPTATIONS, LADY SOUL & FUNKADELIC; THE VELVET UNDERGROUND...& NICO; BLUE CHEER; LET IT BLEED; SPOOKY TOOTH; COLOSSEUM

Although Radio London and *Ready Steady Go!* opened the door and I was in thrall to Otis Redding after his September '66 *RSG* special, sweet soul music and nasty funk took a couple more years to become lifelong obsessions. Thanks to the Stones, black music previously meant Bo Diddley, Chuck Berry, Muddy Waters, John Lee Hooker and Howlin' Wolf. Big L introduced cool soul 45s like Sam and Dave ('Soothe Me'), Joe Tex ('Show Me') and Wilson Pickett ('The Midnight Hour'). On mainstream radio, the Four Tops, Temptations, Supremes and other Motown giants cut through white chart-riding candy-floss with force ten vocal power, transcendent melodies and killer grooves.

I can never pretend to have been among the self-appointed elite who called themselves soul boys. At the time, it seemed like cubs for grown-ups or masons for kids; a clandestine box where you had to wear the right strides, before George Clinton and even Bowie put paid to all that. In '69, I was too far gone in other directions and rarely went to discos as the only local option was Discville (top ten spun by our local Tony Blackburn, although I remember being there jiggling awkwardly to the Isley Brothers' 'Behind A Painted Smile'). There was also the Social Club, which hosted soul bands but had been commandeered by local skinheads who spent most nights pooling their few braincells to get the bottle to beat up anyone on their own who didn't conform to their Hitler Youth uniform, particularly hair length. One screw-faced specimen even beat me up while I was walking home from a friend's house, snarling threats only he considered scary. The import copy of the new Band album under my arm remained unscathed, even if my face didn't. In these times of exploring and battling for new freedoms, skinheads were conformists in their own uniform, moronically acceding to the war generation's violent tendencies by beating up hippies for them, but too thick to see it. The question remains why these Neanderthal racists liked music made by black people.

Until The Funk started gestating in 1969, soul ballads grabbed the most, those soaring, testifying reveries that channeled pure emotion and awoke feelings I didn't know existed. '69 saw soul gird itself for the coming decade with James Brown's new funk, Curtis Mayfield's conscious messages, Sly Stone's superbad apocalypse and George Clinton's acid-funk scuba-diving. While Curtis (my other favourite singer) gave this turbulent time messages of hope and strength as a sweet-voiced ectoplasm who now seems like he was too good for this world, James Brown, Sly and Clinton presented their own black music reflections, distorted and amplified in their larger-than-life images.

Sometime in the eighties I read Val Wilmer's definitive jazz tome *As Serious As Your Life*, where she declares, 'Black music is, with cinema, the most important art form of this century. In terms of influence there is scarcely anyone touched by it.' By then, I was well in there, eternally smitten, on a lifelong mission to discover and track down the endless spine-chilling records released since the 60s through relentless detective work, New York street-prowling and record shop invasions.

It's been life-affirming encountering Stuart Cosgrove's trilogy of books about soul and social upheavals in '67 Detroit, '68 Memphis and, most recently, *Harlem 69: The Future Of Soul*, which positions that year as the one that saw great changes all round, using New York's city within a city as its microcosm. 'The pace of change in black music in 1969 is best described as a big bang, and sudden splintering and diversification of soul music,' writes Cosgrove as he recounts foundations being laid for the coming decade, by the Last Poets, Gil Scott-Heron and Donny Hathaway, whose Afro-Cuban street chant 'The Ghetto' changed black music, while bringing the term into widespread use.

The assassinations of Malcolm X and Dr Martin Luther King, pillaging of ghetto communities for Vietnam bodybag candidates and relentless police persecution ignited seething anger in America's black communities. In November '68, Richard Nixon won the Presidential election, inaugurated in January '69. This nasty little slug enhanced years of encroaching darkness in black ghettos by routinely ignoring their pleas for assistance. Instead, he helped engineer their wipeout by importing hard drugs and upping the draft. Therefore it came as little surprise when, as Cosgrove says, 'a harder-edged social realism began to shape soul' that even infiltrated Motown's hit assembly line.

The Black Power Party for Self-Defence was formed by Huey Newton and Bobby Seale in Oakland to provide a revolutionary alternative to nonviolent means of protest; an underground resistance movement flying militant style and cool uniform of shades, berets and leather jackets. The Panthers attended classes in combat and black history, aimed at offering disenfranchised kids a positive alternative to the aimless, drug-dictated corner and sense of safety for oppressed communities, running breakfast programmes and holding events teaching black history or their own manifesto. Their initial flush until the end of the decade caught the public imagination, predictably greeted with dismay by a white establishment that considered them more dangerous than the hippie plague. FBI director J. Edgar Hoover called the Panthers 'the greatest threat to the internal security of the country' but, unlike the counterculture's stoner elements flaunting old-fashioned greed and sexism under pretences of free love and new utopias, the Panthers stood for well-organised change in the social structure and tried to implement it in a positive fashion. They really would help an old lady across the road, although even that courtly act could mean a trumped-up beating from racist cops.

The Panthers were too much for an establishment that could mentally handle napalming an unruly mob but not get their little brains around the choreographed shows of militant strength. However, dissent in the ranks, often instigated by shit-stirring FBI undercover infiltrators, was creeping in by early '69, lynchpin Stokely Carmichael relocating to Algiers, for one. April would see the high-profile show-trial of the 'New York 21' Panthers (accused of plotting to blow up department stores, police stations and even the Botanical Gardens over Easter weekend) and Bobby Seale among the 'Chicago Eight' charged with conspiracy to cause a riot at the previous year's Democratic Convention. The net was closing in and would bring further fractures like a domino effect. For now, the dogged Panthers still held their heads and clenched fists high.

The first Panther-produced music came with '69's *Seize The Time*, its revolutionary supper club piano ballads written and performed by young LA chapter leader Elaine Brown. After prominent Panthers John

Huggins and Alprentice 'Bunchy' Carter were shot at a meeting on the UCLA campus that January by members of Ron Karenga's rival US party (who were also in the FBI's grip), Elaine sang her songs to grieving Panthers after the pair's funerals. Panther David Hilliard proclaimed 'The Meeting' (written for exiled Minister of Information Cleaver) the movement's national anthem and reckoned she should get on record. With her annotation and cover designed by Panthers artist Emory Douglas, *Seize the Time*'s songs were beautifully framed by veteran jazz arranger Horace Tapscott, including 'Assassination' (written for the murdered Panthers), 'The Panther', 'Into The Silence' ('we'll just have to get guns and be men') and 'The Meeting'. All benefit from Elaine's vibrant voice, showing how music could be an effective medium for this message; in the sublime Paul Robeson sense rather than aggressive confrontation.

Later that year, the Panthers formed their own house band The Lumpen, who rewrote Curtis Mayfield songs as movement anthems and released a single for imprisoned Bobby Seale called 'Free Bobby Now'. 'Everything about my stage production I got from James Brown,' says Lumpen leader William Calhoun. Despite his show-biz tropes, ruthless business sense, human failings and sometimes patchy albums that could swing between hoary standards and epoch-making funk templates, James Brown is still the original embodiment of rags-to-riches success and black empowerment. His white-hot performances presented black music with its dance-oriented past and coming future as he introduced rhyming over grooves that would birth hiphop. As author Rickey Vincent says in his exemplary *Party Music: The Inside Story of the Black Panthers' Band and How Black Power Transformed Soul Music*, 'James Brown was the most prominent popular entertainer to openly promote and celebrate black pride,' whose late 60s music 'was the single most unifying facet of popular black culture of the time.' Rickey (whose radio show I was honoured to be invited on in 2014 to talk about my George Clinton book) points out how 'Papa's Got A Brand New Bag' ('65), 'It's A Man's Man's Man's World' ('66), 'Cold Sweat' ('67), 'Say It Loud (I'm Black and I'm Proud)' ('68) and '69's 'Mother Popcorn' 'pushed an assertive, black masculine aesthetic into popular music in ways never heard in America...James Brown was at the center of a process of identity formation for a generation (black and white) that was beginning to understand on an intuitive, visceral, personal level what freedom was really about.'

I'd seen the now legendary *Ready Steady Go!* in March 1966 that saw Brown unleash the devastating soul power that had slaughtered the Apollo Theatre on '62's seminal live album and was now gripping London's mod dancefloors. My proper J.B. initiation happened after starting at Aylesbury College in 1970 and playing records at lunchtimes over the common room sound system; my first DJing experience. One of the 'suedehead' contingent (ie mods) brought along some of J.B.'s choicest UK Polydor 45s, and asked if I could remove the Velvet Underground's *White Light/White Heat* and stick 'em on. I was then floored by the skin-tight syncopated grooves, chanted messages, sizzling energy and rubber band bass-lines of 'Say It Loud' and 'Sex Machine'; so much so I was never the same again (the little room where the deck was got quite steamy, adding another lingering funk association!).

Brown would be prolific in '69, releasing four albums that probably boasted five pure funk tracks between them, but what tracks these were. His funky turning point had come with 'Papa's Got A Brand New Bag' defying structural norms by being written on the one and three as opposed to two and four, deploying gospel-style vocal refrains over its pulsing rhythmic thrust. Sax titan Maceo Parker had joined the band that could turn on a dime if Brown twitched his nose, along with his drummer brother Melvin.

Brown refined his new formula on 'Cold Sweat', 'Out Of Sight' and 'Licking Stick', stripping his music down to high-tensile, pulsating grooves while injecting his songs with the spirit of the time. It took the June '66 shooting of James Meredith when walking his one-man March Against Fear from Memphis to Jackson to turn Brown into a politicised tornado. Working independently of organisations, he wanted to draw attention to the vengeful white-on-black violence escalating against civil rights advances. Brown visited Meredith in hospital, recalling in Denise Sullivan's *Keep On Pushing*, 'I was greatly affected by that visit and afterward, I intensified the pledge I had made to myself... It was no longer going to be enough to change the music of a generation; I had to try to change people's way of thinking as well.' Resolving to use his celebrity status 'for the good of my people,' he wrote and recorded 'Money Won't Change You' and 'Don't Be A Drop-Out' and, after striking up a relationship with Vice President Hubert Humphrey, advised the White House on race issues.

When Dr King was assassinated at the Lorraine Motel in Memphis in April '68, it sent the US into panic over potential rioting. Brown was booked to play Boston's Garden and persuaded the mayor to let him televise the show to keep the heat off the streets. Boston remained peaceful that night. He then debagged his credibility with a misfire 45 called 'America Is My Home' and his tour of Vietnam army bases was condemned by anti-war protesters as it had been revealed how black soldiers were being sent on the most dangerous combat missions and suffering disproportionate fatalities. Cast as a lackey of LBJ's government, Brown was shunned by communities who didn't appreciate him supporting the forces responsible for their neighbourhood's decline and young men's decimation. According to band colleague Hank Ballard, Brown was advised by gun-toting Black Panthers to show he was down with the movement. His answer was 'Say It Loud, I'm Black And I'm Proud', a turning point for black music that became everything from political slogan to declaration of defiant empowerment as the word Black was reclaimed from a derogatory term used by whites. Rickey Vincent calls it 'the most important black popular music recording ever released.'

Written by Brown and bandleader Alfred 'Pee Wee' Ellis, 'Say It Loud' held the R&B top spot for six weeks and reached ten in the main chart, gripping feet with its churning funk and giving the Black Power movement its anthem with the deafening hook, bolstered by a mixed-race choir of local LA kids. His opening declaration 'With your bad self' gave J.B. yet another nickname.

'Soul music and the civil rights movement went hand in hand, sort of grew up together,' said Brown who, for reasons known only to his bad self, then released *James Brown Plays Nothing But Soul*, consisting of jazzy organ instrumentals, before the single appeared like Santa's street-wise elves dropping their keks amidst seasonal chestnuts on December '68's *A Soulful Christmas*. In March '69, the song finally titled its own album, appearing alongside a clutch of slow-burning ballads, although the funk rears like a hippo's boner on 'Lickin' Stick'. Starting this year with January's scorching 'Give It Up And Turn It Loose' then 'I Don't Want Nobody To Give Me Nothing (Open Up The Door, I'll Get It Myself)' as 45rpm fire-bombs, Brown kept black flames burning but, although influencing countless others, would later downplay 'Say It Loud'. 'The song is obsolete now,' he insisted in his autobiography. 'But it was necessary to teach pride then... People called 'Black And Proud' militant and angry – maybe because of the line about dying on your feet rather than living on your knees... The song cost me a lot of my crossover audience. The racial makeup at my concerts was mostly black after that. I don't regret recording it, though, even if it was misunderstood. It was badly needed at the time. It helped the Afro-Americans in general and the dark-skinned man in particular. I'm proud of that.'

As always happens after a big record, more black pride outings started appearing in '69, but while political funk and social liberation raged throughout the US, Brown released May's *Getting' Down To It* (tackling Sinatra-style balladeering on standards like 'Strangers In The Night' but slipping in 'Cold Sweat'), before two in August that basked in the new dance craze celebrated on *The Popcorn*, which matched the title track with funky instrumentals like 'The Chicken', 'Soul Pride' released as a single. *It's A Mother* showed his band continuing to develop their virulent strain of subtly-insidious killer funk, 'Mother Popcorn' and 'Mashed Potato', along with nasty live-sounding 'The Little Groovemaker Me', constructing syncopated mosaics of skittering, undulating groove-power forged by master craftsmen funk engineers. The all-round entertainer routines started melting under the syncopated molten juggernaut exploding in Brown's tremulous loins and clued-in consciousness.

By early 1970, Brown's squad included wild space hipster bassist Bootsy Collins, who told me in 1990 when we were sitting in a downtown bar, 'What James Brown meant to me was total bliss. I had never ever seen a black man take care of that much business and have fun at the same time. This cat was so bad at the time; he produced his own records, had his own picture on them, had his own promotion men. These were things I didn't understand, but I realised later how on it this man was.'

March also saw *Cloud Nine* by the Temptations, a psychedelic soul pole-vault from the previous month's *Live At The Copa* that continued through 1970's *Psychedelic Shack* and *Sky's The Limit*. *Cloud Nine* was the first Temps album to feature Dennis Edwards in place of recently-fired David Ruffin, the group's new direction coming from Otis Williams hearing Sly and telling producer Norman Whitfield that funk had come today. Initially, Whitfield was dismissive of what he described as 'a passing fancy' but had the Temps recording 'Cloud Nine's lunging riot of chicka-chicking hi-hats, wah wah action and lyrics about urban childhood hardship by late '68. The new direction was clinched after the single, widely misread as a drug song thanks to declaring 'I'm doing fine up here on cloud nine', hit number six and won Motown its first Grammy. 'I'm gonna love the life I live and live the life I love on cloud nine' gave Primal Scream a future hook.

A few years ago, Topper Headon, The Clash's immortal drummer, explained why the song was his favourite Motown track. ' 'Cloud Nine' actually started me drumming. I first heard it on *Top Of The Pops* when I was about 13 when I was just starting to drum and thought it was brilliant. Then I ended up doing it onstage when I was in a soul band called the G.I.s, who used to do Temptations songs. The arrangement is so good and the words: 'I'm doing fine, on cloud nine!' It's their best song. It was more up my street musically because it had a more funk-rock sound to it, a lot rockier than the stuff they'd done before. If you say to me Temptations, I just say 'Cloud Nine'.'

Elsewhere on the LP, 'Run Away Child, Running Wild' was a cerebral psychedelic doo-wop epic with James Jamerson's vicious bass-line and spaced crawling tiptoe momentum, exploding into bongo fury and scatted vocal interplay; it's desolate inner city funky soul on the button for current times.

Aretha Franklin was well-established as soul's First Lady since 'I Never Loved A Man The Way I Love You' catapulted her to stardom in '67. She'd released two more studio albums in '68 (*Lady Soul* and *Aretha Arrives*), greeting the new year with *Soul '69*'s sublimely jazzy cover versions of Percy Mayfield's 'River's Invitation', Smokey Robinson's 'Tracks Of My Tears', 'Gentle On My Mind', even Bob Lind's 'The Elusive Butterfly'. It showed the lady in fine voice against the Muscle Shoals band and guests including guitarist Kenny Burrell, pianist Joe Zawinul, bassist Ron Carter and David Newman. *Rolling Stone*'s Stanley Booth called the album 'quite possibly the best record to appear in the last five years…excellent in ways in which pop music hasn't been since the Beatles spear-headed the renaissance of rock.' Having said that, the album has been overlooked as a career landmark. Although in fine voice, Aretha's personal life was in shreds as she struggled with her disintegrating marriage, rumoured domestic abuse, charges of disorderly conduct and reckless driving, erratic concerts, snide press and her weight; giving 'Today I Sing the Blues' and 'Tracks Of My Tears' deeper resonance.

A Parliafunkadelicment Thang

This month sees the first high-profile 45 from new crew on the block Funkadelic and first time an 'A Parliafunkadelicment Thang' credit appears on a record label. 'Music For My Mother' sounded like nothing else in black music or rock as it set off its incantatory pulsing hoodoo with alchemical field hollers and fried guitar scratchings glazed in eerie luminescence, topped with sax player Herbert J. Sparkman's hipster space-ghetto-drawl invoking Jim Crow paranoia. The band become a ghostly chorus of siren spirits as Sparky intones, 'I recall when I left a little town in North Carolina/I tried to escape this music/I said it was for old country folks/I went to New York, got slick, Got my hair made, heheheh, No groove, no groove, no groove, no groove, I had no groove, But here it comes! But now, fly on baby…'

In '69 I'd only heard vague rumblings about Parliament and Funkadelic sounded like a great name. When old enough to go to London unaccompanied, I made sure to hit Kensington Market for the first time. Instantly entranced by its bazaar-like hubbub, I made for the record bins and happened across Funkadelic's first album. After gawping at its mirror image cover boasting track titles such as 'Mommy, What's A Funkadelic?' and 'I Got A Thing, You've Got A Thing', I took the plunge and made it the record I went home with; a smart move that ignited a Funkadelic brain invasion that blew my little mind and laid implants that glowed ever-brighter as I succumbed to their dark, opiated shadow world. Dancers got nasty, potent LSD was on the menu and grooves dripped with sweat and other bodily fluids as Funkadelic played the headiest, sexiest, most stoned-out cool music I'd ever heard. It realised everything Hendrix laid foundations for with the Band of Gypsys or, as the afore-mentioned Rickey Vincent says in his Funk bible, 'George Clinton's Parliafunkadelicment Thang captured perhaps the most authentic replication of the Hendrix legacy, recording as Funkadelic…For some, Parliament/Funkadelic was evidence that soul had reached its apocalypse.' Guitarist Eddie Hazel seemed to be transmitting from somewhere behind Jimi's left shoulder, the only successor to my all-time hero after he passed away. Funkadelic still sounds like they picked up Jimi's cosmic baton then sold it for drugs as thunderous blues-rock riffs raged against booming monster-funk with lyrics mirroring the darkest recesses of American society. I had to know more but nothing was forthcoming just yet.

For now, Funkadelic was a gang of fried black rock marauders who didn't give a shit, until along came '71's *Maggot Brain* then '75's *Chocolate City* playing over the in-house system at, of all places, Noel Redding's King's Road record shop, I returned to Clinton's doings and they became another keen hobby, especially after he landed his *Mothership* as Parliament in '75. While living in New York in the 80s, I embarked on a quest to track down every Parliament-Funkadelic-related album and single Clinton had steered (and pretty much succeeded!), collaring George himself for the first of several encounters in '89; at the Warner Brothers offices, where he commandeered a boardroom and dumped half Columbia's national export on the glass table. From there, I saw him at Harlem's famous Apollo Theatre, in London and even DJed for him, including '94's monumental double-header with Primal Scream at Brixton Academy and ten years later at the Forum.

In 2014 I wrote *George Clinton and the Cosmic Odyssey of The P-Funk Empire*; the first major book about the crazy world Clinton built around himself. Here I recounted the incredible tale of the stoned freewheeling gaggle who, gleefully brandishing their acid-fuelled 'free your mind and your ass will follow' manifesto, embodied black power in its most uncut form, reflecting the turmoil of their ravaged country and providing a fun escape route for the beleaguered ghettos. Growing up in the New Jersey industrial city of Newark (after being born in a North Carolina outhouse), George worked his way up to part-owning a ghetto barbershop in nearby Plainfield after becoming renowned for his hair styling expertise. While his R&B vocal group the Parliaments rehearsed in the back room, his community hotbed became a magnet for juvenile delinquents and budding musicians. After the Parliaments flunked their 1962 Motown audition (for resembling the Temptations too much), George landed a songwriting gig with the label's Jobete publishing arm in New York's Brill Building. The Parliaments released singles on Detroit-based independent Revilot, scoring a top 20 hit in 1967 with gospel-soul anthem 'Testify'. After their prestigious headlining show at the Apollo degenerated into disastrous shambles, the Parliaments binned uniforms and dance routines, their stage act getting wilder as they toured clubs and colleges with a band formed around around 17-year-old barbershop kid Billy 'Bass' Nelson. He recruited childhood guitarist friend Eddie Hazel, joined by keyboard prodigy Bernie Worrell, rhythm guitarist Lucius 'Tawl' Ross and drummer

96

Ramon 'Tiki' Fulwood. The band developed their own look with oversized diapers, tie-dyed long johns, superfly street clobber and bags their old suits returned from the cleaners in. The group became heavily influenced by Clinton's old gig circuit buddy Jimi Hendrix and LSD, offering themselves as guinea pigs for Timothy Leary's acid tests at Harvard University.

'Jimi Hendrix was the king of it at that time,' recalled George. 'I knew him as Jimmy James when he was with King Curtis and he wasn't playing like that. He went over to England and did *Are You Experienced*. I was like, "Hey shit! He's doin' it!" As far as that style, we was already doing it ourselves anyway.'

Any Motown ambitions were replaced by Sly and the Family Stone's psychedelic soul, Hendrix's interplanetary soul shocks and blues-rockers like Cream, Vanilla Fudge and Blue Cheer. Sporting a slashed sheet pulled over his Mohican-topped head, George might dive naked into the audience to slap punters upside the head with his todger (including, it's said, his old boss Berry Gordy). 'I was naked, probably,' he struggled to recall. 'I probably poured some wine over my head, then it dripped all down my dick, and as I run across all the tables in there – I don't know if Berry was there, but I know the family was – I would run up and down the table, up the bar, and wine would drip down so everybody say it looked like I peed in everybody's drink. But I was too out of it to even know if I did or not.'

The rock element became properly amplified after the Parliaments were supported by Vanilla Fudge at a Connecticut college. When their equipment was delayed, they borrowed the Fudge's Marshall amps, triple-stack speakers and elephant-size drums with wall-shaking results. Within weeks, the Parliaments sported the same setup. That's when, as George put it, 'We just went totally loony. We'd always be tripping. Everybody in the audience was tripping. You'd see some pimp walking around tripping. That was the funniest shit in the world. He's supposed to be all cool and he's wandering about saying "beeeeeautiful…" '

Despite the global surge of peace-loving consciousness, little had changed in the ghettos, where life was dominated by drug-copping and racist police. By summer '67 there were riots exploding in inner cities, hitting George's Plainfield doorstep, although his barbershop remained unscathed. The Parliaments relocated to Detroit, welcomed by the draft dodgers and radicals attracted to its tolerated revolutionary electricity.

Detroit's riots drove away Motown but fuelled the incendiary rock 'n' roll of the MC5 and Stooges. While east and west coasts were exploring ragas and whimsy, Detroit rock reflected the city's radical no-bullshit attitude. The Parliaments became punks of funk with their unholy psychedelic rock 'n' soul hybrid. Revilot released one final Parliaments single, 'A New Day Begins'/'I'll Stay', licensing it to Atlantic subsidiary Atco in May '69 and making the R&B Top 50 before folding. The Parliaments name and catalogue was cast into legal limbo while they waited for their contract to run out but, for now, the Parliaments were in frozen recess. George simply suggested the backing band make records under another name with Parliament's singers 'guesting'.

The name Funkadelic arose out of stoned banter while the group was driving home from a gig. Laughing at old doo-wop band names such as the Del Vikings, the giggling crew pondered a 'Del' for the psychedelic era. According to Billy in Rob Bowman's liner notes to *Music For Your Mother* compilation, Eddie said something like, 'the Del Funkloroids or some shit like that. We all laughed and I said "no, like Funkadelic." It came out of my mouth, that's the truth...As soon as that name came out, man, there was a little silence and then George started talking about "well yeah, y'all ought to call yourself Funkadelic and we'll have Parliafunkadelicment Thang"...Not even ten minutes later he started talking about the whole concept - a label called Funkadelic, the group Funkadelic and the whole conglomeration/production situation, Parliafunkadelicment Thang. It all came out in that car the same day.'

Their first vinyl appearance under the name, then still in transition, was a one-off that year on the short-lived Funkedelic (sic) label set up by George and Golden World's Ed Wingate. Produced by Mike Terry, the A-side is the supercharged southern-fried funk of 'Whatever Makes My Baby Feel Good', credited to singer Rose Williams, George Clinton and the Funkedelics. The B-side's instrumental is funky and dynamic with a blistering Hazel guitar groove. Detroit record distributor Armen Boladian knew the Parliaments through handling Revilot and started Westbound Records to release the new project, starting with 'Music For My Mother'. Radio stations refused to play it, fearing it might spark more rioting. Boladian later admitted the song 'was just totally against the grain of what was happening in those days...But, believe it or not, the record got played and the record sold. It was not a huge record, but it was certainly the kickoff of what was to come.'

Funkadelic soon slipped out another Westbound 45 that also appeared on the album. Written while he was with Golden World, George's 'I'll Bet You' had been covered by the Jacksons but was now dunked in a subterranean vat of steaming funk, Tiki laying down heavyweight beats under sinister blues riffage and Billy's malevolent rumble, while the singers let fly in the vocal group style, but looser and wilder. The track's big moment is the first savage, scything note of Eddie's solo combining with the vocalists' blood-boiling screams.

Two versions of the single were issued, featuring different B-sides; one in August '69 with the bluesy vamp of 'Qualify And Satisfy', then 'Open Our Eyes' the following month; a soaring, Hazel-sung cover of Leon Lumpkins' 1958 gospel classic made famous by his Gospel Clefs - almost a straight piano gospel workout until Eddie weighs in with his firefly wah-wah over roaring sound effects. Such an impassioned spiritual outing was possibly the last thing anyone expected on a Funkadelic record but can only be a tribute to Professor Lumpkins, the great Newark religious song composer (despite the 'p' ironically missing from his name on the label credit). The single reached 22 in the R&B charts and 60 in pop.

Following that first album, all bets were off as Funkadelic upped their fried funk game through classic albums that enlivened the first half of the 70s. There are too many incredible tales to tell here but they're all in that book I waited 44 years to write.

Soft Velvets and a Desolation Angel

'If you want to write the story of the Velvet Underground...you first have to look at New York City, the mother which spawned them, which gave them its inner fire, creating an umbilical attachment of emotion to a monstrous hulk of urban sprawl. You have to walk its streets, ride its subways, see it bustling and alive in the day, cold and haunted at night. And you have to love it, embrace and recognize its strange power, for there, if anywhere, can you find the roots.'

So wrote Lenny Kaye in the *NY New Times* underground mag around the mid-70s, when the Velvet Underground were on their last legs, reproduced in that October's *Zigzag* as one of the first in-depth features on the band that had been either ignored, hated or shunned during its actual lifetime, only to be hauled out as the true precursor to the punk revolution of a few years hence. Lenny knew; as he says, 'The Velvets are probably the most creative band in America today, dealing in an area which most other groups avoid studiously: life.'

After January '68's demented speed-fest *White Light/White Heat*, the Velvets had managed to be even more shocking on their last album by simply pulling back and going softly reflective on cohesive songs. Of course, it wasn't that obvious; just a Lou Reed trope manifesting that would continue through until his death in 2013; no two albums were the same, the change often unexpected, every one a chapter in his story.

As I said earlier, my lifelong New York obsession probably started with the city's ultimate band. After school between '67-'69, I often walked around the corner to my schoolmate Graham's house, where we'd sit in his bedroom and religiously devour our latest vinyl acquisitions, before discussing them endlessly. An original mono pressing of the *The Velvet Underground & Nico* was a particular fave. I still have it, complete with Eric Emerson's later airbrushed-out head hovering over the band on the cover.

The Velvet Underground & Nico appeared while the world was going technicolour in spangled 1967, recorded nearly a year earlier yet no record label would touch it before it spooked the one they landed. Although barely recognised in the band's four-year supernova lifetime, the album sent gradually swelling shockwaves that have resonated ever since. It now stands as one of the most influential all-time milestones; certainly more than the innovative but firmly-of-its-era quaintness of *Sgt. Pepper's*. Like Suicide ten years later, New York's true originals often found it hard to break into the outside world, even if the city routinely called the shots in art, cinema, literature and musical movements including bebop, doowop, rock 'n' roll, avant jazz, punk, later disco and hiphop.

New York punk's 70s uprising recognised the Velvets as radical sonic revolutionaries; the city's ultimate motherlode. Since then, the album has lost none of its unique supernatural power or enigmatic lyrical mystique, catching this disparate ensemble in its first flush peak as Tin Pan Alley songwriter Lou Reed joined avant-classical electric viola-player John Cale to thrust minimalist punk attitude into rock 'n' roll, bolstered by skin-tight guitarist Sterling Morrison and androgynous Maureen Tucker pounding her upturned bass drum with mallets, their scabrous gutter groove bathed in the surreal, speed-driven excess of Warhol's multi-media Exploding Plastic Inevitable onslaughts. It was worlds apart from the hippie culture the Velvets despised; wilder and more dangerous than anything going on in California or London.

'Heroin' blew my little mind clean out of its socket. At 13 in '67 I didn't really know what Lou Reed was singing about, smack being the domain of jazz artists, although I'd started reading Burroughs. It was the sheer noise and calm-to-storm intensity that gripped me then, and still does, John Cale's hot-wired electric viola screeching like a Black and Dekker power drill sawing through a log and, most definitely, the brain (or, as he put it, a B52 bomber). Mo Tucker's blood-bubbling tom tom pulses perfectly controlling the velocity, its importance felt when she drops the beat for a few seconds as they take off on the coruscating grand finale, leaving the scything melee flying through the air rejoicing in the rush as Lou howls 'When that heroin is in my blood, and the blood is in my head, then I'm as good as dead' before she piles back in so they can finish the job. The song's indescribable aural cleave was surrounded by other forbidden delights, including the clamouring street scenarios of 'Run Run Run' and 'I'm Waiting For The Man' treading turf rarely mentioned on record before. 'Up to Lexington and 125, feel sick and dirty, more dead than alive' marks the first time cold turkey had been graphically displayed in a rock 'n' roll song, perfectly complemented by the jittery, juddering backdrop. Later I found it the perfect description of how I felt myself while falling victim to New York City around 1988.

The album's a non-stop tour-de-force; nerve-shredding viola gouging 'The Black Angel's Death Song', razor-edged S&M chiller 'Venus In Furs', Nico's majestic cavernous melancholy on 'All Tomorrow's Parties' and her opiated ballads 'Femme Fatale' and 'I'll Be Your Mirror', the Exploding Plastic Inevitable-style fried blow-out of 'European Son' bringing proceedings to a glass-shattering close. While enduring their personal nightmare of playing to California's hippie crowds, the Velvets found an unexpected fan and ally in former Sun Ra and Dylan producer Tom Wilson, re-recording a couple of tracks and adding paranoia classic 'Sunday Morning', conceived for Nico until Reed claimed it for himself. Wilson signed the Velvets to the Verve label he was running for MGM and it finally appeared in March '67.

After Nico (more on her later) and Warhol had gone, the Velvets produced the blacker-than-black gutter roar of *White Light/White Heat*; released in January '68 and contender for my favourite album of all time. No rock band ever sounded this extreme, cataclysmic or malevolently evil, its amphetamined proto-punk and twisted lyrical vignettes enough to get it banned and totally ignored by *Rolling Stone*. The title track and nerve-shattering 'I Heard Her Call My Name' were sheer amphetamine psychosis, nailing an intense sonic overload that hasn't been topped since. The epic 'Sister Ray' was the crowning killer; a raging, churning tour de force where Cale tortured his keyboards into a screaming cauldron of pure noise while Reed, inspired by Hubert Selby's *Last Exit To Brooklyn*, sang about a night involving sailors, transvestites, shooting smack and an orgy raided by cops. I always remember first hearing it in a listening booth at a sedate High Wycombe music shop, Cale's demonic organ mutilation surging over the violin counter. Always gave it a blast before going off to sit my O levels in 1970 - possibly why I flopped so miserably at everything except English.

Nothing could top that and, anyway, Reed wanted to rise above making cult albums that didn't sell. The Velvet Underground appeared on the import lists I got from One Stop Records to pore over and sigh. There were also music paper ads just listing the tracks. One was called 'Jesus'. It was the most shocking, perplexing stroke they could have pulled, because they appeared to have gone soft and accessible.

Of course, being the Velvet Underground this was not the whole story, but try and imagine what it was like. While the debut had twisted rock 'n' roll apart to open its horizons with avant-garde experimentalism and New York underbelly narratives, *White Light/White Heat* napalmed it with the most extreme noise onslaught rock had seen. When both failed to sell, Lou Reed decided to pursue a more accessible, song-based direction, while the increasingly-restless Cale still craved carnage. The band wasn't big enough for both of them so Lou, still shaken by Warhol being shot by Valerie Solanas that June, sacked Cale (getting Sterling Morrison to do the deed, estranging him for years). He replaced him that September with eerily similar and conveniently subservient clone, 21-year-old Boston singer-bassist-organist Doug Yule, shortly before recording the third album in November, breaking with tradition by recording in Los Angeles and producing themselves.

Choosing to bask in the sun rather than glimpse its reflection in the gutter, it seemed to represent a clean break from mind-scrambling mayhem. The Velvets looked worryingly normal and happy in sensible pullovers on the cover, this positive new attitude emblazoned on tracks called 'Beginning To See The Light' and afore-mentioned 'Jesus'. The pastoral, acoustic-brushed sound was a startling contrast to what had gone before, subtle double guitar interplay replacing howling cacophony. It also boasted some of Reed's strongest songs, including 'Candy Says' (sung by Yule, about Warhol superstar Candy Darling,), smokey vamp 'Some Kinda Love' and hypnotic 'What Goes On'. Inspired by a girlfriend at Syracuse University, 'Pale Blue Eyes' stands as possibly Reed's most intoxicating love ballad. The only brain-twister was spoken word knees-up 'The Murder Mystery', different voices in each channel.

In retrospect, Lou's desire to emphasise his pop-slanted tender side was a master-move. Now in complete control, with a surrogate who could sing his songs if directed, he could explore other facets of his musical apprenticeship, such as doowop and romantic ballads. The mind boggles at what might have happened if they had carried on down the sewer mined on the second album. Instead he dumped the dazzling Cale, seeing him as competitor rather than collaborator, to take the commercial route. By opening the curtains to let the sunshine in, he actually induced the demise of the band the following year after The Velvet Underground sold even less before they bid farewell with the tortuously-mangled *Loaded*, completed by others after Lou had quit.

Having said that, The Velvet Underground's inevitable *Super Deluxe* reissue shows a thing of rare beauty over three different mixes; the commonly-heard 'Val Valentin' mix, Reed's intimate 'Closet Mix' with vocal upfront and 'Promotional Mono Mix'. There are also 'lost' Velvets tracks recorded in '69, including groove-driven live faves such as 'Foggy Notion' and curios like the original 'Andy's Chest'. The set also includes the full November Matrix shows that partly appeared on '74's *1969: The Velvet Underground Live* album (including a jaw-dropping 37 minute 'Sister Ray' and hair-raising 'White Light/White Heat' that showed they'd lost none of their live fire as they toured America's hipper clubs, also including Cleveland's La Cave and Boston's Tea Party).

Mo Tucker's vocal on 'After Hours' was the Velvets most honestly fragile statement. I'll never forget seeing her sing it with the Reed-less lineup at our Friars club in November '71; alone centre-stage as the only surviving remnant of the once magnificently ground-breaking elemental force that was the Velvet Underground. Lou himself sang those first album classics at Friars in August '72. Now festooned in glitter and makeup reflecting his *Transformer*-period dalliance with Bowie, he still oozed New York charisma as the strength of his songwriting was carried with another band. That night marked the only time I ever met Lou Reed. He smiled and was very pleasant as he signed my ticket (maybe because I was sporting my latest Ken Market haul of black satin jacket, green satin loon pants, liberal slap and eye-liner).

Only later would he acknowledge Cale's assertion that the Velvet Underground 'never really fulfilled our potential.' In some ways, he tried to do that with 1975's *Metal Machine Music* but, as he said, these were all different chapters in the same book.

Nico

After leaving the Velvets, Cale would go on to record his first solo album, 1970's *Vintage Violence*, after joining Elektra as a staff producer/arranger. One of his first projects was Nico's astonishing *The Marble Index*, which sneaked out in late '68 or early '69 but took some months to filter through. I managed to track down a copy around the time *The Velvet Underground* was released and it totally demolished me.

The difference between the two albums was striking. While Reed was cooing what he considered more accessible songs, Cale took Nico to a place he envisioned the early Velvets could have evolved to. According to *Transformer*, Victor Bockris's definitive Reed biography, Cale marched up to Lou with *The Marble Index*, which he arranged in modern European classical fashion after Frasier Mohawk produced the smack-sodden sessions, and said, 'Listen to this; this is what we could have done!' There wasn't much Lou could say, so he didn't.

I'll never forget that day I clocked the black-haired Nico glaring from the cover among the gaily-coloured record bins. It was an image so striking I bought it on the spot without a moment's hesitation (and Helen used it on the front of the French edition of her wonderful Ibiza history *Shadows Across The Moon*, in which Nico figured due to her lifelong relationship with the island). The design perfectly heralded the bleakly-beautiful mood of tracks like 'Frozen Warnings', 'No One Is There', 'Facing The Wind' and jangling, relentless terror of 'Evenings Of Light', which dissolves into Cale freaking his viola into a white noise holocaust. Although arcane folk melodies lace Nico's luminescent cathedral vocals, nothing had ever sounded like this. This music was way beyond *Chelsea Girl*'s baroque ballads, glazed in her harmonium and coated in astral barbed wire deep-fried in a startling new alien tundra.

After 1970's *Desertshore* broadened a similarly-audacious sonic palette to include heart-shredding ballads, Nico remained a fascinating but increasingly ghostly presence in my musical nut-gathering, her ethereal dark magic always haunting. I saw her perform in June '74 at a gig at London's Rainbow Theatre headlined by Kevin Ayers, promoting his *The Confessions of Dr. Dream and Other Stories*, which featured Nico on its epic title track. The bill was completed by Brian Eno and Cale, Mike Oldfield and Robert Wyatt in the backing band, but it was Nico who played the most captivating set, sitting imperiously in black with just her harmonium as she performed her chillingly-dramatic interpretations of The Doors' 'The End' then 'Deutschland Uber Alles'. Three weeks later, she did it again on a sunny Saturday afternoon at Ayers' Hyde Park free concert; a strange experience indeed.

'The End' provided the title track for the Cale-produced album she released on Island. Although gripped by heroin, she still unfurled her unique natural magic on the impossibly desolate 'You Forget To Answer', written when she had failed to contact her former lover and original artistic motivator Jim Morrison by phone then found out he'd died. Nico showed up in London again in '78, playing London's Music Machine at the invitation of the Adverts, but amidst those awed by her returning presence lurched the sub-species of pug-ugly bottle-throwing punks who also abused her opening for Siouxsie and the Banshees that September. I stood on the stage at Hemel Hempstead Pavilion, watching her sitting alone and bewildered as these Neanderthal cowards pelted a lone woman with abuse and missiles. She fled the stage in tears.

Around that time, I spent a memorable evening with the lady herself. The interview appeared in the June '78 *Zigzag* - so last minute I wrote it on the page by hand. We met at Bizarre Records shop owner Larry Debay's Highgate house. When I arrived, Nico was up the pub, so Larry scooted off to get her. Waiting felt weird after spending the week in a state of feverish anticipation, tinged with some apprehension after ploughing through my Nico cuttings, although practically every writer who voiced pre-meeting apprehension said it was unfounded. Larry returned with Nico, sporting black cape, rust-coloured Cossack-style trousers and her trusty boots ('I like boots to be strong, in case I am dropped in the middle of nowhere and have to walk'). She wanted to talk alone so we went to her room, where she plonked herself on the bed and patted it with a smile. 'Come and sit down,' boomed that voice. She smiled and laughed a lot, though still retaining this detached charisma. This is beyond surreal, but we get along like a house on fire.

At one point a dramatic arm gesture sends the shade flying off the small standard lamp by her bed, revealing a little tin inscribed 'HEROIN' when she moves the bedspread with her foot.

'See what I do?' she asks plaintively. 'These things happen to me all the time. What's the matter with me?' The voice alternates between little girl amusement and strident statement. There are long periods of silence. She talks about leaving Island Records and her next album, *Drama Of Exile*. I wonder what made her write.

'Events. Like when I meet someone that strikes me as a personality. Like the Sphinx, right? The Sphinx. I can actually meet the Sphinx because there's the Sphinx in many persons that I've met. Then also, of course, the one in Egypt made out of stone, and I see real similarities. Things like that make me write songs; similarities. And Genghis Khan. I met a young English boy who looked...He was very much a Mongol. His name is David Brown (laughs). He lives in Spain. And I wrote this song, 'Genghis Khan', thinking that he was really Genghis Khan because he looked so very much like the way I imagined Genghis Khan to be. That's how I write songs.'

Suddenly, Nico's harmonium filters through the door; one of her stoned French friends is attempting 'Don't Let Me Misunderstood'. She leaps up crying 'I won't let them play my organ!' On returning she tells me it was a gift from Patti Smith: 'The last one has been stolen from me just a month ago and Patti Smith bought me this one here. I was down and out in Paris and thought, Well, what was I going to without my organ? And then a musician friend of mine had just seen the same organ as I had before in a small place; the only one in whole Paris.'

Chaos now reigns as Nico has to keep ducking out for refills and hauling zonked French men off her organ. The tape is turned off, we take some Polaroids and I leave, pinching myself I've just hung out with Nico. It will be three years before *Drama Of Exile* appears, fraught with tales of stolen tapes, re-recordings and drug-fuelled skulduggery. Nico would show up in Manchester in the '80s, characterised by the heroin-dominated chaos documented in Faction keyboardist James Young's fabulous book *Songs They Never Play On The Radio*. (One evening in 1985 I was astonished to encounter Nico waiting for the eternal man in a Brixton drugs den; she didn't recognise me but all eyes were focused on the black door.) Her final studio album was 1985's *Camera Obscura*, produced by Cale, although her last recorded statement was *Fata Morgana*, capturing the Faction's mesmerising June '88 performance at Berlin Planetarium.

Now free of heroin, Nico would die the following month after falling off her bike when cycling through Ibiza Town on the hottest day of the year. The tragedy's 25th anniversary was marked on the island that provided her home and anchor by a 2013 event organised by my Helen, featuring James Young. She took him to the alley where Nico met her end and me to the same spot the following year. Helen loved Nico as a strong, enigmatic woman. It was yet another element that bonded us.

Like Calling Up Thunder: Blue Cheer

At this time it was vitally important what LP you carried under your arm in the school playground, getting so ridiculous that I would've walked around brandishing Ken Dodd for a laugh. The epitome of cool was some guy in the year above parading about with Blue Cheer's classic debut, *Vincebus Eruptum*, all silver, black and shiny on thick import cardboard; the man of the moment as he strutted around with it under his arm. When someone had the bright idea of starting a record club at school, members chipping in to buy singles to be loaned like a library and played in the music room at lunchtimes, this guy brought along his *Vincebus Eruptum* and set controls to stun. As windows rattled and teachers spluttered into their lunch-time tipples, Cream-hardened kids vibrated with delight at the psychotic guitar solos seemingly double-tracked with little regard for what the other channel was doing, while the hysterical-sounding singer pleaded with his doctor for a painkiller 'SHOT inside of me' over earthquake bass and avalanchal drumming. It was pummelling mindless heaven for a restless teenage

107

brain then, and still is now as Blue Cheer gouged a venerated hole in my cerebral makeup, scarring me for life.

Named after a potent brand of Owsley acid and managed by a Hell's Angel called Gut, Blue Cheer had formed in '66, solidifying at singer-bassist Dickie Peterson, guitarist Leigh Stevens and drummer Paul Whaley by '68. Thanks to an over-worked stack of Marshall amps, they achieved infamy as America's loudest band, accompanied by lurid tales of bleeding ears, heads sliced with low-flying cymbals and all-round dark vibe. They claimed to be angry about the Vietnam War, but hard drugs were later blamed for their wanton nihilism.

Simeon Coxe once told me about the time Blue Cheer supported Silver Apples in Chicago. 'That was astonishing. I can't tell you how many Marshall amps they had stacked on top of each other. It was a big auditorium type of place. They launched into their set and it was so loud the audience left and went out on the street. They were listening to it through the walls and it was still too loud. Danny and I were stuck in the place because we were going to play next. We were behind the curtain and it was just a wall of sound. The drummer was screaming at the others 'Turn the fuck down! Turn the fuck down!', over and over and over again while he was pounding like crazy on his drums. They had a hit called 'Summertime Blues' and they did it but you could not tell which one was that one and which one was the other one. They billed themselves the loudest rock 'n' roll band in the world so they had to prove it every time they went out.'

'Summertime Blues' made number 14 on the Billboard Hot 100, the album number 11. After equally-merciless second album, *Outsideinside*, Blue Cheer underwent lineup changes that saw Stevens, suffering from deafness, replaced by Randy Holden from Californian psych-rockers the Sons of Adam and Other Half, lasting long enough to record side one of the optimistically-titled *New! Improved!*, released this month. Bruce Stephens joined for side two along with keyboardist Ralph Burns Kellogg. The band seem to have stepped back from the extreme noise abyss into the hard rock burgeoning with Iron Butterfly and Steppenwolf, including a cover of Dylan's 'It Takes A Lot To Laugh, It Takes A Train To Cry'. The transformation continued with December's even lighter *Blue Cheer*. Now they were just another US rock band.

Stones and Other Trivia

Work is stepping up on the Stones' new album. They return to 'You Can't Always Get What You Want', adding session singers Doris Troy, Madelaine Bell and actress Nannette Newman to the soaring chorale along with 35-strong London Bach Choir, arranged by Jack Nitzsche. Speaking in *Rave*, a hip teen monthly I'd been getting for years, producer Jimmy Miller said, 'The important thing about *Let It Bleed* is the amount of work Keith did.' He described it as the album that saw Keith take control of the Stones; partly due to Brian's absence from the sessions. Feeling sidelined, when he did turn up he was invariably fucked up and overhears Jagger threatening to throw him out of the band. Brian should've done a 'No Expectations' on 'Love In Vain', although it does feature Keith at his scathing blues-slide best on his Gibson Hummingbird acoustic. Keith had got the track, recorded at Johnson's second session on June 20 1937, from a second collection released in '68 that had been on bootleg. Around this time I'd pored over *King Of The Delta Blues Singers*, originally released in 1961 on CBS, becoming increasingly fascinated by mythical long-lost names such as Blind Lemon Jefferson. But it was Johnson's legend about selling his soul to the devil in exchange for his supernatural guitar skills that proved irresistible to a budding teenage werewolf. This was an arcane lost world which, before the deluge of blues compilations and literature, seemed as mysterious and forbidden as the dinosaurs or fall of ancient Rome. The song about following his lover to the railway station was said to be inspired by Johnson's lover, Willie Mae Powell. Keith and Gram Parsons had explored adding country chords and flavours, enhanced by a visiting Ry Cooder on mandolin later in the month. Cooder also revisited the Stones' version of 'Sister Morphine'.

Elsewhere, The Who have recorded their rock opera about deaf, dumb and blind boy Tommy (inspired by Townsend's childhood abuse, he revealed many years later) and trailer it with the clanging 'Pinball Wizard'. Paul McCartney marries Linda Eastman (a lovely devoted couple when we adjourned to a table at the *Back To The Egg* launch at Abbey Road a few years later), followed by John and Yoko tying the knot in Gibraltar and hosting their 'Bed-In' at the Amsterdam Hilton.

Even though I'm not yet old enough to go, the UK has a thriving gig circuit, as listed in the back of *Melody Maker*. For instance, this month sees Led Zeppelin, Pink Floyd and Spooky Tooth at Van Dykes in Plymouth. Sadly, I will never get to see Middle Earth as this last vestige of London's '67 underground presents its last event at London's Royal Theatre with Caravan, Pete Brown's Battered Ornaments and Writing On The Wall. For just a little while longer, TV is still the lifeline, whether Julie Felix's *Once More With Felix*, BBC2's *Colour Me Pop* (where you can catch the earnest likes of Ten Years After, Free or Caravan), whoever's on *The Golden Shot* or even catch The Who on *Today With Eamonn Andrews*. Fresh from stunning the nation's front rooms with his *All My Loving* documentary, Tony Palmer made a film around Cream's farewell shows at the Royal Albert Hall the previous November; the result is 50 minutes of band interviews (Ginger on good form) and explosive workouts around live faves. Though employing psyched-up camera antics, it's a better document of the band than the soggy *Goodbye* LP. Tony was also the producer of the afore-mentioned *How It Is*. The first show featured Yoko Ono, Henry Moore, Alexis Korner and Victor Spinetti and subsequent programmes welcomed Kenneth Williams, Joe Cocker, the Nice, Fugs and Small Faces. Sadly, after five months, Palmer bowed out and the show got shunted to a late-night spot as *How Late It Is*; past my bloody bedtime!

This month sees the launch of *Creem* magazine from a head shop basement, originally intended to support and mirror Detroit's music community as an underground rock magazine, partly through features and reviews sent in by readers. Pete Frame had it delivered as a member of the Underground Press Syndicate but you wouldn't see it in London shops yet (he very kindly gave me his '69 and '70 issues). Dave Marsh thrilled with his reports and Lester Bangs started here. 15 years later I'd be writing for them.

In these pre-*Zigzag* times, it was down to *Rolling Stone* to give in-depth accounts and reviews of what was happening. They sold it in the local newsagents where my mum worked, despite a cover featuring Jim Morrison emblazoned; 'For: Lewd and Lascivious Behaviour in Public by Exposing His Private Parts and by Simulating Masturbation and Oral Copulation. A Felony.' Yes, Jimbo was in trouble again but this time it looked serious after he faced charges arising from a drunken display inspired by attending a Living Theatre show the previous night. This saw him tear off his shirt and pour champagne over his head while crowd-teasing and bellowing about revolution at Florida's Dinner Key auditorium in front of 10,000 baying devotees. Jim faced a felony and misdemeanours for indecent exposure, open public profanity and public drunkenness. This could mean doing hard time at the notorious Rainford State Penitentiary and the end of the Doors. Accounts varied on whether the king flashed his lizard, most saying he didn't. Manager Bill Siddons described it as 'just another dirty Doors show', although remembers Jim muttering 'Uh-oh, I think I exposed myself.' Speaking in the *New York Times*, Jim declared, 'When I sing my songs in public, it's a dramatic act, but not just acting as in theatre, but a social act.'

RECORDS

Spooky Tooth: *Spooky Two* (Island)

Almost like he was breaking in the massed gospel blues-rock wall-of-sound template he would deploy with the Stones on *Sticky Fingers* and heavier still on *Exile On Main Street*, Jimmy Miller produced one of the greatest albums of the era with the band brought to Island and mentored by Guy Stevens. It's another case of the planets being in the right place as weighty riffs churned, guitarist Luther Grosvenor excelled himself, and the double-fire blues-wailing of twin keyboardists Mike Harrison and Gary Wright drove each other to heights of apoplectic frenzy, framed in richly-woven textures and accentuated by heavenly gospel chorales. Each of the eight tracks was stone killer perfection; the cliffhanging 'Waitin' For The Wind'; dense gospel swell of 'Feelin' Bad'; pain-soothing massed-soul bubble-bath 'I've Got Enough Heartache'; sinister blues howl of 'Evil Woman' giving Luther space to shine; swirling desperation building to cloud-bursting drama on 'Lost In A Dream'; searing bombast of 'That Was Only Yesterday'; proto-metal riiffage of 'Better By You, Better Than Me' and dark shuffle of 'Hangman Hang My Shell On A Tree'. Something different and special I would go back to for years afterwards.

Colosseum: *Those About To Die Salute you* (Vertigo)

Bond refugees Jon Hiseman and Dick Heckstall-Smith form Colosseum with bassist Tony Reeves, organist Dave Greenslade from Chris Farlowe's Thunderbirds and guitarist James Litherland. Heckstall-Smith says the Colosseum concept started in the GBO; 'when Jon and I began to want to have a group in which there were no drug addicts or other timewasters.' The name came when Hiseman and wife saxophonist Barbara Thompson were on holiday in Italy, looking down at the ancient Roman landmark. On returning he rounded up his old mates Reeves, Greenslade and Heckstall-Smith. If anything, Colosseum achieved much of what Bond was trying to do, first single (a cover of his) 'Walking In The Park' swinging like a warthog with blazing testicles, its riff pumped into a monolithic skyscraper as each member lets fly, from guitar-organ skirmishes to Heckstall-Smith's sax battling trumpeter Henry Lowther. 'Mandarin' is an instrumental featuring bass solos, Heckstall-Smith igniting its potent meltdown of riproaring sax riffs countered by Greenslade's swinging Hammond. 'Beware The Ides Of March' is a lustrous instrumental version of 'A Whiter Shade Of Pale'. As Hiseman declares in *Zigzag*; 'I consider the people in my band to be the best in the country on their instruments...Colosseum may never be a world shaking band, it may never be as big or popular as many bands, but I believe this is the only band in England...What I set to do with Colosseum was to beat the star plus rhythm section...without being bigheaded, I've got the only band in the country.'

Quicksilver Messenger Service: *Happy Trails* (Capitol)

Described by Pete Frame as one of the greatest albums of the era and nearly all recorded at the two Fillmores, QSM's second stands as the definitive document of the classic San Francisco ballroom sound and fulfilment of their heady legend. Side one stretches Bo Diddley's 'Who Do You Love' to 25 minutes before the epic, live in the studio 'Calvary' - their sonic painting of the crucifixion, representing the condemnation, journey to the cross and incoming angels. After that sending emotional sparks keening like ectoplasmic static over its majestic sweep, *Happy Trails* closed with Gary Duncan's unwitting recording of the Roy Rogers cowboy song. The album will forever remain firefly flash guitarist John Cippolina's finest 45 minutes. Now the band would splinter, Nicky Hopkins' piano only partly elevating December's *Shady Grove*, before being ruined by self-aggrandising Dino Valenti on his return from jail.

The Byrds: *Dr. Byrds & Mr Hyde* (CBS)

Produced by Dylan-Cash studio cohort Bob Johnston, the Byrds are down to sole original member Roger McGuinn, plus mercurial guitarist Clarence White, drummer Gene Parsons and bassist John York (replacing recently-departed Chris Hillman, who'd gone to the Flying Burrito Brothers). As schizophrenic as its title suggests, the (short)

112

album veers between quintessential Byrds-lite ('Bad Night At The Whisky', 'This Wheel's On Fire') and country doodles ('Old Blue', deceptively vitriolic 'Drug Store Truck Drivin' Man'), the only unifying factor McGuinn singing lead every track. It makes nowhere in the UK. Even a non-album cover of Dylan's 'Lay Lady Lay' fails to take off. 'This is not one of our best,' confessed McGuinn to Pete Frame.

Free: *Tons Of Sobs* (Island)
Produced on a shoestring by Guy Stevens before he formed Mott The Hoople, Free's debut ranks among the rawest of Britain's blues boomers, with none of the band having turned twenty years old. As yet unfogged by drugs, guitarist Paul Kossoff is on stinging form, Paul Rodgers belts out future classic 'The Hunter' and bassist Andy Fraser's elastic four-string lyricism locks beautifully with Simon Kirke's percussive wallop. They'd improved immeasurably by October's self-titled second album. I believe I saw them but can't swear on it.

Mike Bloomfield: *It's Not Killing Me* (CBS).
As a big fan of Bloomfield with the Butterfield band, Electric Flag and Super Session with Al Kooper, I was a tad disappointed when that blistering guitar seemed muted as the vocals on his first solo album. He helped redress the balance by uncorking a couple of killer solos on *Live At Bill Graham's Fillmore East* and reunited with Butterfield for a solid Chess Records hook-up with Muddy Waters and Otis Spann called *Fathers And Sons*. Soon heroin would claim his spark and he'd be found dead in his car in '81.

Bee Gees: *Odessa* (Polydor)
Ambitious concept double album inspired by a vanished ship in 1899, *Odessa* was such a departure for the hit-making BeeGees it's not received well and led to Robin splitting for a solo career. 'First Of May' is its only big hit but the album has since been reappraised as a period classic of extreme visionary depth.

13th Floor Elevators: *Bull Of The Woods* (International Artists)
My entry into the weird and wigged-out Elevators acid-scape came with stumbling on 1966's first album, *The Psychedelic Sounds Of...*, in a charity shop around fifty years ago for 50p. After *Easter Everywhere*

and a live album, the band is on their last legs when they record this final death gasp, only featuring Roky Erickson on four tracks but guitarist Stacy Sutherland supplying more. The Elevators had disintegrated by the time this dark dreamy curio was released, leaving an obscure legend that would only grow in years to come.

Family: *Family Entertainment* (Reprise)

Before the departures of bassist Ric Grech (to Blind Faith) and saxophonist Jim King, Family consolidated the promise shown on *Music In A Doll's House* with solid songs like 'The Weaver's Answer', 'Observations From A Hill' and 'Hung Up Down', Roger Chapman's goat-like warble bleating over Tony Cox's string arrangements, the ubiquitous Nicky Hopkins and Glyn Johns' deft capturing of a shit-hot band that would soon be no more. Gets to number six.

Scott Walker: *Scott 3* (Philips/Fontana)

It was obvious Scott was busting to escape teen-mag pinup oblivion when he started singing Jacques Brel songs, like '67's 'Jackie', on prime-time TV and faced 10,000 screaming fans at the NME Pollwinners Concert with a heartfelt 'Amsterdam'. Three Brel songs, including charged Rod McKuen collaboration 'If You Go Away', join the drone dissonance underpinning Wally Stott's vibrant orchestral arrangements on Scott's transformative third album, other highlights including heart-breaking 'Big Louise', later covered by Marc Almond. A fearlessly beautiful move.

Aylesbury Grammar School;
class of '69

Moody teenager, smiling Wendy

115

Psychedelic poster - 1967

Psychedelic poster - 1968

116

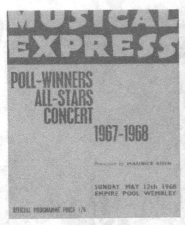

NAME ...Christopher... Nuds......

ADDRESS ...178. Churchill Ave,.....
.....Aylesbury.........
..........Bucks..........

NO ....10019.....................

DATE OF ENROLLMENT October 1964

ANNABELLE SMITH,
93-97, REGENT STREET,
LONDON, W. 1.

Membership card for The Rolling Stones Fan Club

MUSICAL EXPRESS

POLL-WINNERS
ALL-STARS
CONCERT
1967-1968

Presented by MAURICE KINN

SUNDAY MAY 12th 1968
EMPIRE POOL WEMBLEY

OFFICIAL PROGRAMME PRICE 1/6

First gig program 1968

Always meet your heroes; me and Keef in 1980

117

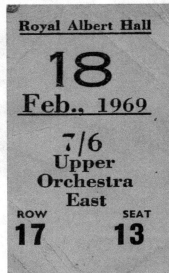

My Jimi Hendrix ticket stub   My RAH programme

RAH soundcheck February 24 1969 *(Pic: Ben Valkhoff)*

RAH soundcheck February 24 1969 *(Pic: Ben Valkhoff)*

Arthur Brown

Velvet Underground on my mind

My promo of withdrawn Marianne Faithfull 45

Kris invents goth as his
posters get darker

'Windmill': the wonderful record
made possible by close friends in
memory of Helen

WINDMILL

SENDELICA
SECRET KNOWLEDGE
THE ORB

GEORGE CLINTON

KRIS & GEORGE, NYC 1994
(Pic: Grant Fleming)

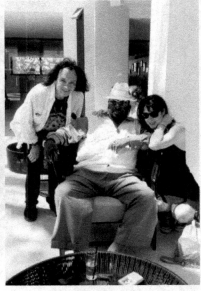

KRIS, GEORGE & HELEN
IBIZA 2014

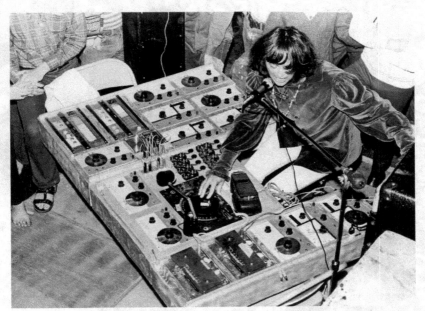

SILVER APPLES, CENTRAL PARK '69

KRIS & NICO, LONDON '78

My original Friars logo   My actual Friars logo

First Friars gig poster

zigzag magazine covers

Graham Bond
demolishes Friars '69

Kris on his 60th birthday
with Pete Frame, Barbican

Another of Kris's
psychedelic posters

Still with smiling dog:
Kris & Jack,
65th birthday, 2019

CHAPTER FOUR

APRIL

ENTER THE ZIGZAG WANDERER; A NEW CLUB IN AN OLD TOWN; TIM BUCKLEY; VILLAGE PEOPLE: IZZY YOUNG, FRED NEIL, PHIL OCHS, TIM HARDIN; TIM ROSE

There's a new monthly music magazine called *Zigzag*, the first of its kind that, ultimately, will change the face of British rock journalism. Back then there were four weekly music papers - *NME*, *Disc & Music Echo*, *Record Mirror*, which I have delivered, plus the jazz-oriented *Melody Maker* and what underground publications I can sneak into the house (*IT*, *Oz*), along with the US's *Creem* and *Rolling Stone*.

Zigzag signals a new era for fan-generated rock journalism, thanks to editor Pete Frame bringing meticulous detail, irreverent humour, unfettered passion and previously-unheard-of personal touch. Heralded by cover star Sandy Denny, the first issue sets out its stall as the first UK fanzine bringing a depth the new music deserves but has never had in this country. *Zigzag* will go on to become central to punk and, although later castrated by clueless publishers, will cling on to the mid-80s before literally turning into *MOJO* after backroom publishing shenanigans few even know about.

Gazing at that first issue, I have no idea *Zigzag* will change my life, in so many ways, and that Pete Frame will become a lifelong friend.

With *Zigzag*, Frame created himself a wide open field in which to run naked wearing a guardsman's busby if he wanted to, everyone invited to join in 'if you have something to say.' He raves about Fairport Convention's *What We Did On Our Holidays* for four pages ('To my mind the record towers like an aardvark over an ant colony compared with all 1969's other releases'), interviews Chicken Shack's Christine Perfect and Blodwyn Pig's Mick Abrahams, remembers Donovan playing 'for a few bob' at the folk club he ran in Luton before reviewing the recently-released *Donovan's Greatest Hits* under his Mac Garry pseudonym. Elsewhere, co-editor Ian Mann examines Leonard Cohen's *Beautiful Losers*, there's a centrefold of 'legendary wild man of St Albans' Ginger Mills and bits on Led Zep, Ramblin' Jack Elliott and Creedence. Frame finishes by declaring, 'If you think this magazine is a bit tattier than you would have liked, we agree. The columns are wonky, there are typing errors, and the whole thing is smaller and a lot less polished than we wanted.' Who gave a toss? Certainly not kids like me, who love Peel but feel the music he plays is woefully under-represented in the existing press. Suddenly we have his literary lifeline counterpart.

Frame arrived as a larger-than-life whirlwind of ideas and passion carried from his teenage years as an original rock 'n' roll tearaway (as recounted in his fantastic book *The Restless Generation*). He started his folk club in '65, putting on Bert Jansch, John Renbourn and that unknown Donovan. 'I was already completely loony,' he confessed as we sat in Aylesbury's historic King's Head pub which, at various times, has entertained Oliver Cromwell and an unknown XTC playing in this very bar. (At this point I should point out Aylesbury is a historic market town with ties to the English Civil War, surviving in this 15th century pub, dominated by the clock tower in the Market Square that Bowie immortalised in 'Five Years').

'I was training to be a chartered surveyor but had always been far more interested in rock 'n' roll than motorbikes and women,' chortles Frame. 'I thought I'd better be in a band but I was fucking hopeless. When the underground press came along I thought maybe this was where it's at. The very first piece I ever wrote got accepted by *International Times*: about a power trio called Hurdy Gurdy (written under a Swedish pseudonym). Donovan wrote 'Hurdy Gurdy Man' for them. They were going to record it then Donovan turned round and said, 'Sorry I'm gonna record it myself!' I wrote this article and it got published in *IT*. I thought, That's it, I'm a writer now!'

Pete subscribed to Boston folk magazine *Broadside* (whose layouts inspired his initial *Zigzag* artwork). Founded in 1962 by folk-activist couple Agnes 'Sis' Cunningham and husband Gordon Friesen, it predated punk-era fanzines as a hand-drawn, photocopied platform for folk music. In his early Village days, Dylan was an active contributor, contributing compositions under the name Blind Boy Grunt.

'There was this bloke who later wrote for it called Peter Stampfel,' continues Pete. 'He became a big mate of mine just through writing letters, turning me on to Country Joe and The Fish, Buffalo Springfield and all these sort of people. He would send me tapes. He also told me about John Fahey. There was all this great underground music around and the only guy playing it was John Peel on Radio One. But it was a very innocent, positive and uplifting time when anything seemed possible. You could do anything you wanted to, so I thought, Right, I'm going to start my own magazine! I started *Zigzag*, which was the very first rock magazine in this country by decades. A few came along which didn't last long but *Zigzag* was the first.

'Originally it was just me and various friends. There was a great anti-establishment feeling about everything. We all believed it was an alternative society - which was a load of bollocks! But I wanted to be part of that camaraderie of people spreading the word. *Zigzag* definitely did that. It brought together a whole body of people. Many readers are still my friends, and still write to me. They used to make pilgrimages up to my house.'

The name was derived from Captain Beefheart's 'Zigzag Wanderer' and the rolling papers. 'Also, I heard that if you approach a stranger in a zigzag line it means you come as a friend. I thought it summed up the whole camaraderie of *Zigzag*. I dropped out of work and did it full time because I thought lying on the floor with headphones on listening to Captain Beefheart and Quicksilver was better than catching the 7.55 to St Pancras every day.'

Pete was the first writer I'd encountered who wrote from the heart with an eloquent flourish when describing something he liked, and a master of the piss-taking insult. At school then college, I harboured an increasing desire to write for *Zigzag*, which went through various changes and editors over the years until Pete returned in the mid-70s. By then I was working on Aylesbury's local paper the *Bucks Advertiser* and we would meet for a drink every lunchtime, hatching plans to take over the world that first manifested in a local scene fanzine called *The Aylesbury Roxette*. Pete invited me to front a band he had put together to play songs he'd select from his enormous collection of 60s psychedelic and garage-punk, many appearing on Lenny Kaye's definitive *Nuggets* compilation. My old school friend Colin Keinch was on guitar and my fellow cub reporter Fraser Pearson on drums, joined by lead guitarist Robin Boult (who went on to play with Fish) and future *Zigzag* editor Paul Kendall on bass. Pete christened us The Aylesbury Bucks and we'd rehearse weekly at his ancient country pile in the nearby village of North Marston, charging through the Standells' 'Dirty Water', Strangeloves' 'Night Time' and Yardbirds' 'Psycho Daisies', me howling like a gnu on heat. I'd never sung before, just played bongos until my hands bled behind local pop star wannabe loony John Otway before he sneaked off with Wild Willy Barrett without telling me. The Bucks played local gigs in late '76 before mutating into the punky Vice Creems, who released two singles, recorded with and supported The Clash and opened for the Adverts and Lurkers, but that's another story.

Suffice to say, *Zigzag* became my '69 bible, first place I read about new bands like Mott The Hoople and, looking at those old issues now, a brilliant reflection of what was happening beyond record company boardrooms and the scantily-flippant music press of the time. I never would have believed that, by '76, I'd become a contributor, let alone take over as editor the following year. I still don't.

A Club is Born

One day after chemistry class, Mr Pike says he's starting a rock club in Aylesbury with a guy called Dave Stopps. By now, my psychedelic posters can be found hanging on the back wall of the chemistry lab, meticulous tapestries of exotic females and stained-glass swirls that consume most of my after-school hours and had recently attracted swarms of admiring females when I allowed them to decorate a mate's birthday bash at a local hall. Robin asks if I'd like to design the new club's membership card. It's to be called Friars and will also change my life in several ways.

What's now a world famous club that recently celebrated its 50th anniversary, actually started life as the germ of an idea Robin came up with made reality, starting with the school dances he ran in '67. Better if he tells how several disparate elements came together to create the club...

'I used to go to the Ram Jam Club in Brixton. The first time I had been in London in the afternoon and Cream, who'd just formed, were advertised. There was a phone number so I went into a call-box in the west end. I said 'Where are you?' 'We're in Brixton High Street.' 'How do I get there?' The tube only went as far as Stockwell then. He said, 'You could go to Stockwell then walk up the Stockwell Road to

Brixton.' So, I got a tube, walked up Stockwell Road and found the Ram Jam Club, which was a doorway with a guy stood over it. I went in, got to the top of the stairs where there were a couple of guys taking the money. One looked at me and said, 'Are you the guy who rang up?' I said 'Yes.' I gathered later that the chances of a white man coming out of Stockwell tube station, walking to Brixton and arriving alive were very small. It was called the Front Line then; people had guns and stuff. But at that time I didn't care. I went to a lot of black clubs for black music, which I liked, and never had a problem. They were surprised to see me as you wouldn't have got up there normally. There was hardly anybody there, perhaps a couple of dozen. Clapton was there with his hair.

'I saw Otis Redding at the Ram Jam in September '66. It was a very small, low stage and he played there with his full band. It just changed my life forever, really. He's the greatest artist of all time in my book. To see this guy at close quarters was something else. He was on his knees with the microphone. He drew you in so you were a part of it. It was just absolutely incredible. The sweat came off him. He was not that far away from being a preacher. It all stems from southern gospel, which is where a lot of music came from. It was like he was talking to me. The next week I saw the Ike and Tina Turner Revue on the same stage with a 12-piece band. Tina Turner was wearing a fur coat when they came onstage through the fire door. She's wearing high heels and a tight skirt, dancing backwards...ah! Those two things together were just indescribable - in a little club. Then another night Nina Simone played. She would perhaps play the Festival Hall. The only reason she played the Ram Jam was because it was a black place and she wanted to play to black people. At that time, Brixton was black, very violent and touchy. The trouble was the black audience in Brixton weren't her audience, so people were talking and she was not at all pleased.'

Then there was the fabled Mothers club at Erdington, near Birmingham.

'I drove up to Erdington on a Friday night, which was when John Peel played music. There wasn't a band on. I joined and got a membership card. It was upstairs, a rectangular room with a stage at the end. We all sat on the floor, as you did, and he played records. It was a real hippy thing. You couldn't really describe it, everybody was just there together. Just the feel of the music, it was just absolutely amazing. When I got back to Aylesbury, I thought there could be something like

131

that here. Put what I saw at the Ram Jam with what I'd seen at Mothers and I began to understand what a club could be. There were loads of little clubs at that time.'

Robin's club dream catalysed by meeting Friars promoter David Stopps when he booked the local Smokey Rice Blues Band for the '68 school dance and found he was their manager.

'I ran school dances as soon as I started teaching at Aylesbury Grammar School. A pupil called Dennis Cutton in my A level chemistry set was the drummer in the Smokey Rice Blues Band. At that time, we alternated with the (girls') high school for the Christmas dances. I booked Smokey Rice and that's the first time I met David Stopps. He appeared at the High School door and said, 'I'm their manager.' I got to thinking. I'd been to these clubs and there was some wonderful stuff happening. Dennis gave me his phone number so I got in touch with David, we met up and I said, 'Why don't we start a club in Aylesbury?' I felt sure there was an audience. I'd been running these coach trips to the Saville, people were interested.'

As it happened, two of Robin's pupils, Adrian Roach and Jerry Slater, were already planning 'more of a folk type club' in the town. 'Bear in mind they were sixteen and we had a tutor group magazine, so Adrian had interviewed Marc Bolan.' These two were a year above me and I found it immensely exciting that Roach spent an afternoon with Marc and Syd Barrett was there having afternoon tea. The ever-resourceful, or maybe fearlessly cheeky, Adrian had gone on that Hendrix trip and somehow ended up sitting between Janis Joplin and Eric Clapton.

Another pupil, stellar guitarist Steven Rennie (whose sister has been my first girlfriend this year, although I got dumped pretty sharpish), suggested to Robin he check out Aylesbury's Ex-Servicemen's Club, which had a little hall with a bar. 'So I went along one afternoon and talked to the person. They didn't have anything on Monday night and it seemed possible. I came up with the idea of Friars partly because there had been a friarage in Aylesbury. It lent itself to an image and the first handouts had the image of a friar. I then went to David with more ideas and he came on board. There were three of us; John Fowler, myself and David. David got fifty per cent, we had twenty five. Bear in mind I had a full-time job and David didn't. Adrian, Jerry and a guy called Terry Harms were involved as well. The six of us had a meeting and signed some sort of agreement because Adrian and Jerry were going to form their club and were now merged. That was the right thing to do and it worked. It all came out of these earlier experiences that I'd had going to clubs.'

The DJ would be Andy Dunkley, who Robin had seen at the Roundhouse's Sunday all-dayers; 'Looking back, that was outrageous really, but a tremendous atmosphere. Andy was playing amazing music and I thought he was absolutely right for Friars. So I went up to Andy and said I was starting a club in Aylesbury; would he be interested in DJing? He said yes. That's how it started. The membership card was based on Mothers' with your design on the front with rules and stuff, which were identical to Mothers.'

This is where I came in. When I got home from school, I got some white cardboard and drew rough templates. I only had one ink pen and a bottle of black Indian ink. I started playing with designs, binning several before happening on the word 'FRIARS' with the 'F' a reversed-colour leaf through the other letters. On the back the pen blobbed and formed a kind of ink devil. Playing with it to disguise its blob origin, I left it as it was. I've since been asked many times what the symbol meant and usually say it's a frog in a boat or something. This modified blob would go on to appear on the back of over 80,000 membership cards.

Robin said I could come with him and David to see a printer in the village of Haddenham on a Saturday morning to explain its presentation. We went in Dave's gold Ford Zodiac. In complete contrast to Mr Pike's cool, sober front, in keeping with his position as Aylesbury Grammar School chemistry teacher, Dave, as we knew him then, was the quintessential hippie promoter with long black hair and beard, exuding good vibes, mad schemes and the flying-by-the-seat-of-the-pants enthusiasm that still carries him as he presents Friars events in today's very different world.

It was all terribly exciting; my first art commission and, even better, ground floor involvement in Aylesbury's answer to Middle Earth and those clubs I saw in the *Melody Maker* gig guide every week. With *Zigzag* too, there really was something in the air.

Strange Feeling

Fifty years later, thinking back to that exciting Saturday, the thing I recall most is gazing at Robin's just-acquired copy of Tim Buckley's *Happy Sad* on the drive home. On the front, Tim is looking down, deep in thought, described by Frame in *Zigzag* as a mind contemplating a sinkhole of melancholy. On the back, he gazes into the camera, his wild, curly hair framed by sunlight creating a rainbow effect. The album was on Elektra so tracks and credits were listed in that distinctive typeface. Only six songs, all tantalisingly long, some familiar from the Peel session Tim recorded on his visit the previous October.

After Robin let me borrow it, I spent the rest of that pivotal day immersed in Buckley's timestoppingly beautiful world. Since then, I've held the belief he's the single most charismatic, jaw-dropping and often criminally misunderstood singer to emerge from that time; my favourite male vocalist next to Otis Redding and Curtis Mayfield, charged with that same deep soul, coupled with an ever-restless muse that refused to stand still. Most early 60s male folk troubadours looked like a hardy, beer-loving bunch as they earnestly bellowed spirited Leadbelly covers and political broadsides. Even on the cover of his self-titled debut album, Buckley had seemed different, his classically-perfect face staring out from under his thick black eyebrows with a mixture of Bambi-eyed innocence and steely defiance, fronting rather than selling the album's mix of LA folk-rock and the dreamy ballads he would soon call his own.

Although Tim Buckley had arrived, few took much notice, although Peel was already a fan. Then came '67's psychedelic magnum opus *Goodbye And Hello*. After that, each successive Buckley album posed fresh challenges and opened up heady new avenues. Tim seemed to be shooting for the moon with not a care he was blasting his career in the foot. He saw himself as a jazz singer making jazz albums; the best vehicle for the astonishing five octave voice that poured molten honey over everything he sang and was never the same in any two performances. The Hendrix of the voice.

Tim came out of LA's vibrant Sunset Strip folk scene after being taken on by Mothers of Invention manager Herb Cohen, who had promoted LA clubs including the Purple Onion, Unicorn and Cosmo Alley. He saw the frizzy haired kid radiating enigmatic charisma with a thrillingly-expressive voice filling the vacancy for LA's answer to Dylan.

In New York, where the folk boom raged in Greenwich Village, Jac Holzman had started Elektra Records in 1950 to release global folk music, operating on a shoestring with a record store. By '66, Elektra was becoming one of the most influential record labels, upping gear in '62 after Dylan turned the folk movement into an epidemic, although, according to New York Folklore Center owner Izzy Young, Elektra rejected Dylan before he signed with Columbia. Undeterred, Holzman signed Greenwich Village's finest, including Koerner, Ray and Glover, Fred Neil, Tom Paxton, Phil Ochs, David Blue, Judy Henske and Judy Collins, before tapping the electric rock scene that made it the world's coolest label, starting with the Paul Butterfield Blues Band and LA's mysterious Love.

Considering Elektra a suitable home for Buckley, Cohen sent Holzman a six-song 10-inch demo acetate that Tim had recorded. Within a week, Holzman had secured 18-year-old Tim to an album deal, announced in *Billboard* with fellow new signings the Doors. By happy coincidence, Tim's new muse and girlfriend Jane Goldstein's father needed her to deliver a Volkswagen van to New York so the couple drove cross country. Arriving in Greenwich Village, they found an apartment on Thompson Street and themselves in the thick of clubs such as the Gaslight, Gerdes Folk City, Café Wha? and Café Au Go Go. Cohen landed Tim a weekly spot at the Night Owl, at 118 West Third Street, near the corner of MacDougal Street. The little club could hold 100 punters and had proved a valuable base for the Lovin' Spoonful, Mamas and the Papas and many more.

For three years from late '86, I went to that address every day to work at Bleecker Bob's Records, which had taken over the space earlier that decade. Sometimes on dead nights (it didn't close until 1am), I would imagine the cramped little record shop as a bustling club, along with the legends that had graced its portals. Ben's Pizzeria was still next door, the ornate Cafe Regio's from *Shaft* around the corner on MacDougal and there was Café Wha?, where Linda Keith had taken Chas Chandler to see hot young guitarist Jimmy Hendrix around the time Buckley arrived.

Tim didn't attract large crowds but those who caught his solo sets were struck by the soaring purity billowing from the thin figure with an untamed afro hunched over a huge 12-string guitar, seemingly caught in perpetual circular motion. His vulnerable lizard prince persona enraptured female fans who gathered at his feet. Tim took to the Village scene with wide-eyed gusto, soaking up the hustle and noise of a new culture. He saw his heroes perform at the clubs, notably doomed Tim Hardin and Fred Neil, who was also managed by Cohen and signed to Elektra. Possessing a richly expressive voice, Neil's substance-besieged blues, folk and jazz on *Bleecker & MacDougal* showed Tim how far he could take his own music. One evening at the Night Owl, he met a lifelong friend and collaborator after being introduced to folk-blues guitarist Lee Underwood.

After Tim and Jane settled in a Bowery apartment with the Night Owl residency building an underground buzz, he was told he could record his debut album - in LA. August saw him record 14 songs with Elektra staff producer Paul Rothchild and engineer Bruce Botnick, strings arranged by Jack Nitzche. The most compelling, future-presaging tracks are ballads; glimmering 'Song Slowly Song', luminescent waltz of 'Song Of The Musician' and accelerating 'Strange Street Affair Under Blue'. Although Tim was on a leash, it was startling to encounter a voice that could soar from sensual moan to falsetto in the twist of a gnat's penis.

Back in Anaheim, Tim's long-suffering ex-wife Mary, who he married young, gave birth to the son later known as Jeff. Focussing on his music rather than domesticity, Tim would carry that guilt for the rest of his life. In turn, this abandonment would have a profound effect on Jeff as he grew into the supernova talent who perished in a dark Memphis river in 1997.

By Christmas, Tim was back in New York, opening for the Mothers of Invention in a nine-night stint at the Balloon Farm on St Mark's Place; a psychedelic club that had opened at the same Polish National Hall where the Velvet Underground accompanied Andy Warhol's Exploding Plastic Inevitable. Tim remained in New York through early '67, playing Village clubs and upstate colleges with his band and, acting on a tip from his friend Jackson Browne, opened for newly-solo Nico at the Dom, the basement bar below the Balloon Farm. His burgeoning sound was further hot-wired when six-foot African-American conga player Carter Crawford Christopher Collins joined after clicking with Tim at a college show. Holed up in the infamous Albert Hotel, Tim wrote new songs, including 'Buzzing Fly', on acid.

Tim's first landmark New York show took place in March at Izzy Young's fabled Folklore Center on 110 MacDougal Street, where he had put on concerts and sold musical instruments, sheet music, books and albums since 1957. If Dave Van Ronk, according to Dylan in *Chronicles Volume One*, was 'the king of MacDougal Street', Izzy was its instigator, agitator and tireless dynamo, his Center the most vital element in New York's folk music revolution; its corner shop and social networking hub for local musical activities. 'Everybody would just live in the store,' Izzy told me in 2010 from the current Folklore Center in Stockholm that he was still operating as he turned 90. 'That's why it was hard to make a living because they weren't buying things, just meeting people and listening to free music. You've got to be an immensely strong idiot to do what I did! There always was a big cultural centre at Greenwich Village. A lot of writers and artists lived there because it was cheap. You sort of knew everybody on the street. I probably would have been more in if I'd drank but I didn't drink, but I went to all the clubs where they had jazz music. The folk music clubs charged too much money for me! So I was living in my own world.'

After negotiating four stone steps past a window sporting Izzy's hand-written sign announcing FOLK MUSIC BLUES FOLK DANCE, visitors entered a seven by thirty feet space housing his shelf-buckling collection of magazines, books, song sheets and self-compiled folk catalogues, records adorning one wall, stringed instruments the other. Izzy pinned up flyers, lyrics and photos of the local singers who hung out there. In *Chronicles*, Dylan describes the Center as 'the citadel of American folk music,' with, 'an antique grace...like an ancient chapel,' and Izzy as, 'an old-line folk enthusiast...In reality, a romantic. To him, folk music glittered like a mound of gold.'

As the downtown folk scene's irrepressible dynamo, Izzy is one of the unsung giants of 20th century American music. 'A different kind of public came to my concerts than went to the clubs. The people who came to my store were cognoscenti and musicians. My store was like a private theatre. There was always a terrific atmosphere, because I didn't cheat anybody and never signed a contract. I didn't give a shit about money; I was just having a good time. I didn't do auditions; I found out by talking to people. If I liked someone I would say, 'Let's do a concert!' They could get 50 dollars; more than off the street.

'Tim Buckley just walked into the store and we talked for maybe six hours. I took care of him and his girlfriend; we had bagels and lox. I said, 'Let's do a concert.' I'd never really heard Tim Buckley before, but knew all about him. That guy was determined to do the best concert he ever did. Tim Buckley wanted to tell a story but knew he couldn't at these gigs where he was playing half an hour. That didn't mean shit but a concert in my store meant something.'

The Center started getting cramped after 40 punters paid their dollar admission to witness concerts in its setting of casual intimacy, names who appeared including Sonny Terry and Brownie McGee, Emmylou Harris, Tom Paley, Gus Cannon and Mance Lipscomb. Izzy rarely recorded these nights, explaining, 'If I did that I would have been just like everybody else. Somehow it was keeping it pure. People remember a concert forever.' As can be heard on Tompkins Square's *Live At The Folklore Center, NYC: March 6, 1967*, the tapes were rolling that night Tim perched on a stool and sang songs from his debut album and upcoming *Goodbye And Hello*, along with never-recorded beauties. They show an immensely powerful talent in its first flush, already striking into unchartered waters with vocal acrobatics. He had started performing his magnificent version of Fred Neil's 'Dolphins', which he witnessed its composer recording in a Hollywood studio around that time. That experience never left Tim, along with learning Fred would never sing a song the same way twice.

Interviewed by Izzy, Buckley said, 'I'm always trying to stretch myself, explore. I love to see change.' He carried that ethos into his next album. Out of the Modern Folk Quartet and producing the Association, Jerry Yester had heard Tim singing at Herb Cohen's house in early '66. Cohen felt he would be perfect to produce the album, which Tim and lyricist Larry Beckett were planning as an ambitious work in keeping with the psychedelic explosion gripping the world. Sessions commenced at the same Western Recorders in Hollywood used by Brian Wilson for *Pet Sounds*. Post-*Sgt. Pepper's*, nothing was sacred when it came to sounds and sources; the perfect climate for Tim to make his grand statement and dispel his troubadour folkie image. His band joined by the legendary Wrecking Crew, Buckley and Beckett took to their big budget studio like kids in a candy store, coating tracks in soft focus shimmer and dark drama. There were two anti-war songs, 'No Man Can Find The War' Beckett's blistering attack on complacent millions watching Vietnam on TV and Tim's desolately-poignant 'Once I Was'. Buying the album in '69, my immediate favourite was 'I Never Asked To Be Your Mountain's bubbling cauldron of congas and slashing twelve-string over which Buckley purges Mary and his infant son from his tortured soul with quivering pleas and demonic yelps. Throbbingly cataclysmic, it captured the turmoil bubbling in his besieged psyche and pointed at future directions. The spellbindingly evocative 'Morning Glory' brings down the curtain. For hours I would luxuriate over every luminescent strand in the LP's psychedelic tapestry and swoon to Tim's voice. If even today the album encapsulates that whole era, it was already time to move on.

Tim and Jane relocated to 613 1/2 Ocean Park Boulevard, on Venice Beach, dropping acid and strolling by the waves. One morning, Tim took new Beckett lyrics that used the mythological femme fatales in Homer's *The Odyssey* as inspiration and wrote spectral ballad 'Song To The Siren'. That November, he unveiled the song on the final episode of the Monkees' TV show, having befriended Michael Nesmith at the Troubadour's hoot nights. Although Tim appeared in the same teen mags that featured pinups of Jim Morrison, *Goodbye And Hello* only made 171 in the *Billboard* top 200, selling a disappointing 50,000 copies. Tim wasn't bothered, being more concerned with the new music he was about to create, '68 marking the start of his transition from bright record company hope to serious artist forging his own path. That April, he made his UK concert debut, sharing a bill at London's Royal Festival Hall with the Incredible String Band, intuitively backed by Collins and Underwood. The trio also recorded a Peel session that included 'Sing A Song for You'; the gentle ballad that would close *Happy Sad*.

Talking to *Record Mirror*'s Norman Jopling during the visit, Tim described his mission as 'breaking down – or trying to break down – prejudice between black and white. Everywhere I go in America, I meet prejudice. This is often aimed towards me, prejudice towards my hair, my clothes, the fact that my conga player is a negro, every possible kind of prejudice.' He promised, 'My most important songs – or those which are most important to me – will be on my next album. I'm not bothered about what I've already done – only what I'm doing or am going to do. There are more jazz-influenced things that I'm doing now, and on stage we do completely different things to the albums.'

On his return to the US, Tim buried himself in jazz furnished by Lee Underwood, devouring Miles' *Kind Of Blue* and Porgy and Bess, Thelonious Monk, Charles Mingus, Bill Evans, Cecil Taylor, Gabor Szabo, Roland Kirk and revelatory throat singer Leon Thomas, his old style a speck in the rear view mirror as he based his new music on jazz improvising. Tim recruited stand-up bassist John Miller for the lower-level fluidity that was perfect for the jazz harmonies and loose rhythms imbuing his new sound. After Beckett was drafted, Tim was free to compose lyrics for the musical explorations swelling in his soul. Unencumbered by singing someone else's lyrics, he fantasised about making his own music of the spheres. In mid-1968, Tim and Jane moved to 19550 Pacific Coast highway, in the idyllic, secluded community of Malibu with a private beach. After Elektra started bellowing for a new album, sessions had taken place at New York's Mayfair Studios in March with Underwood, but the impersonal surroundings resulted in stilted performances of 'Song To The Siren' (shelved until 1970's *Starsailor*), 'Sing A Song For You', 'Danang' and 'Buzzin' Fly'.

Tim returned to the UK in October to headline the Queen Elizabeth Hall, flaunting his rapid evolution with the elemental performances captured on the *Dream Letter* album. Backed by Underwood, David Friedman's vibes and, after budgets didn't extend to Collins and Miller, Pentangle string-bass maestro Danny Thompson, he stretched *Goodbye And Hello* songs, future album tracks and some that would never see a studio. The second set trailered *Happy Sad* with episodic ballad 'Love From Room 109', 'Strange Feelin''s jazzy vamp based on Miles' 'All Blues' and unbearably-poignant 'Dream Letter', merging with also-unrecorded 'Happy Time'.

As '68 gave way to '69, Tim forged new musical visions with two fingers raised at Elektra and the world; a renegade on a mission to demolish barriers between folk and jazz. Interrupted from producing a Pat Boone album (that weirdly featured the first cover of 'Song To The Siren'), Yester returned with former Spoonful guitarist Zal Yanovsky (who Yester had replaced in the band), but any producer was superfluous as, shacked up in Elektra's LA studio, Buckley, Underwood, Miller, Friedman and Collins dissolved into the heady miasma of glimmering dreamscapes, languorous ballads and speaking-in-tongues hoodoo that formed *Happy Sad*, using spontaneous, jazz-style improvisations, best take rather than overdubbing. Yester only had to turn on the tape and let it roll. It took a week, compared to the previous album's month.

'I really loved doing that album,' said Tim. 'It was really a break-out time for me musically, and we had a ball doing that…it was really a labour of love - the way it should be.'

That cover photo set the scene for side one's three lengthy higher plane drifters; 'Strange Feelin'', 'Buzzin' Fly' and ten-minute 'Love From Room 109 At The Islander (On Pacific Coast Highway)'

140

conjoining 'Danang' and 'Ashbury Park' from earlier sessions into a time-stopping exercise in pastoral reflection, underscored by ocean sounds recorded outside Tim's house to hide tape hiss after an error by Botnick. Side two started with Buckley's voice resonating with a lower, richer tone on 'Dream Letter', 'Gypsy Woman''s 12-minute conga blowout unleashing caterwauling vocal gymnastics skydiving over Friedman's bass marimbas and Collins' hoodoo percolating. The closing 'Sing A Song for You' is the only throwback to earlier folk styles.

Even Holzman admitted Tim now saw himself as a jazz musician and 'a different light for himself.' Tim declared 'I can see where I'm really headed, and it will probably get further and further from what people expect of me.' *Happy Sad* made 81 after decent reviews. Pete Frame's heartfelt two-page write-up in *Zigzag* cited its 'vivid and enveloping dreamland...words of sophisticated, soft, satin magic,' and 'works of breathtaking beauty.' Summing it up as 'A treasure of incredible rare aesthetic excellence', Pete signs off calling it 'A love record - to absorb in solitude. To just lie and listen to over and over.'

That's exactly what I did that weekend in April '69 when my whole world seemed to have shifted up a notch towards an ecstatic new one.

Village People

Apart from Elektra, other 50s-established NYC folk labels that continued to operate included the Solomon brothers' Vanguard, Moe Asch's Folkways, Riverside and Tradition. Of course, the turning point for the downtown folk scene came on January 24, 1961 when Robert Zimmerman blew in from Minnesota, in search of the ailing Woody Guthrie and determined to make a splash. By '63, Dylan had made Greenwich Village the place to be during the first half of the decade. It had previously been a more insular community, dominated by venerable Pete Seeger. After Dylan's rise, clubs and coffeehouses magnetised the likes of Tom Paxton, Phil Ochs and Peter, Paul and Mary. By '63, the Village was a musical boom town, Dylan unintentionally leading the charge, like the Beatles were with Liverpool.

Despite being invaded by the rampant gentrification affecting much of New York City, Greenwich Village still looks pretty much the same as it did last century. Only the signs and store-fronts have changed,

141

along with the rents. In the early 60s, the Gaslight on MacDougal Street was a major folk niterie. The liquorless, low-ceilinged basement opened in '58 after local scenester/entrepreneur John Mitchell dug out the floor by hand, becoming the local beatnik watering hole before folkies took over. The cellar became a lesbian bar during the 1970s, then industrial-upholstered Scrap Bar the following decade when I became a regular. Just around the corner working at Bleecker Bob's, I would often negotiate those same steps into its dark confines, unaware then of the history dripping off those exposed brick walls. As MacDougal's neighbourhood bar, next door's Kettle Of Fish was a natural attraction for folkies fleeing the hothouse Gaslight. When Dylan met Hendrix here in '66 the stoned pair just giggled, while local legend has Bob engaging Warhol in a fist fight over Edie Sedgwick. Dylan played his first professional gig at Gerdes Folk City on West 4th Street. John Mitchell opened The Commons coffeehouse on narrow MacDougal offshoot Minetta in '58. The Bitter End on Bleecker Street kicked off in '62 with wildly-successful hootenannies and is still operating. Opening in '58, designed and fitted by future 'Voice of Woodstock' Chip Monck, the Village Gate at 158 Bleecker was a jazz mecca, presenting Miles, Coltrane and Hawkins. Café Au Go Go opened at 152 Bleecker Street in '64. The teeming coffeehouses included Café Figaro, Café Bizarre (where Warhol first saw the Velvet Underground) and many forgotten hole-in-the-wall joints.

Stratospheric force of nature Judy Henske spent time in the Village during this boomtown period when recording her two albums for Elektra that Ace Records asked me to annotate in 2016. Over fifty years later her voice still explodes with joy and wonder remembering. 'When I lived in the Village, it was just fabulous. There wasn't any time of the day or night that you couldn't go somewhere and be talking to someone about something wonderful. The bars closed at four and opened at six. You had enough time to go home, have a shower, change your underwear then go back and start your next day. It was the most fun. There was always somebody to talk to. The Village was really different because LA is really big and everything is really scattered; in the Village everything was just there. It was like a million ants on a postage stamp. You'd go out of your place – I lived at 350 Bleecker – and there'd be ten different people that you could talk to about ten different things. Everybody was so smart. I think you know when you're having the time of your life and I certainly knew. It was the time of my life and it was fabulous."

From the mid-forties, Washington Square Park attracted artists, radicals and musicians to Sunday afternoon gatherings. When 1961's singing permit was denied by the parks commissioner, Izzy Young led weeks of (successful) protest, including the famous 'folk riot' of April 9, 1961. Izzy is the single figure who helped Dylan most during his Village scuffling days; his first New York mentor, surrogate manager pitching him to uninterested record labels and friend, extending his hospitality and priceless books and records to the upstart troubadour. Dylan was a regular face at the Center, where an on-the-spot audition for Dave Van Ronk landed him his first paying gig at the Gaslight.

'He was just hustling, like everybody else,' Izzy told me. 'He would play in the store for anybody who was there, like Dave Van Ronk, Reverend Gary Davis…and his playing wasn't that hot then! He used to hang around and be a pain in the ass. He was a hustler, always asking me questions, wanting to meet everybody. I didn't think he was so interesting in those days, but I did know he was intensive. He ransacked the shelves, read all the magazines. He would go through them regularly and consistently; more than anyone I ever met. He was always listening to the people in the back room and would play with every single person there ever was. He would sit in the back there and type. I didn't think anything of it! Someone sitting in the back typing wasn't anything noticeable, but he was writing those songs.'

On November 4, 1962, Izzy promoted Dylan's first concert, at Carnegie Hall's intimate Chapter annex, losing money after only 52 punters turned up (haggling with Dylan to pay him ten bucks). 'He was jumping around the stage like Ramblin' Jack Elliott does, shaking his boots. He practically fell off the stage he was so relaxed! The concert wasn't that good, but he did have some interesting songs.' Dylan had just signed to Columbia and recorded his debut album two weeks later.

Fred Neil was one of the Village's most talented but frustratingly-difficult artists, considered the best by his peers but reluctant to record, let alone promote his albums. His rich baritone could send send shivers down men's spines and tears down women's faces; a massive influence on Buckley, Gram Parsons, Steven Stills and Pete Stampfel, but Fred didn't sit comfortably in the commercial world. He was a long-time heroin addict, which obviously impacted on his work ethic. Just the few albums he did make were enough to cement a legend. I once asked

Frame for his opinion of the folk scene when I was compiling an album that never saw the light of day. He immediately said, 'If I could distil everyone on your list down to one name it would be Fred Neil.' When I asked his favourite Neil track, he replied, ' 'Bleecker and McDougal'! When I first went to New York in 1970, that was the first landmark I made for and had my picture taken there. It was fantastic, but I never got to interview Fred. He was a junkie and every time we asked to interview him they said he doesn't talk to magazines, so there you go.'

Bleecker and McDougal is often held as the forerunner of the folk-rock movement, with tracks like 'Other Side To This Life' (covered by Jefferson Airplane, Lovin' Spoonful and the Youngbloods), 'Morning Dew', 'Blues On The Ceiling' and 'The Water Is Wide'.

In '69, Neil got flush with royalties from 'Everybody's Talkin', a track from 1966's *Fred Neil* that provided Harry Nilsson with a worldwide smash after its appearance in the *Midnight Cowboy* movie released that May. One of the late 60s' biggest films, it starred Jon Voight as a Texan cowboy who tries his luck as a male prostitute in New York, meets down-and-out Ratso (Dustin Hoffman) and finds the city a cruel, unwelcoming place. Fred had moved to Capitol and knocked out the song in the bog when another track was needed. Having a massive worldwide hit meant he didn't have to work again.

After the success of 'Everybody's Talkin', Fred moved to Florida to spend the last 30 years of his life amongst his beloved dolphins. Here he befriended Cathy, the dolphin who played Flipper in the popular TV series (one of my favourite childhood TV programmes; I can still sing the theme song). He died of natural causes in July, 2001.

Tim Hardin has been one of my precious favourite singers since hearing 'Hang On To A Dream', a minor UK hit in '66. His tender, weary slur resonated deeper than the rest, gracing 'Lady Came From Baltimore', 'Black Sheep Boy', 'Reason To Believe' and 'If I Was A Carpenter' with a fragile, damaged tremor that hit my young heart like opiated honey. Hardin was a stone junkie who'd picked up a hefty habit after joining the Marine Corps at 18 and spending 1959 as a military advisor amidst the poppies of Vietnam. 'Listen, troop ships have got the biggest holds in the world, right?' he told *Zigzag's* Connor McKnight. 'Because many are barracks. Well, raped of beds, showers, stalls and everything else, they could be sent straight to Marseilles with a skeleton crew of 38 cats. I was the only cat hip enough to steal 40 pounds for myself. I took it straight down the gang plank in Hong Kong, switched it to heroin and spent the rest of my Marine Corps days cool. Then I got back to the States and got a big surprise.'

Hardin landed in New York after being discharged in 1961, pursuing an acting career at the American Academy of Dramatic Arts before being expelled for truancy. He started playing his supernatural haunted blues and standards such as 'Staggerlee' and 'Hoochie Coochie Man' at Village niteries. After producer Eric Jacobson signed him to Columbia in mid-'64, Hardin recorded traditional folk-blues songs on electric instruments, beating Dylan but not satisfying Columbia enough to release them. The story's often told of how he composed his most revered songs during an eight month period starting in late '65 at the LA home of Lenny Bruce. After he met muse and on-off lover, actress Susan Morss, their relationship, besieged by Hardin's drug addiction, dominated the rest of his life, inspiring many songs, including 'Lady Came from Baltimore'. Signing with Verve-Forecast in '66, he recorded *Tim Hardin*, which included 'Reason To Believe' (later covered by Rod Stewart), 'Misty Roses', 'Don't Make Promises' and 'Hang On To A Dream'. Although recorded with a small band, including drummer Earl Palmer, Hardin got a shock when the finished product appeared with string arrangements overdubbed without his knowledge. This then-obligatory practice happened again on *Tim Hardin 2* after Hardin sent half an hour of unadorned new songs to New York but the baroque orchestration couldn't smother the strongest songs of his career, each a perfectly-crafted gem of simple, broken-voiced radiance, including 'If I Were A Carpenter', 'Lady Came from Baltimore' and 'Black Sheep Boy'. The late Joe Strummer, whose love of folk music started with his college Guthrie fixation, selected 'Black Sheep Boy' for one of his *London Calling* radio shows for the BBC World Service. Joe described this as the work of a genius, and did not use that term lightly. It melts my heart every time I hear it (makes me think of Joe and dead friends). I also love the line in 'Tribute To Hank Williams' that goes, 'Goodbye Hank Williams my friend, I didn't know you but I've been to places you've been.' There was a time in New York City when that resonated particularly deeply with me too.

A July '68 UK tour didn't get past one Royal Albert Hall show, the rest cancelled due to 'pleurisy'. September's *Tim Hardin 3; Live In Concert* had been recorded at New York's Town Hall with a jazz-inflected small group, Mike Mainieri's vibraphone like a lighthouse sending shimmering globules over moonlit waves washing over a shipwreck. Here I was loving Hardin and Fred Neil in my early teens, little knowing the precarious high-wires these men's creative paths were balanced on. As with any great artist whose brilliance shines brightest when the balance of chemicals and circumstances are just right, tales circulated of Hardin playing an incredible four hour live set without once opening his eyes, or singing beautifully to Fred's guitar and John Sebastian's harmonica at the Night Owl, then turning in a somnambulant clinker the following week. He released cover versions, demos and out-takes on *Tim Hardin 4*.

By '69, Hardin had returned to Columbia, reaching number 50 with stand alone single 'Sing A Song Of Freedom' (ironically a Bobby Darin song which could have been a return gift for 'If I Were A Carpenter', marking Hardin's only protest song). Hardin appeared at Woodstock but smack and stage fright meant Richie Havens bagged his Friday opening spot so he missed the movie and soundtrack. Later emerging filmed evidence showed he still played a captivating ghostly slur of a set. By now, the Hardin family were living in Woodstock, resulting in that year's ambitious *Suite For Susan Moore and Damion; We Are One, One, All In One* on which he openly confesses his love for his wife and two-year-old son using songs and spoken word; a supreme romantic statement or blatantly soppy, depending on your standing or even the Hardin-like condition I was in when, one Saturday night in 1985, alone with my own recently-born son in the early hours, I whacked it on to see if I could appreciate it in the spirit Tim meant it then blubbered like a baby as I looked down at the recently-born Daniel Lee Needs. Susan and Damion had already fled back to LA by the time it was released, leaving Hardin alone in Woodstock with his habit. From here, alternating between US and UK methadone programmes, Hardin recorded three more albums, sold his songwriting publishing and moved back to LA to be near Susan and Damion, bloated but clean. Trying again with Susan, heroin re-entered the relationship, and he fatally overdosed in December at 39.

'He's the one bloke I wish I'd interviewed,' says Frame. 'I used to absolutely adore 'Black Sheep Boy'; fucking amazing that was (starts singing). I can sing all these bloody songs but I can't sing any that came out in the 70s! The vibrancy was extraordinary. All these guys were writing their own songs and doing all sorts of stuff for causes; the civil rights movement, war in Vietnam. They were doing amazing stuff and were so talented.'

Phil Ochs was another firebrand 60s folkie on his last legs by the time '69 rolled around with the sombre *Rehearsals For Retirement*. Another non-New Yorker drawn to the Village in the early 60s, Ochs was a walking paradox whose songs were fiercely political but, as he told many, his goal was also money and stardom; 'the first left-wing star', driven by a combination of ego, ambition and long-running rivalry with Dylan. Ochs was jealous of Bob's mystique, command of words that could cause ructions and resented his withdrawal from the political front line in '64. While Dylan could sail along, safe in the furore he could ignite with the flick of an eyebrow or by sticking a toilet brush in his back pocket, Ochs battled to make the next big statement on whatever was happening in the world.

Rehearsals For Retirement is a morose album, as indicated by its cover depicting his headstone, which reads: PHIL OCHS (AMERICAN) BORN: EL PASO, TEXAS, 1940; DIED: CHICAGO, ILLINOIS, 1968. Its aural grieving asks 'Doesn't Lenny Live Here Any More?', laments the hateful Nixon on 'Another Age' (Ochs pledging 'allegiance against the flag') and references Chicago's 60s-snuffing park riot on 'William Butler Yeats Visits Lincoln Park and Escapes Unscathed'. It was Ochs' poorest seller yet. After 1970's ironically-titled *Greatest Hits*, which contained the chillingly-prescient 'No More Songs', this once incendiary commentator repaired to his brother's house in Far Rockaway, continued drinking heavily, was diagnosed with bipolar disorder and, in April '76, hanged himself.

Whatever demons and contradictions riddled Ochs until his suicide, he was unflinchingly topical, tempering his acidic activism with wit and (often gallows) humour, writing hundreds of songs relating to anything from civil rights to the Vietnam war, including 'I Ain't Marching Any More', 'Crucifixion', 'Draft Dodger Rag', 'There But For Fortune', 'The War Is Over' and 'Outside A Small Circle Of Friends'. In many ways, Ochs was the most rebellious, punk-like Village person; in contrast to, say, the affable Tom Paxton, who was happy to be making a living. That just wouldn't do.

Long Time Man

Tim Rose was another former Village folkie who shot himself in the foot - in his case, with torrents of alcohol and another less-than-successful album in '69. It was my pleasure to spend two long London afternoons with the unrepentant exile in 2002. After having his career revitalised by Nick Cave's cover of Rose's 'Long Time Man' on *Your Funeral...My Trial*, resulting in supporting the Bad Seeds at the Royal Albert Hall and recording 1999's *Haunted*, Rose had released his late-period classic *American Son* and, curiously, was being helped out by my old friend Robin Pike at this time. This led to that afternoon's meeting in a Great Portland pub to conduct one of the first in-depth interviews Tim had ever been asked to do. Neither of us had any idea it would be his last major interview.

I found a man who could laugh with self-deprecating resignation at the colossal balls-ups he made that poleaxed a career that had started so brightly 30 years earlier. The mane of hair was white and glasses were propped on his nose, but Rose still growled with an arrogance and intensity that must have been awesome when he was the young man in a black t-shirt, cigarette clasped in his jutting jaw, on the cover of his self-titled debut album. Compared to Village contemporaries, Rose carried a dark edge that was one of the factors that attracted him to Cave and me in '67. I loved how his songs often built to a throat-shredding, blood-letting scream-up.

That first album remains one of the era's most powerful, moving and resonant statements, a personal favourite since hearing his versions of 'Hey Joe', the one that blueprinted Hendrix's hit, and 'Morning Dew' on Radio London. Rose relished growling and howling through gritty murder ballads, ominous nuclear warnings and desperate love songs in the summer of love, his barely-containable primal roar taking folk music to extreme levels of passion and intensity. Charismatic and talented, he should have been huge but fucked things up with drunken behaviour while subsequent albums were hampered by bad song choices and ill-fitting window dressing, starting with '69's *Through Rose Coloured Glasses*.

Rose started exercising his latent talent after meeting fellow Virginia resident Scott McKenzie (later of 'San Francisco' fame), the pair joining future-Papa John Phillips in the Smoothies, who became the Journeymen. Everything changed when Rose met Cass Elliott at a party. Describing her as the funniest, most talented person he had ever met, they hit it off and took to the road as the Triumvirate, then Big Three after gaining guitarist James Hendricks in Omaha, Nebraska. The Big Three were embraced by the Village scene, playing its clubs then making two albums before Rose found out Cass and James had secretly married (so Hendricks could beat the draft). Rose then formed the Feldmans with Jake Holmes and Rich Husson, who alternated at the Night Owl with the Lovin' Spoonful. He was spotted in '66 by Columbia Records' David Rubinson, who signed him on the spot.

Rose's first single, 'I'm Bringing It Home', produced by Nashville veteran Bob Johnston with Area Code 615, bombed. He was better left alone with minimal embellishment, allowing his wracked rasp the space to wrench every drop of emotion from songs that usually focussed on the bleak end of romance, death and murder. That lonesome, tortured first album was recorded with session band including drummer Bernard 'Pretty' Purdie and bassist Felix Pappalardi. Stark and powerful on 'I Got A Loneliness', unusually poignant on 'Fare Thee Well' and ravishingly melancholic on 'Eat Drink And Be Merry (For Tomorrow You'll Cry)'; there's a cover of Gene Pitney's 'I'm Gonna Be Strong' and his brooding, wailing rearrangement of folk standard 'It Makes A Long-Time Man Feel Bad' into 'Long Time Man' is one of the great prison songs. 'Come Away Melinda's haunted post-nuclear bleakness graced CBS's pocket-friendly *The Rock Machine Turns You On* sampler.

'Hey Joe' was a delicate subject. Tim claimed he first heard it as an Appalachian mountain ballad called 'Blue Steel .44' as a kid then rewrote it. Garage band the Leaves had already released a breakneck pileup through the song as 'Hey Joe, Where You Gonna Go' in November '65 that reached the top 30, claiming they'd learned the song now figuring in any self-respecting garage-rock band's set from Dave Crosby, who got it from Dino Valente (Crosby also taught it to Byrds roadie Bryan MacLean, who brought it to early Love sets and their March '66 first album). 'Hey Joe' had actually been written by coffee-house singer Billy Roberts, who assigned it to Valente to give him an income after he'd served time for drugs. Roberts got the song back after legal wrangling.

Sources vary on how Hendrix first heard 'Hey Joe'. Some say on the Cock 'n' Bull jukebox, others that Chas Chandler had it lined up as Jimi's debut UK single then was stunned to hear it already in his set at Cafe Wha?. Whichever, Rose was so miffed he failed to cash in, recalling, 'I was doing the Saville Theatre one afternoon in 1967 with Fleetwood Mac, Ten Years After, Incredible String Band and Tomorrow. I had a band consisting of Aynsley Dunbar and Ron Wood. There was a woman there who wanted to interview me for *NME*. Her first question: 'What do you think of Hendrix doing your song?' I said, 'Oh yeah, Hendrix plays a nice guitar. It's a Gibson, isn't it?' That was a snotty, shitty answer. 35 years later I wouldn't have said that. I wanted to distance myself from any attempt to connect me with Hendrix, to my detriment. I should've made hay there, just as I could've done when Jeff Beck covered 'Morning Dew' on *Truth*, or the Grateful Dead covered it after they worked with me in San Francisco. I was jealous when I should've been grateful. It would've opened a few doors but I wouldn't let it.'

'Morning Dew' was a post-apocalyptic ballad written by Canadian folk singer Bonnie Dobson. After hearing the latter's version, Rose rocked it into a blisteringly-dramatic nearly four minute crescendo and claimed the songwriting. In 2014, I had the honour of writing liner notes for Ace's reissue of Bonnie's first two 1960 Prestige albums. A lovely soul, she harboured no bitterness, pointing out Rose had actually heisted his arrangement from Fred Neil's version on *Tear Down the Walls*. Some singer-songwriters are lucky enough to write that one song that places them in a hall of fame where the tune gets remembered more than its composer but 'Morning Dew' has served Bonnie well after she spent years clawing back her credit, royalties and establishing herself as much more than a one-tune wonder. She even returned to record an album in 2014, *Take Me Out For A Walk In The Morning Dew*.

After hitting New York in '61, Bonnie recorded *Dear Companion* and *She's Like A Swallow* for Prestige before *Bonnie Dobson At Folk City* featured the first version of 'Morning Dew', composed during an all night songwriting session after a show at LA's Ash Grove in '61 inspired by seeing Stanley Kramer's post-apocalyptic movie *On The Beach*. After recording an album for RCA ('Morning Dew' credited to her), Bonnie settled in England in '69, going back to university to study for a degree in politics, philosophy and history, ending up head administrator for the Philosophy Department at University of London's Birkbeck College. She was still active at 73, revelling in curling the undimmed purity of her voice around songs she started out on and began writing in the early sixties. 'It was so different then,' she sighs. 'It was just me and my guitar and I was just doing what I would normally do if I was standing on stage at some folk club. It's hard to imagine that now.'

When Tim Rose made his '67 UK visit, he played the Saville and Middle Earth, sang 'Morning Dew' on *How It Is* and recorded two amazing Peel sessions. His backing band included John Bonham; already on the booze that would finish him off. Rose sometimes opened for the Doors in the US. 'We had the same agency and they liked working with me. By the time I met them they'd had the hit. I remember being asked to an Elektra party at the Hilton in New York. They were very shy, very accommodating, as you are the first time out. Who was to know what would happen a year later?' Rose was supporting the December '67 night Jim Morrison got hauled in by cops in Newhaven, Connecticut, maced onstage after he'd been caught in an uncompromising position with a female fan backstage. Tim told this story with suitable dramatic pauses and relish of someone who knows the listener is hanging on every word.

'I finished my set and was talking to a couple of guys in the band and Jimmy was well out of it by then. This was an afternoon show so the kids could come: 12, 13 years old. Jimmy's reputation had preceded him. The place is full: three thousand people, mainly girls under fifteen…and about a hundred cops. After my set, I was standing on the side of the stage watching to see what happened because I knew he was drunk. After every song the drummer would look at me and Ray would look across from the keyboards and go like, 'Here we go again.' Jimmy starts and the chief of police comes up to me and says, 'Are you the guy who just sang?' 'Yeah.' 'Do you know this guy?' 'Personally, yes, but we wouldn't have gone to each other's weddings.' 'What's he going to do now?' 'I have no idea but I know it's not vicious and he's not going to hurt anybody.' He said, 'Well, this is Connecticut and we've heard about him.' So Jimmy starts one of those things: 'We know what you want.' The band's going, 'Jimmy, watch it.' Then they're yelling at him and you see the cops from the back of the hall running up. He got so far and undid the zipper. When he did that the chief of police and four cops ran on and got him off the stage and he starts to fight these guys backstage. It wasn't a noble act. It wasn't even rebellious. It was fucking out of control. It would have been fine if he'd done it with eighteen or twenty year olds. He had the crowd in the palm of his hand. The man looked like Jesus Christ. He didn't need this. It was in Miami that he took out his dick. I saw him do that offstage when we went to see a band at the Troubadour in LA. There was a balcony. He didn't like the act that was on on so he took out his dick and started pissing on the audience.

'Morrison did publicly what I was doing privately. My attitude privately wasn't that different from what Jimmy was doing onstage, but I did it to the wrong people, just as he did to the wrong people. I think it killed him because he didn't understand and didn't know the difference. He thought it was his art that people were rejecting but it wasn't at all. It was just his outrageous fucking behaviour but with all the drugs and alcohol he couldn't differentiate, so he died a hero's death. But he didn't die a hero's death. Cass didn't die a hero's death. She had a great fucking voice but she died because she killed herself. These people were greats. But you go back to the tragedy of youth, the tragedy of art. I don't buy all that. It makes great press but we're feeding it. If you're an artist and you're making money people will feed your habit. Nobody cares about you personally as along as you keep producing. You don't listen to people who really love you.'

Tim spoke from his own experience as a hard-drinking hellraiser. Sitting in the pub sipping coke, he squarely blamed alcohol for his career never reaching its full potential.

'No shit! How else would I be acting like that? I was an alcoholic. I had alcoholic behaviour even when I wasn't drunk. My whole career had been coloured by this kind of alcoholic behaviour. I thought drinking was a harmless, we-are-rebels kind of thing which started the first time I tasted tequila when I was with The Big Three. I puked my guts up and thought, 'This is great!' Some out there are gonna say, 'Yeah, well youth be served.' Yes, but assholes aren't. Youth may be served but assholes are devoured. I was an asshole. I'm not gonna apologise to anybody. That's what I was. Myself and Aretha (Franklin) were invited to Clive Davis' house on Central Park West two days after he got married. I got so drunk I tried to pick up his wife. I thought, 'He'll never notice.' Mickey Kapp from Kapp Records walked over and said, 'You may as well take your nuts and cut 'em off because you've just ruined yourself at CBS. Don't think Clive don't know what you're doing.' From that day my career at CBS was fucked. I was doing it all wrong. I went to San Francisco where 'Hey Joe' was number one and picked up Clive's secretary there, a beautiful girl. I got pissed off with her one night and left her on the Golden Gate Bridge, by a cabstand. Of course that got back to the office the next day, so who's going to be a hero? She was pretty influential. Everything that got to Clive went through her. I did it all wrong. I was treading on a lot of people's toes. I was shagging my producer's secretary. People were sensitive to these things.'

Tim's hardheaded approach wasn't able to stop his music falling victim to the afore-mentioned over-production using orchestras and choirs. He always sounded better raw and unadorned, like late Johnny Cash. Instead his post-debut albums were diluted by what Tim described as 'corny arrangements...I allowed myself into a game where if you don't do what the producer says you don't get to do your record. The only one that wasn't like that was the first.'

Through Rose Coloured Glasses might have been adorned with string quartets but contains one of his strongest anti-war statements in the desolate 'Maman', Rose berating injustice and the soldier's plight over solitary drum tattoo. Other highlights included strong originals like 'Roanoke', 'When I Was A Young Man', lovelorn 'Angela' and 'The Days Back When'. He also tackles early Bee Gees composition 'Let There Be Love'. Fluff like 'Hello Sunshine' are disposable.

More albums filtered out during the two decades after 1970's *Love: A Kind Of Hate Story*. We have Nick Cave to thank for many things but bringing Tim back from obscurity for his last years among us was wonderful. I only saw Tim in concert once, at a concert hall in Blackheath he held rapt with still-burning intensity, blossoming in virtuoso attacks on his guitar. We even talked about working together in the studio. Then came the phone-call to say he'd died on the operating table during routine surgery.

Such a waste, in so many ways.

Country Pie

Bob Dylan releases *Nashville Skyline* and Radio Luxemburg is playing 'Lay Lady Lay' through the static. Forget any ten-page analysis of his latest lyrical stand or motives, at the time it's Bob's new nasal croon - practically unrecognisable from the pungent amphetamine sneer of three years earlier - that elicits most comment. Just like he'd rode his electrification of folk from the tentative amplified jangle of *Another Side...* to towering majesty of *Blonde On Blonde*, Dylan had embarked on another cycle after the low-key outlaw serenades of *John Wesley Harding* saw him step back from being reluctant spokesman for his generation by embracing then-uncool country music. *Nashville Skyline* took it further with eight love songs, both happy and sad. He duets with Johnny Cash on 'Girl of the North Country' (one of several the pair recorded together) when the man in black wasn't yet hip (although he will be after February's set recorded at San Quentin prison, led by the smash 'A Boy Named Sue').

'I Threw It All Away', 'Lay Lady Lay' and 'Tonight I'll Be Staying Here With You' are mystical love songs beautifying country's redneck conservative image into heart-grabbing relevance. Like he'd shredded folk's cosy cardigans, Dylan reinterpreted country for modern times, defiantly throwing his counterculture icon crown into the air for some earnest troubadour to scoop up and abuse. Bob had done his time and now craved a quiet life after his speed idol years, knowing that 'Once I held mountains in the palm of my hands' could apply as equally to his old image as lost love; *Nashville Skyline* was cleverer than anyone thought. Now Dylan could do anything, including getting out of the presumptuous Woodstock festival held under his very private nose by agreeing to play his first full gig for three years on a tiny British island that August.

As a suburban teenager with not much money, it was down to wisdom received from 'experts' (reviewers) to get the vibe around a new album and see if it was worth splashing out on. *Nashville Skyline* was sniffily dismissed by those craving 'Like A Rolling Stone' retreads, a steel guitar too far that even lacked the arcane gold prospector mystique surrounding his backing group The Band, who not only pioneered Americana but today's hipster chic (albeit without the ridiculous sculpted beard-short army hair combo favoured by gleeful barbers that looks too conservatively sad to make it as a cutting edge young look).

RECORDS

The Beatles' new 45 'Get Back' also strips away the mystery, unwelcome responsibilities imposed by others and frivolous musical trappings; in their case to get down to some infectious boogie, Lennon playing the country-tinged guitar solo after George's temporary walk-out (fans had no idea of the internal shit and bickering going down with the Fabs). My mate Dave has it on a turntable in the garden when we

154

go over to his house in a nearby country hamlet. I get so carried away I career through his glass kitchen door and cut my wrist (still bear the scars). A contagious little ditty, grown from a jam at Twickenham studios while filming *Let It Be*, 'The Beatles as nature intended' trumpeted the press ads, continuing, 'It's the first Beatles record which is as live as can be, in this electronic age. There's no electronic watchamacallit." (Apart from Glyn Johns grafting the coda from another take, that is).

With its ready-made video from the rooftop knees-up, the single became the first Beatles single to come in at number one, staying there for six weeks. Now it could be relevant again for all the wrong reasons; in his 1980 *Playboy* interview, Lennon recalled Macca staring at Yoko when he sang 'Get back to where you once belonged', even though his lyrics started life sending up racist MP Enoch Powell. Now it could Donald Trump's next campaign song.

Loved the B-side, 'Don't Let Me Down' more. One of Lennon's love songs for Yoko, I loved Lennon's rooftop performance as dowdy nowhere men jostle behind him, their snickering at the weirdos probably swelling into threats in the pub afterwards. They could never know the pure, defiant love Lennon is expressing or even have a clue about the world it was spawned in. Much of the population then was like Alf Garnett minus the comedy aspect, hence Powell being allowed to exist, even applauded. That John chose a gorgeous classic pop melody, nuanced by Paul's harmonies and George's sensitive guitar, as the joyous vehicle for his simple message adds to the song's power as one of the lesser-recognised Beatles B-sides.

Meanwhile, Lennon's old hero Elvis Presley binned the dodgy movies and rode the impact of '68's TV comeback special into American Studios on his Memphis doorstep, capturing a starburst of late period classics including 'In the Ghetto', 'Suspicious Minds', 'Don't Cry Daddy', 'Kentucky Rain' and Martin Luther King-inspired 'If I Can Dream'. Written by Mac Davis for Sammy Davis Jr, 'In The Ghetto' is a masterpiece of melodramatic social comment, hitting Curtis Mayfield territory in relating the plight of a boy born to a mother with more kids than she can feed. He grows up starving, steals, fights, gets a gun and nicks a car, only to be shot and killed as his own child is born; in the ghetto, thus continuing the cycle. The song provides Elvis's first UK hit for years, reaching number two (evocatively covered 15 years later by a respectful Nick Cave).

Blossom Toes' gargling anti-war stonker 'Peace Loving Man' and the Misunderstood's shuddering psych-blues tear-up 'Children Of The Sun' prick the ears on Peel (thanks to his evangelical ravings, I bought heavily into Misunderstood mystique; 'I Can Take You To The Sun' still sends tingles)… On the symphonic soul front Sonny Charles and the Checkmates' 'Black Pearl' is one of Phil Spector's greatest (but most overlooked) productions. I will track down the mothership album *Love Is All We Have To Give in New York* 20 years later.

Dusty Springfield: *Dusty In Memphis* (Atlantic)

Dusty was my favourite British female singer through the 60s thanks to hits like 'I Only Want To Be With You', 'You Don't Have To Say You Love Me', 'Going Back' and countless TV appearances (including her own show on which she duetted with Hendrix on Inez and Charlie Fox's 'Mockingbird'). There was obviously a deeper talent here that had been restrained by Tin Pan Alley; intoxicatingly illustrated when she signed to Atlantic, home of her beloved Aretha, and went to American Recording Studios in November '68 to work with Jerry Wexler, Arif Mardin and Tom Dowd, along with crack band including bassist Tommy Cogbill, guitarist Reggie Young and Elvis's backing vocalists The Sweet Inspirations. Dusty later confessed to feeling over-awed and insecure at recording in the same studio with the same team that produced so many towering recordings but rose to the occasion, recording her final vocals in New York and draping the honeyed grit of her unmistakable voice over future hit 'Son of a Preacher Man', along with songs by Goffin and King, Mann and Weill, Bacharach and David and Randy Newman. And who can resist her version of 'The Windmills Of You Mind'? Elegant, evocative, emotional, the album's a major step in her artistic evolution. Yet *Dusty in Memphis* took a while to sink in with critics and sold poorly, only later recognised as her greatest album.

Chicago Transit Authority: *Chicago Transit Authority* (CBS)

After being taken to Columbia by Blood, Sweat & Tears producer James Guercio, future yacht rock supremos Chicago Transit Authority hit big with their self-titled debut double-album. First appearing under CBS's latest marketing campaign as 'Revolutionaries', CTA's original mission fuses brass-forged jazz with intense rock and soul, living up to their original protest manifesto with tracks like 'Prologue: August 29, 1968' and 'Does Anybody Really Know What Time It Is?' Hendrix is an early fan of guitarist Terry Kath, who stretches out noisily on 'Free Form Guitar', while their scorching version of the Spencer David Group's 'I'm A Man' is a sensation in underground clubs and proto-discos with its Latin percussion hoedown. 'We're a contemporary conglomeration of all idioms,' declares trombonist Jim Carter. 'Call it contemporary rock, borrowing from jazz.' The album goes top 20 on both sides of the Atlantic. By 1970's second double album they've become Chicago. By the time Kath fatally shoots himself by accident in '78 they've smoothed into power ballads and AOR stardom.

Al Green: *Green Is Blues* (Hi)

The beautifully-controlled velvet tones of the man now often called the last great southern soul singer find their natural studio conduit in producer Willie Mitchell and his Hi Rhythm Section, achieving subtle transcendence with familiar covers, including Jerry Butler and Curtis Mayfield's 'I Stand Accused', Gershwin's 'Summertime' and Smokey's 'My Girl', although early compositions such as 'Tomorrow's Dream' and Dixon's 'What Am I Gonna Do With Myself' point at oncoming greatness.

Albums I can't buy and hear later include Taste's self-titled Polydor debut. Peel's had sessions and played LP tracks by superb singer-guitarist Rory Gallagher and his Belfast-spawned power-blues trio, including psych-tinged 45 'Blister On The Moon' and standards such as 'Catfish' given a good shaking.... Peel also hammers Leonard Cohen's second album *Songs From A Room* (CBS). After his lushly-garnished debut, Leonard and producer Bob Johnston strip down his sound to focus on his sonorous monotone and the words of Cohen classics such as 'Bird On The Wire', 'Seems So Long Ago, Nancy' and 'Story Of Isaac'. Peel goes nuts, saying Cohen's name three times every time he plays the album, which goes to number two on the UK charts.... The Isley Brothers release the transformative *It's Our Thing* (Epic), led by their title track hit and delving into Sly-style funk on further singles 'I Know Who You Been Socking It To' and 'Give The Women What They Want'. Soon younger brother Ernie will step up brandishing his sizzling, Hendrix-propelled guitar.... Zappa's Mothers Of Invention drop their double album soundtrack to a proposed science fiction film (that never happened) called *Uncle Meat* (Bizarre/Reprise), further refining his tape-speed experiments and studio exploration using an

even wider smorgasbord of classical, jazz, blues, doo-wop and rock....
The Moody Blues continue their portentous concepts in *On The Threshold Of A Dream* (Deram), trailered by wistful single 'Never Comes a Day'. Side two concludes with 'Dream Sequence', in which Graeme Edge's hilarious poem 'The Dream' leads into Pinder's precious 'Have You Heard? Parts 1 and II'.

CHAPTER FIVE

MAY

BLIND JOE DEATH WALKS AMONG US; ROBBIE BASHO; SLY & THE FAMILY STONE; THE QUIET GENIUS OF CURTIS MAYFIELD; THIRD EAR BAND; TRAFFIC JAM; THUNDERCLAP NEWMAN

1969 was a good year for devotees of John Fahey, the idiosyncratic guitarist who revolutionised steel-string acoustic picking then invented the movement he called American Primitive. In '69, most only knew of Fahey's existence from Peel's championing of the early albums with surreal titles whose impenetrable liner notes did little to alleviate the mystery around a man who could've been an obscure twenties blues eccentric or, as it turned out, the unpredictable virtuoso from Takoma Park, Maryland now recognised as one of the 20th century's greatest innovators.

Fahey was also one of 20th century music's great characters; a romantic academic punk who built his own mythology when he released 78s under the guise of old bluesman Blind Thomas in 1958 and first album as another persona called Blind Joe Death. When people started noticing his blinding guitar playing, John Fahey stepped forward. Although he came from the blues, Fahey created musical genres only he seemed to understand, unintentionally setting trends then disparaging the eager disciples who followed. Although helping instigate the 60s blues revival, he despised with year zero venom the comfortably-elite folkies and loathed hippies drawn to his phantasmagorical annotations. Hailed new age pioneer, Fahey lurched into ear-bleeding racket. The only label he embraced was his own American Primitive but then couldn't abide the earnest strummers who adopted that tag either.

Any of Fahey's early albums can still induce dropped-jaw disbelief at his unparalleled displays of effortless sizzle, letting fly like he doesn't have enough fingers to cope with the music gushing out of his brain, fielding lightning runs, drone clusters and breathtaking acrobatics.

159

Fahey's personal life uncannily mirrored the trials and hardships of his original heroes, dogged by woman trouble, illness, alcoholism, poverty and homelessness while beneath the other-worldly beauty of his guitar excursions bubbled inner turmoil and anger stretching back to childhood. That oblique humour was often present, his mood often sailing with the female besotting him. Fahey saw the guitar as an extension of the soul, his mission to turn it into a one-man orchestra. From austere hymnal to Delta moan or even coruscating racket, Fahey's playing possessed an astonishing purity and majesty that resonated like nobody else, every note and curl a lava fragment from the same volcanic psyche. Some were just prettier than others.

The UK's first taste of Fahey was Peel playing what Broadside of Boston's Phil Spiro described as his 'finest knife piece' on *Top Gear* in '67, purring 'If you're very good I'll invite you for tea and play 'The Death Of The Clayton Peacock', which would be the nicest thing that could possibly happen, and then we'll go and feed the ducks.' Spellbinding; who was this bloke who'd just out-freaked and out-beautified everything else on that show armed with just a guitar and bottleneck? I was transfixed every time I heard Fahey. Never heard guitar playing like it; dazzling and impossibly-atmospheric with something dark and sinister lurking beneath the floorboards. Putting on a Fahey album felt like entering another world, his earlier ones now sounding like sepia snapshots from a bygone time of old time deep south reverie, the later works challengingly evocative.

Fahey later became a lifelong obsession as I tried excavating his convoluted catalogue from every corner of the planet, finding him lodged in my brain whenever I've entered a record shop over the last 50 years, New York proving the most fertile hunting ground. Then I got to write about him, starting with *Zigzag* at the height of punk (as the original provocateur who launched one of the first independent labels). Nearly 40 years later I tried to unravel Fahey's impossibly-convoluted catalogue as one of the first things I did for *Record Collector*. In 2012, Ace Records asked if I would compile a consummate career-spanning compilation but we couldn't even find, let alone clear, all the tracks in that esoteric tangle of around 40 albums released between 1959 and 2001 when Fahey passed away; a minefield of aliases, re-recordings, reissues, limited pressings and red herrings. I praised the Great Koonaklaster when Claudio Guerrieri's awesomely-exhaustive two

160

volume *The John Fahey Handbook* appeared to finally explain everything, down to run-out groove widths.

Before '69, Fahey's British releases were confined to '65's *The Transfiguration Of Blind Joe Death*. Now his UK catalogue swelled with the releases of late '68's *The Yellow Princess* and '67's *Requia*, plus first two albums *Blind Joe Death* and *Death Chants, Breakdowns and Military Waltzes*. Further Fahey furore was stoked by the man playing his first UK tour.

John Fahey was born in February 1939 in Takoma Park, Maryland, where he spent his formative years. His father, Aloysius, who worked for the Public Health Department, and mother Jane both played piano so Fahey appreciated classical music from childhood, playing clarinet at eleven in his school band at Junior High, where the music teacher told him he could never be a musician ('I never forgot that'). After the soundtrack to *The Thief of Baghdad* on a 1948 cinema trip sparked his love of music, he became gripped by hillbilly and country music he heard on the radio and on family trips to the New River Ranch in Rising Sun, Maryland, witnessing the Stanley Brothers and Bill Monroe. After noticing girls flocking around guitar-toting guys in the park, he saved 17 dollars from his paper round to buy a Silvertone guitar from the Sears-Roebuck catalogue, teaching himself to play from Pete Seeger's guitar instructional book, all the time plotting his own compositions. First song he wrote, in his mid-teens, was 'On The Sunny Side Of The Ocean'.

Fahey got heavily into bluegrass after hearing Bill Monroe's 1941 version of Jimmie Rodgers' 'Blue Yodel No. 7' on the radio, his quest for the record leading him to befriend Washington DC record collector Dick Spottswood. The pair started going on record-collecting trips, canvassing door-to-door in Maryland, Virginia and North Carolina. One such jaunt turned up a 1929 Columbia 78 of Blind Willie Johnson's 'Praise God I'm Satisfied'. Accounts liken its impact on him to religious epiphany. He became obsessed with country blues, learning to pick off old records as canvassing continued, accompanied by fellow local record collectors, including Henry Vestine and Joe Bussard, sometimes deep into the south. Fahey gathered key early influences including pre-war finger-picker Sam McGee and Kentucky country blues pioneer Sylvester Weaver, who inspired him to tackle slide. While he studied crackly old 78s by Barbecue Bob, Mississippi John Hurt and Flamenco ragtime maestro Blind Blake, his early guitar foragings were also

161

informed by classical music and Episcopalian hymns he sang at church, resulting in the cross-cultural pollination blossoming by his first recording session, where he blueprinted his extended suites with 'The Transcendental Waterfall'. 'I was thinking mainly of Bartok as a model, but played in this finger picking pattern,' he told *The Wire*'s Edwin Pouncey in '98. 'Everybody else was just trying to copy folk musicians...I was never trying to be a folk. How can I be a folk? I'm from the suburbs, you know.'

Music also helped Fahey escape childhood trauma that included, as he told Pouncey, childhood sexual abuse from his father. 'Mainly it's a parental situation. I was writing these things as an escape, as a possible way to make money...I was creating for myself an imaginary, beautiful world and pretending that I lived there, but I didn't feel that beautiful. I was mad but I wasn't aware of it. I was also very sad, afraid and lonely.' After his parents separated in the mid-50s, Fahey lived with his mother on New Hampshire Avenue. He enrolled to study philosophy at the University of Maryland, befriending future Takoma partner Eugene 'ED' Denson and budding guitar iconoclast Robbie Basho, before switching to D.C.'s American University to study philosophy and religion.

Fahey and friends such as flautist Nancy McLean and organist Anthony 'Flea' Lee hung out and jammed at the local St Michael and All Angels Episcopal Church. After Pat Sullivan became first of his lifelong string of all-consuming girlfriend/muses, the pair played guitars together for hours. Fahey dedicated 'A Raga Called Pat' to her, declaring in a '92 interview, 'She was the only person who understood what I was doing...I would never have become a good guitarist or anything if it hadn't been for her.'

Folk giant Mike Seeger introduced Fahey to singer-guitarist Elizabeth 'Libba' Cotten, then working as his family's domestic in D.C.. She was in her 60s when her massively-influential *Folksongs And Instrumentals With Guitar* was released in '58 (including her signature 'Freight Train'). The pair jammed together, Elizabeth teaching Fahey slide techniques and open chords that had previously baffled him as few blues musicians stuck to rigid playing conventions. Her single string picking, adapted from south-eastern country ragtime, is a noticeable influence.

Blues legend Charley Patton was the single most inspirational figure in Fahey's life. An abrasive shouter and story-teller with a hard, ricocheting guitar tone, he started playing in public around 1897, a favourite at juke joints on the huge plantations, singing blues, gospel and pop hits, adding moves like playing his guitar behind his head. Beset by drunkenness and woman trouble, Patton played dives for thirty years, recording 52 epoch-making sides for Paramount between 1929 and his last New York session in 1934, three months before he died from a congenital heart condition. Credited with teaching Son House and John Lee Hooker guitar, Patton sang about events and characters on his home turf, including police harassment on 'Tom Rushen Blues', plantation owners on 'Joe Kirby', jail on 'High Sheriff Blues' and 1927's floods on 'High Water Everywhere'.

The latter song was Fahey's port of entry into Patton's music around 1958 after he bagged a copy on a North Carolina canvassing trip. The 78 prodded Fahey to raid Spottswood's Patton stash, feverishly absorbing the idiosyncrasies, harmonies and dissonant embellishments, beginning the obsession that would pepper his repertoire and fuel his UCLA Master's thesis. Published in 1970 by Studio Vista Books (when I was lucky enough to unearth a copy in the Oxfam shop), it's a remarkable piece of research into blues and music theory, assisted by future room-mate Al Wilson. Fahey describes Patton as, 'the greatest blues singer I've ever heard…actor, hypnotist, clown, preacher, wealthy magician…a pioneer in the externalisation through music of strange, weird, even ghastly emotional states…a pilgrim of the ominous.'

When recounting the stories of Fahey, the Stones and other blues pilgrims it should be remembered that when these artists were on their evangelical blues missions there weren't compilations or any internet to conjure obscure recordings with a click. These artists were unknown, except to scholars like Fahey and friends, who performed as great a service establishing their legacies as Harry Smith's celebrated *Anthology of American Folk Music*. Pre-war country blues was an impossibly obscure field in a market dusting itself off after the rock 'n' roll revolution its electric descendant had helped birth. Even in '69, few knew about Patton, Son House, Skip James or Bukka White, although we got Robert Johnson's astonishing album on CBS. Before Fahey, my blues foragings were Stones-motivated and of the electric Chicago variety (Muddy, Jimmy Reed, etc). Fahey was exploring a rawer, more primitive, darker new world.

Joe Bussard of Frederick, Maryland, began record hunting in the late 40s, building up the largest collection of 1920s-30s blues, folk and gospel 78s in the world, over 30,000 crammed into the basement where he also recorded visiting pilgrims like 19-year-old Fahey, whose guitar-playing was already beyond his years. Between 1956 and 1970, Joe's Fonotone was the last record label releasing 78s as he taped then cut them as ten-inch records on his lathe, typing labels and sticking them on the disc. Sometimes, he ran off ten or twelve inch 33rpm EPs or LPs, switching to seven-inch 45rpm records until 1985, when he offered compilations on cassette. Fahey started releasing Fonotone records in early '58, continuing sporadically for the next seven years. Thankfully, these super-rarities were assembled over five CDs on the superlative *Your Past Comes Back To Haunt You* bookset that shows how later Fahey standards such as 'In Christ There Is No East Or West' and 'The Transcendental Waterfall' were blueprinted in Joe's basement. Fahey's first recording was 'Takoma Park Pool Hall Blues', a skeletal rework of Blind Willie Johnson's 'Dark Was The Night, Cold Was The Ground'. Like anything he covered, it was pillaged then adapted his into his rapidly-evolving personal soundscapes, celebrating the 'buried tune', twisted into something new; as can be heard on his scintillating versions of 'John Henry', 'Poor Boy Long Ways From Home', the Staple Singers' 'Uncloudy Day' and Robert Johnson-derived 'On Doing An Evil Deed Blues'.

October '58's session marked the birth of Fahey's first musical persona, created after Bussard prodded him to 'sing like an old black guy and sing rough as hell and we'll call you Blind Thomas.' Fahey's Blind Thomas output was Patton heavy, the closest he got to straight replication, sometimes including his drunken singing as he commenced debunking blues mythology and starting his own with this anonymous test-driving; at the same time he was honing his own compositions during long hours as night manager at Langley Park's Esso gas station, where he worked for three years. After school friend Dalles Sherwood heard him playing, she suggested making an album. In April 1959, Pat Sullivan recorded Fahey playing Fonotone items and his compositions at St Michael's Church. He decided to release it himself, explaining, 'I thought I'd be wasting my time to go to commercial record companies and make demos for them because, don't forget, I was doing what I was doing and nobody understood what I was doing.' Raising the necessary $300 from most likely his mother, Fahey had a hundred albums pressed

164

at RCA Custom Recorders (some damaged in transit); one side rubber-stamped JOHN FAHEY, the other BLIND JOE DEATH. As Fahey told Edwin Pouncey, 'I wanted to die. Blind Joe Death was my death instinct. He was also all the negroes in the slums who were suffering. He was the incarnation, not only of my death wish, but of all the aggressive instincts in me.'

Calling his label Takoma, Fahey sold his album at work, gave some away, sneaked them into thrift stores, taking three years to shift them. Now it's one of the most highly-sought private pressings in the world. Blues scholar Sam Charters famously wrote Fahey a hissy letter in response to the album, primarily because it had the audacity to be instrumental; there hadn't been albums of just acoustic guitar before. Eventually, there would be different incarnations of the set through reissues, Fahey re-recording tracks in April '64 and for stereo in '67.

In 1962, after graduating with a B.A. in Philosophy of Religion, Fahey ended up in Berkeley, California (where Ed had settled with new wife Pat Sullivan, who returned to Fahey). In 1963, he enrolled to study philosophy at the University of California, but found time to track down long-lost blues legend Booker T. Washington (or 'Bukka') White with Ed by going on a line in 'Aberdeen, Mississippi Blues'. Fahey sent a random postcard picked up by a relative working in the postal service, who forwarded it to Bukka, who was then working for a Memphis tank company. After he replied, Fahey and Ed travelled to Memphis, producing Bukka's *Mississippi Blues* and releasing it on Takoma Records. The pair made the label official with Fahey's *Death Chants, Breakdowns and Military Waltzes*, recorded in two whiskey-fuelled autumn days at Sierra Sound Studios. It sold out in months after Fahey hooked up with record distributor Norman Pierce, who ran Jack's Record Cellar in San Francisco and started a buzz in Boston by sending up a batch. Fahey got his first press review from Phil Spiro, who called him 'The most inventive, original guitarist working in the folk idiom today.'

Fahey joined the Master's programme of Ethnomusicology at UCLA's Folklore and Mythology department at the invitation of new head Donald Knight Wilgus. Wilgus persuaded Fahey to move to LA, where he began his Patton thesis. 'I wanted to find out what it was about Patton that was so exciting,' he explained. 'Because to me he was the most exciting guitar player and blues singer I ever heard. So in order to to find out what he was doing I had to really analyse what he did.' Fahey took music theory advice from new room-mate Al Wilson, who he named 'Blind Owl' after his near-sightedness and introduced to old mucker Henry Vestine and vociferous man mountain Bob Hite, resulting in the formation of Canned Heat. Fahey played with them too, until they bought amplifiers and turned into a serious band. Wilson was a prodigious supernova talent who mastered Fahey's Indian veena as easily as Brian Jones did the sitar. While doing the heavy analysis for Fahey's Patton thesis, Wilson even taught Son House his own songs after the blues legend was rediscovered - on the same day Fahey and crew tracked down the mysterious Skip James.

Accompanied by guitarist Bill Barth (later of the fabled Insect Trust), Fahey set out to find Nehemiah 'Skip' James simply to learn about his unearthly tunings. Skip was then known only to the few who had heard his eerie falsetto on sides cut for Paramount in 1931, including 'Crow Jane', 'Cypress Grove' and 'I'm So Glad'. Fahey, Barth and Vestine doggedly tracked him down to a Tunica, Mississippi hospital. After paying his bills, they brought him to record at Silver Springs, Maryland's Adelphi Studios (engineer Gene Rosenthal's basement) and perform at the Newport Folk Festival. The simultaneous discovery of Son House is credited with starting the sixties American blues revival. Unlike fishing buddy Bukka, Fahey failed to connect with Skip and described him as 'a hateful old creep' (Skip passed away in late '69).

Fahey and Barth recorded *Dance Of Death and Other Plantation Favorites* at Silver Springs in August '64 (released September '65), continuing to explore blues and Appalachian folk forms, along with raga-esque excursions. The title track became one of Fahey's best known songs after being used for the desert rumpo scene in Michelangelo Antonioni's late 60s hippy-trip movie *Zabriskie Point*. In June '67, having just married Janet Lebow, Fahey went to Rome to work on the soundtrack but was only shown the sex scene and, according to his bride in biography *Dance Of Death*, found himself facing a creative block, although Fahey's self-mythologising always had him decking Antonioni in a restaurant after an argument stemming from the director's hatred of America, resulting in none of his soundtrack being used. That nice Pink Floyd were less trouble.

In June '65 sessions arranged by Barry Hansen, Fahey recorded at the home of Robert Riskin, owner of McCabe's Guitar Shop in Topanga

Canyon, accompanied by banjo-player L. Mayne Smith (from UCLA's Folklore program) and second guitarist Mark Levine. These joined tracks recorded during Fahey's Boston visit the following month at MIT radio station, Cambridge to produce *The Transfiguration of Blind Joe Death*; initially a 50-pressing promo on Boston's Riverboat Records (partly set up by future London underground dynamo Joe Boyd, then a Harvard student). Released in February '67, this sparkling distillation of Fahey's ever-increasing powers became his first UK release when it appeared on Transatlantic the following year. There it is in the record bins of the Chelsea Drugstore in *A Clockwork Orange*, as selected by Stanley Kubrick (who had HAL the mad super-computer singing 'Bicycle Made For Two' in *2001: A Space Odyssey* - coincidentally a track on the album).

'When *The Transfiguration Of Blind Joe Death* came out, I sent away for it from America,' recalls Pete Frame. 'It had that book in it. That was like a turning point album for me. It had music, lettering, art, mythology: everything I was interested in was in this one fucking record.' One day, Beautiful Linda Getchell herself appeared on Pete's doorstep.

Al Wilson wrote liner notes for the album under the name Charles Holloway. It would be some years before I learned of this Fahey-Wilson relationship. Fahey contributed to the 'Pathenogenesis' collage on Canned Heat's *Living The Blues* in '68 - albeit inadvertently as, during hard times before Heat's success, Wilson recorded several ragas and presented them to Fahey for Takoma. Instead, a clip from his 'Raga Kafi' introduced 'Pathinogenesis', followed by Wilson's dense, dirt-slow ragas amidst other members' soloing.

When I caught Canned Heat live at a rain-battered 1970 Hyde Park free concert sharing a bill with the fierce Eric Burdon and War, Wilson had overdosed in his sleeping bag nine days earlier. Fahey paid belated tribute by including another section of 'Raga Kafi' on '92's *Old Girlfriends & Other Horrible Memories*, which he called 'Fear and Loathing at 4th and Butternut'; a moon-howling serenade with Wilson roaring through chromatic harmonica. Wilson was one of the few musicians Fahey respected; enough to cite the 'spellbinding beauty' of his work and homage his old friend and sparring partner in this testament to their mutual visions stretching way beyond the blues.

Released in July '66, *The Great San Bernadino Birthday Party & Other Excursions (Vol. Four)* led with its monumental 19-minute title

167

track. That June, after completing his Patton thesis, Fahey gained his Folklore masters degree at UCLA. He recorded 'A Raga Called Pat' at Sierra Sound Labs, overdubbing sound effects from Folkways' *Sounds Of A Tropical Rain Forest* and self-explanatory *Steam Railroading Under Thundering Skies* over a guitar improvisation he recorded that month at LA's Ash Grove. Fahey predated turntablism by years, running records backwards and forwards at different speeds under his playing (including a toad!). The first two parts of 'A Raga Called Pat' joined unusually intimate outings, old and recent, on July '67's *Volume VI Days Have Gone By*, including Fahey classics 'The Portland Cement Factory at Monolith, California' (the album's original title) and haunted 'Joe Kirby'.

The set boasted another striking cover design by Tom Weller, the Country Joe and the Fish artist who came up with Fahey's trademark sleeves, starting with psych-swirls before the 16th century skeleton-dominated designs adapted for the first three albums' stereo versions from Arthur M. Hind's 1963 tome *An Introduction To A History Of Woodcut*. In 1987, I was over the moon to unearth a cache of Fahey Takomas at New York's Sounds record store. This one still had its booklet, boasting notes by Elijah P. Lovejoy (Fahey), ending 'Evilones will tell you he is wierd (sic), but his heart is pure.'

In December '66, Fahey signed to Vanguard, where earliest critic Sam Charters was A&R man and had signed Country Joe and the Fish, then managed by Ed Denson. With Charters producing, Fahey entered Hollywood Sound Recorders on January 24, 1967, recording guitar tracks that would be sprinkled over his next three albums, plus experimental outings including the 21-minute 'Requiem For Molly' suite that appeared with boggling effect on November '67's *Requia And Other Compositions For Guitar Solo* (released in the UK in '69 by Sonet). Fahey had recently been dumped by girlfriend/muse Molly Greenbaum, making the suite his astonishing eulogy to their deceased relationship with its demented mosaic of sound effects, Nazis, brass band marching music, fairground organ and Fahey caught picking 'California Dreamin' at the Ash Grove in mid-'66. The track is intended to depict Molly's mental unravelling 'and the reaction of another person in observing this process, for which he was perhaps, to some extent, responsible.'

Claudio Guerrier's remarkable handbook pinpoints what was used in each part; including Charles Ives, 'Deutschland Uber Alles' and the only known copy of Charley Patton's 'Circle Round the Moon' (unearthed by Fahey on a trip) on part one; Hitler, Nazi marching music, cows and easy listening from an old radio compilation on part two; Fahey picking 'California Dreamin' accompanied by ducks and assorted animals on part three and bellowing rooster, seals, squawking baby and screaming woman on four; effectively predicting sampling, 20 years before it caught on. Elsewhere sees guitar pyrotechnics of bristling dexterity. 'When The Catfish Is In Bloom' (title mutated from Jimmie Rodgers' 'When The Cactus Is In Bloom') starts like an Indian raga before Fahey unleashes a torrential display of molten virtuosity. The song started life as 'Fare Forward Voyagers' at August '65's ill-fated New York demo sessions for Elektra (which became part of *The Voice Of The Turtle*'s 'A Raga Called Pat Volume III' collage a year later). The demo journeyed on to collide with its inner raga on the stunning 24-minute title track of '73's *Fare Forward Voyagers*. 'Requiem For Mississippi John Hurt' heists Patton's 'Jesus Is A Dying Bedmaker' and, as was always the case, the album closes with a hymn, 'Fight On Christians, Fight On'.

As Charters went through the tapes, which furnished the next two Vanguard albums, the record's title changed from *Voice Of The Turtle* to *The Yellow Princess*, and finally *Requia*. It was followed by '68/69's actual *The Yellow Princess* (already a must-have import before its UK release in early '69). Perhaps his greatest album, it's led by the majestic title track (inspired by a magnificent, golden-sailed clipper ship Fahey saw in Virginia in 1953) showing him in full sail on a second version, re-recorded for this album at breathtaking full throttle as he improvises on a passage from Camille Saint-Saens' *The Yellow Princess Overture*. I never fail to flop down knackered when Fahey drops anchor at the end.

It's followed by further glistening displays and sonic expansions, weird excursions, such as the eerily atmospheric 'The Singing Bridge Of Memphis Tennessee', achieved by recording freight cars passing over a railroad bridge, overlaid with electric bassoon and Fahey's 1927 78 of Big Boy Cleveland's 'Big Boy Blues'. As an alien concept for Fahey, some rock band interaction came through co-producer Barry Hansen, who was on the same UCLA course and, living next door near Venice Beach, witnessed his unique technique develop at close quarters. Hansen went on to become early mentor-producer for psych-jazz wonders Spirit, who he hooked up with Fahey by bringing bassist Mark

Andes, his guitarist brother Matt and keyboardist Jay Ferguson to play with drummer Keven Kelley (who flew fleetingly with the Byrds on *Sweetheart Of The Rodeo*) to create the stately 'March! For Martin Luther King'. Fahey's reverential wordless eulogy achieved dignified homage by simply evoking a feeling in support of the recently-assassinated civil rights leader. Spirit also figure on the haunted 'Dance Of The Inhabitants of the Invisible City of Bladensburg' (recorded the day after Bobby Kennedy's assassination with title derived from Rimsky Korsakov's 'The Legend of the Invisible City of Kitezh').

Remaining on import for years, *The Voice Of The Turtle* remains Fahey's most elaborate but infuriatingly-puzzling album, coming in several versions. The original release was the only one where track listings matched the record, collating 1927 blues 78s, field-recorded fiddle duets, Bussard recordings, 1962 church tracks, musique concrete and Gregorian chants. The 20-page book contained photos and Fahey's extravagantly garnished autobiography laced with the mythology of Blind Joe Death. We learn Death was cursed to travel through Africa before coming to America on a slave ship, working on a cotton plantation and influencing Charley Patton, WC Handy and Son House before settling in Takoma Park, where he taught a small group of folk musicians. Fahey calls 'The Story of Dorothy Gooch' an 'American Primitive tone-poem'; his first use of the term that would later be used to describe his music. Later issues contained different music - despite identical track listing! When Takoma realised the records were costing more to make than they were being sold for it was replaced with a single sleeve version without booklet.

Impressed by 'White Christmas' selling annually, Fahey released his first seasonal album, *The New Possibility; John Fahey's Guitar Soli Christmas Album* in late '68, a strangely gorgeous thing that became Takoma's biggest seller. Much to his horror, he found himself adopted by the hippie movement, playing San Francisco venues with Quicksilver Messenger Service. 'I was never a hippie,' he hissed. 'They picked up on my music and thought I was one of them. They thought I shared their value system and I took LSD and so forth. But they bought my records and I had to play for them. Secretly, I always hated them.'

Fahey was going to start '69 with a third Vanguard album called *Ephalamium*, maybe with orchestra. Instead, he rode interest from the UK prodded by Peel and his albums being released here by making the afore-mentioned visit. Along with colleges and clubs like

170

Birmingham's Mothers, his highest-profile show was on the afternoon of the 18th at the Camden Fringe Festival on Parliament Hill Fields. Headlining were Procol Harum, along with Soft Machine, Blossom Toes, Forest and the ubiquitous Third Ear Band. The only review I've seen reported Fahey playing a shortish set, quite pissed and falling off his stool. He also failed to impress London's folk-guitar cognoscenti at Soho's Les Cousins and, on the 25th, played an afternoon Superfreak show at the Roundhouse supported by Al Stewart. It's often mistaken for the benefit held that evening for the families of Fairport Convention drummer Martin Lamble and Richard Thompson's girlfriend Jeannye Franklin, both killed in a van smash after a gig at Mothers. Hosted by Peel, the bill included Pink Floyd, Blossom Toes, Eclection, Family, Pretty Things and the Deviants.

An idea of Fahey's set at the time is given on 2004 CD *The Great Santa Barbara Oil Slick*, recorded at San Francisco's Matrix, showing him on sparkling form ripping through 'When Springtime Comes Again', 'Joe Kirby Blues', 'Requiem For John Hurt' and 'The Revolt Of The Dyke Brigade'; living up to his claim, 'I just go out and sit down and I hypnotise them.' The best account of Fahey on that UK tour was given to me by my old friend (legendary road manager for The Clash) Johnny Green, who says he caught him in the back room of Magdalen College, Oxford. 'Steppenwolf were on in the main room, but we didn't want to bother with them. John Fahey was just fantastic. He walked on, wearing a plaid shirt, and next to him had a packet of twenty Embassy, box of matches and a can of Coca-Cola. He was playing these long raga things then he'd stop, take a drink of Coke then light a cigarette. He sat on his stool and never spoke. No one made any requests. He would smoke the whole cigarette and just look at us looking at him. This lasted for about four or five minutes, then he would say the next one, play it, stop and smoke a cigarette. This went on all the way through the set.

'It was fucking unbelievable! Never before or since have I seen anything like that. I'd seen Bert Jansch and Davey Graham but he blew me away. It was so minimal but friendly. He let the music do the talking. There was no bullshit. Afterwards I went up to him with my then-wife, a hippy chick with long blonde hair, lace and beads. We shook hands and he turned out to be an amazing bloke. I said, 'Can I come and live with you?' He said, 'Sure', and told me the airport, flight, time and said, 'I'll see you at the airport.' Next day I woke up and thought, What happened there?'

After Fahey signed Leo Kottke to Takoma, '69's *6 & 12 String Guitar* became its second biggest selling album. The Minneapolis-based guitarist sounded like a more easy-to-digest Fahey; virtuoso playing without the edge, unpredictability or surreal genius. As his boozing got out of control, Fahey started facing his psychological demons, requiring hospitalisation in a Santa Monica clinic in 1970, followed by years of psychoanalysis as he dealt with repressed childhood trauma and deep-rooted depression. His first *Rolling Stone* piece was headlined 'Why Fahey wants to kill everybody' and leads with his quote, 'I just want to make a whole bunch of money so I can pay my psychiatric bills.' He reveals he's a member of the International Turtle & Tortoise Society and wants to kill those who run his favourite creature over on the highway - 'That's one reason I want to kill everybody.'

There are still many shapeshifting records to come because, as Fahey said late in life, creating music 'is a joy and a comfort and a wonder and a miracle and when it's happening there's nothing better.' I could now grab them as they came; '71's marvellous *America* sound painting; '72's evocative dixie-dabbling *Of Rivers And Religion* (credited to John Fahey and his Orchestra); '79's dazzling *Visits Washington DC*, 1980's hymns album *Yes! Jesus Loves Me* and '83's awesome *Railroad 1*. If you'd told me then I'd be called to write the liner notes for Ace's reissues of the last three nearly 30 years later I'd have rogered the nearest turtle.

Fahey stories were always welcome and renowned UK singer-guitarist Michael Chapman had some belters from touring Europe and the US together in the mid-70s and 80s. 'That was a gruesome twosome if ever you met 'em!' guffawed the veteran guitar maestro who's still in action today and made his entrance in '69 with the impressively idiosyncratic *Rainmaker*. 'We were described as the two grumpiest guitar players you're ever gonna meet! John was always strange, in the least. The picture of a naked Fahey sitting at the dinner table wrapped in a genuine Nazi flag isn't all that great. He would have so much to drink that, at a certain point, he would just have to take his clothes off. He didn't care where he was. Apparently he's done it in restaurants but this was at his house; full of cardboard boxes because he was moving from East Los Angeles to Oregon next morning.'

When he got to Salem with new muse Melody in '81, Fahey recorded *Railroad 1*, his last Takoma album and great tribute to

America's awesome man-made artery that harnessed the railroad fascination that had gripped him since childhood. Fahey was at the peak of his powers, often threatening to run off the rails but never missing a beat. 1984's *Let Go* became the first of six panoramic sparklers for Massachusetts-based Varrick Records, although Fahey had been diagnosed with chronic fatigue syndrome/Epstein-Barr disease. The next few years were his least productive as he split with Melody while battling alcoholism. By the early 90s, he was living in welfare motels, surviving by selling classical albums he found in used record shops, or staying at the Union Gospel Mission, washing dishes. *Spin* writer and longtime fan Byron Coley found him at a motel in '94, his career-reviving feature depicting Fahey living in hand-to-mouth chaos while writing and pursuing abstract painting. His resuscitated profile further enhanced by *The Return Of The Repressed* anthology and Fahey returned to his guitar after finding himself revered as a pioneer in alternative/Americana circles.

Dean Blackwood, an attorney who'd worked at Sub Pop, saw the *Spin* feature, contacted Coley for Fahey's number and asked if he'd like to record for his Perfect label on which he released Fonotone-style 78s. This appealed to Fahey, who allowed engineer Scott Colburn to record him in his motel room, resulting in feet-refinding spider-drone *Double 78*. Blackwood became his manager and, inheriting money after his father's death in late 1994, Fahey asked him to run Revenant Records as an outlet for raw American music. In the meantime, Fahey released the grinding, experimental *The Mill Pond*, another menacing hotel room recording, its claustrophobic gush working for Fahey as both cataclysmic exorcism and annihilation of past glories.

'97's *City of Refuge* (titled after the Blind Willie Johnson song) congealed more hotel room scrabblings into electrifying nightmare-blues. Fahey disowned his past with punk-style disdain; 'I despise all 'revivalists' of folk music, and I despise all New Age music...In all my music I have never tried to do anything except express emotions, sometimes very dark emotions, depression, hatred, etc, in a coherent, musical language. In the current season the only people who understand me and with whom I have anything in common are punks and alternatives and industrial and no wave and antifolk, etc...My category is alternative, period.'   Fahey stripped his playing to its bare-boned soul and blasted the Wyndham Hill brigade with teeth-rattling, anti-ambient racket. *Womblife* navigated a slow boat through heaving electronic swells, gamelan chimes and subaquatic ambience that, midway through 'Sharks', sounds like Fahey's ghost picking in the subterranean depths as behemoth swells swirl around. He started playing electric guitar because acoustic felt 'like razor blades cutting into my left fingers.' This prolific time also saw the traumatic creation of *The Epiphany of Glenn Jones*, Fahey planting a massive, gaudily-painted art deco ceramic object he called the Great Koonaklaster in the studio for inspiration. He formed The John Fahey Trio with guitar-organist Tim Knight and guitarist Rob Scrivener, their cacophonous improvisations inspired by German demolition merchants Einsturzende Neubauten. The final album completed during Fahey's lifetime was *Hitomi*, its avant-blues seething in clouds of reverb, reflecting his love of guitarist Loren Connors, Brooklyn's 'Venusian blues' genius.

Although Connors started building his own tortuous catalogue in the late 70s, Fahey didn't appear to discover him until two decades later, when he became, as Byron Coley puts it, 'one of Death's chosen few.' In the 'passing it on' fashion often mentioned by Keith Richards as he bigged up old blues artists who'd influenced him for others to discover, it took Fahey's ravings to bring Connors into my own world, ashamedly over twenty years since he'd started building another formidable catalogue begging to be tracked down, veering close to Fahey's in terms of tiny pressings, cassettes, aliases and one-offs.

After moving to New York in 1991, Connors released scathing, emotionally-charged tone sketches and desolate laments on increasingly wraith-like albums, now countless and still swelling. I instantly fell in love with his spectral space-blues vapour trails and, as so often happened, had to have 'em all. That's why I'm banging on about an artist who didn't start recording until a few years after the supposed premise of this book. If my rampant collector mentality got under way in '69 and I now have every Sun Ra album known to earthlings, Connors remains about the only figure left who rekindles those same feelings of relentless discovery and frustrated craving that started gestating in my brain 50 years ago and the obvious successor to Fahey. Crucially, he's no flagrant imitator, with troubles and unknown sonic terrain of his own to struggle with. He's up there with my favourite living guitarist and rarely covered in the magazines I write for - another reason for including him here - because I can, plus he carries '69's exploratory spirit like no one else.

Connors recorded with Fahey around 2000, as evidenced on 2005's magnificent *Sails* as the pair swallow-dive around 'Dark Was The Night, Cold Was The Ground', the Blind Willie Johnson song that informed Fahey's first Fonotone single over 40 years earlier. After Fahey's death, Connors and Christina Carter recorded the darkly-translucent *Meditations On The Ascension Of Blind Joe Death*, the most 'in-spirit' tribute he received.

On Monday, February 19, 2001, Fahey went into Salem hospital complaining of chest pains and discovered he'd suffered a heart attack. After a sextuple-bypass his kidneys failed. After a second heart operation, he was placed on life support for two days, which was switched off on Thursday February 22. When Dean Blackwood spoke to Fahey the night before he died, he thought he might not pull through but, if he did, wanted to end his 'self-imposed isolation from past music and friends.' The memorial service was held in Salem, attended by around a hundred ex-wives, old girlfriends, friends, business people, musicians and the odd bum. Fahey's first release on his Revenant label appeared two years later, the unearthly *Red Cross* presenting material he'd been working on, including its title track named after Rev Moses Mason's 1928 sermon 'Red Cross, Disciple Of Christ Today', dedicated to Guitar Roberts, aka Loren Connors.

After his death, Fahey was revered as the extent of his genius started sinking in, his universal influence placing him alongside the one-off maverick trailblazers who helped shape modern music, such as Hendrix, Brian Jones, Tim Buckley and Jim Morrison; those whose careers took off in a 60s starburst before they fought to continue realising their creative visions while battling personal problems and retro-clamouring audiences, iconic status following untimely death. Fahey was an idiosyncratic behemoth the like of which will never walk the Earth again.

I'm writing about him from the perspective of both lifelong fan and that 13-year-old kid who still remembers that fateful '67 day when Peel brought him into my life. '69 was the year Fahey became flesh and his records purchasable in the UK. I could never have imagined then that, 40 years later, I'd be writing his liner notes or compiling a career-spanning Fahey compilation that would be impossible to realise. Fahey's probably cackling wherever he is (but would appreciate how I've just reworked its notes for this book).

Bashovia

'My philosophy is quite simple: soul first, technique later,' declared Robbie Basho somewhere along the path of the brief but intensely personal journey that established him as one of the greatest (but most overlooked) American acoustic guitarists to come out of the 60s. Although usually bracketed as American Primitive, Basho rapidly became a trailblazer rather than follower after meeting and playing with Fahey while studying at the University of Maryland; first of Washington DC's new folk gaggle to appear on Takoma. As a contemporary rather than acolyte, Basho sounded least like Fahey than any other guitarist on the label, or the many who've ridden under the American Primitive flag since, their earnest replications missing the point. As epoch-making US acoustic guitar giants go, there's Fahey and Robbie Basho.

Tapping into the spiritual essence of different cultures to broaden the horizons of accepted music and his own restless muse, Basho was soon navigating a higher plane as, along with Davy Graham and Sandy Bull, he explored world music improvisation, hitting transcendental heights during lengthy ragas and other-worldly beauty in reflective stretches, calling down the angels when he started unleashing vocals that became another vehicle on which to strive for the spiritual catharsis he craved.

In 2013, Ace also asked if I fancied writing liner notes for two 70s Basho albums they were reissuing: '72's *Voice of The Eagle* and '74's *Zarthus*. Researching uncovered an incredible back story that ended in tragic early death. Born in 1940, he was orphaned early, adopted by Dr Donald Robinson of Baltimore and named Daniel Robinson Junior. Growing up in Annapolis, he went to catholic schools and military academy before attending the University Of Maryland between 1958-62. Working in Ocean City clubs to fund college, Basho met a sailor back from Mexico, who sold him his century-aged Mexican 12-string guitar for $200. After getting into country blues with Fahey's crew, he began delving into classical, oriental and improvisation, a Ravi Shankar album providing his raga epiphany before he started running with the infinite possibilities of the guitar. Using open or exotic tunings of his own devising, he developed his coded 'Esoteric Doctrine of Color & Mood For Twelve and Six String Guitar'.

Robbie followed Fahey, Denson and crew to Berkeley, settling into the happening scene that sparked Takoma. In his notes to 2001's Bashovia compilation of Robbie's '67-68 output, Fahey admits to his late appreciation of the guitarist's genius, the set his way of making up for it. 'He was crazy, very hard to get along with,' he told Edwin Pouncey. 'I didn't put out his records, Ed Denson did. I never really liked them until Al Wilson pointed out that there were some really good songs. He is right, there is some great stuff on those records. I never hung out with Robbie personally much. Nobody did. You couldn't.' Fahey recounted how Daniel Robinson transformed into Robbie Basho while spending the night on a mountain top 'ingesting a great deal of peyote', returning next day declaring himself the reincarnation of 17th century Japanese haiku poet Matsuo Basho. While working with Max Ochs on translating Indian ragas for guitar, Basho studied sarod under Ali Albar Khan in Berkeley, where fellow guitarist Hank Mindlin introduced him to spiritual teacher Meher Baba, whose California school he enrolled in. Robbie's ongoing quest took him on a pilgrimage to India in '69.

The raga excursions and spiritual reflections of Takoma debut *Seal Of The Blue Lotus* already set him apart from other guitarists, followed by five more for the label; *The Grail & The Lotus, Basho Sings* (which unleashed his singing voice) then *The Falconers Arm Volumes One and Volume Two*. '71's *Song Of The Stallion* saw him embracing Native American mysticism among Hindi, western classical and American styles.

Between the latter pair came '69's *Venus In Cancer*, which saw a more matured Basho, alone in an idyllic spiritual dimension of his own making, serenading love's glory and mystery with the soaring vocals that were too much for some but spine-chilling in their ethereal purity. That voice, which Fahey described as 'strangely compelling', came from deep in his soul with no regard for restraint, phrasing or timing. Thankfully, he was blessed with a mercurial tone and bottomless power that he could let loose with ecstatic abandon. Basho refused to cage his muse, and let it fly by any means necessary.

The title track immediately puts normal time and bearings on hold as he works around its undulating, stately theme for ten minutes before his voice elevates 'Eagle Sails the Blue Diamond Waters' and 'Kowaka

D'Amour' ends side one with gentle translucence. 'Song For The Queen' is the set's epic, enhanced by guitarist Victor Chancellor, Moreen Libot's viola and Kreke Ritter's French horn as Basho oddly evokes medieval pageantry in its episodic trawl. 'Cathedrals et Fleur de Lis' is glacial, majestic and closest to Fahey's realer world. 'Wine Song (Sweet Wine of Love)' announces he's too far gone for earthly restraints. Poignantly innocent, surgingly emotional, wonderfully naive or unashamedly romantic, I loved this beatific love garden of a world that Basho built for himself; invincible and impregnable to the outside world's harsh, mundane bullshit, even if it was sometimes so beautiful it could make you cry. It still can, especially considering the fate that would befall this strangest of troubadours.

'I don't call a lot of my stuff far out,' he reasoned. 'I just call it a different level of feeling. It's far in, as far as I'm concerned...I spent years on the road singing folk songs that had no meaning. It dawned on me music is supposed to say something. Music is supposed to do something.' Divorcing himself from the gentrifying acoustic mainstream, Basho went where he pleased, declaring his messages like a spiritual escape valve. Immensely touched by the plight of Native Americans, he introduced their music into *Song of The Stallion* and the two I annotated. *Voice Of The Eagle* marked the peak of Basho's immersion in the culture, straddling love songs, ragas and massacre laments, starting with the title track's 'piece of Hopi pageantry, a Hopi raga', as he said in his notes. The eagle is often used in Hopi Indian ceremonials as solar messenger of the gods. On 'Wounded Knee Soliloquy', Basho laments the atrocity of the last major battle of the American Indian Wars in 1890 as 'a poetical feeling for what happened there and afterwards.' Instead of lambasting the US army psycho-meatheads who gleefully massacred warriors, women and children, he delivers a soulful eulogy to the victims with tangible sorrow.

Zarthus saw Basho in his 'Persian period', weaving Persian, Arabic and Western themes on 'Khalil Gibran' and sidelong 'Rhapsody In Druz' (referring to Lebanon's Sufi mountain wise men, who he aspired to). 'I decided to see how high and beautiful I could go,' explained Basho, adding, 'but then you leave the masses behind.' '81's *Rainbow Thunder: Songs of the American West*, '83's *Bouquet* and '84's *Twilight Peaks* were Basho's last albums before he unexpectedly perished on February 28 '86 after his chiropractor accidentally broke his neck trying to perform an 'intentional whiplash' experiment that caused blood vessels to rupture, leading to a fatal stroke. Basho was only 45.

Higher

One good thing about being 14 is not having to differentiate between Basho's spiritual sky-sailing and the butt-shaking ghetto charge unleashed by Sly and The Family Stone, who want to take you higher their own way. Of course, their scenes and audiences are worlds apart from each other but, at this time, everyone's looking for escape and some kind of transcendent elevation. This inability to judge people in musical boxes bears me in good stead for the rest of my life. I still plug into the special qualities and emotional force of an artist or their record; if it don't connect, feels fake, forced or contrived, I don't wanna know. If it grooves, causes a ruckus or makes you cry, I do. That's why a lot of rock's chest-beating Odin's todger cliches leave me cold, marathon guitar solos seem pointless after seeing Hendrix or many of Laurel Canyon's finest feel like they're putting on a beatific face while looking for the next line.

Sly Stone accessed all areas of the turbo-charged rock and soul pantheon before becoming a post-Woodstock superstar was done and he got too dusted. Sly looked like he could have stepped out of a blaxploitation film, except those floodwaters hadn't yet broken when he napalmed both black music and pop charts with 'Dance To The Music' and his livewire, multi-racial space cowboy soul revue hit *Top Of The Pops* in '68. Sly and The Family Stone led a white-black crossover. The outrageous, multi-talented Sly's socially conscious soul train embodied the new possibilities that disaffected elements of all races were looking for and transcended all barriers. Eschewing uniforms, the Family Stone's hyper-active psychedelic soul hit like a high-octane juggernaut and, with sister Rose on piano and school friend Cynthia Robinson on trumpet, brought women musicians to the fore and black music stage shows into the modern age.

Sly's profile rose in tandem with the Black Panthers, who also hailed from Oakland and changed how their generation thought, looked and sounded before outside forces infiltrated. As Rickey Vincent says in *Party Music*, 'It is no accident that the groundbreaking methodology

179

of Sly and the Family Stone emerged from the San Francisco Bay Area…where a black revolution was also taking place. The black working-class neighborhoods in Oakland, Berkeley, Richmond, Vallejo, and San Francisco were ground zero for many of these emergent new lifestyles and visions. Politics and culture were intertwined in a mix of activity, bringing together black activist roots and rocking blues bars, southern folk wisdom, labor union politics, and the illicit economy of the mean streets.'

A prodigy, Sly was a staff producer for Autumn Records by '64, producing white rock bands including the Beau Brummels and pre-Jefferson Airplane Great Society. This was unusual for a young black man then. He became a popular local radio DJ at KSOL, singing his commercials and sprinkling the Stones, Beatles and Dylan among the Motown and Stax. That was unusual too. Sly and the Family Stone formed when his band the Stoners joined forces with his brother Freddie's the Stone Souls. Signing to Epic, they released the water-testing *A Whole New Thing*; a critical success but commercial failure. After label boss Clive Davis told them to produce a hit, they came back with full-throttle killer 'Dance to The Music', an album of the same name flaunting this multi-hued new attack, followed by autumn '68's second set *Life*, keeping tracks like 'M'Lady' and 'Love City' short and direct.

After these ever-heating warm-ups, 'Everyday People' consolidated everything and took it up several notches, Sly and The Family Stone materialising into funked-up Star Trek transportation evacuees ready to take the world, striking a mass communal chord with its plea for peace and equality between all races and social groups, couched in irresistible zest and melodies; 'Different strokes for different folks.' As I wailed along to it, I realised Sly had created the ultimate statement on everything the hippies had been trying to say with what he called, 'a combination of rhythm and blues, jam music, psychedelic music, and rock 'n' roll and hard rock and church music, a lot of it, and on and on. There's no bag. I like all of it.' With the riveting 'Sing a Simple Song' on the B-side, 'Everyday People' held at number one for four weeks between February and March '69. In May came *Stand!*, whose title track and single took a defiant stance while making a glorious noise. Bolstered by Larry Graham's funk-redefining bass slapping Gregg Errico's nuclear beats like George Clinton's todger in Berry Gordy's face, the song encapsulated the band's idealistic mixed-race utopia. 'Sex Machine' presented a black-rock groove jam template, 'Don't Call Me Nigger, Whitey' fearlessly broke a huge taboo in title alone and 'I Want To Take You Higher' unleashed the ferocious stench machine that could slaughter any party with its merciless call-and-response vocals and vivacious solos, delivered like a huge, light-scattered tidal skywave.

George Clinton loved Sly and the Family Stone and remembers hearing an advance tape of the album when hustling at Epic. 'They were a mixed, beautiful group. Black, white and big Afros. They looked like Funkadelic on Motown!' When he heard the music, 'I didn't know what to think. Were they a white group? Their pop songs were as pop as you could possibly get, but the black songs was as black and funky as Ray Charles and James Brown. They had the biggest Afros in the world. 'Sing A Simple Motherfucking Song' was The Bomb. This was it. This song hit me just like 'What'd I Say' by Ray Charles. It was the funkiest thing I've ever heard in my life, from Motown to James Brown to the Beatles. They were the complete package; they could play sing, write and produce, and all superior to anybody I'd ever seen or heard before. I was so into Sly's records that I forgot I had gone up there to sign a deal for myself.' That same night, George caught a Sly gig at the Electric Circus on St Mark's Place, fortified by strong LSD; 'They had the clarity of Motown but the volume of Hendrix or The Who. They literally turned this motherfucker out. That would be the impression that Sly left on me for the rest of my life.'

Next would come Sly's early hours mass destruction of Woodstock and smash hits with 'Hot Fun In The Summertime' and number one 'Thank You (Falettinme Be Mice Elf Agin)' gouging another phase for dirty funk on the 45 it shared with 'Everybody Wants to Be a Star'. If only this success hadn't gone straight to Sly's nose. It would be a different, coked-up devil Sly who emerged in '71 with the sinister freakiness of *There's A Riot Goin' On'*. Forget Altamont, this was when we really knew the 60s and its florid idealism were gone for good. Yet in '69, Sly helped change the face of rock and soul, starting with Berry Gordy playing *Stand!* to his staff and declaring, 'This is the future of black music!'

Here But I'm Gone

Then there's Curtis Mayfield, steering his own, quieter course balancing civil rights anthems and pop success with the Impressions before embarking on his phosphorescent solo career later this year. I didn't discover Curtis until '71's *Superfly* soundtrack and when he blew me away on *The Old Grey Whistle Test* shortly after. Tracking down every record I could, as I've said he became my very favourite soul singer next to Otis, blessed with a supernatural falsetto that could stop the clock and stir the heart.

As '69 broke, Curtis was entering his final spectacular phase with the Impressions, the classic Chicago vocal group who had presented a subtler but no less powerful alternative to James Brown's force ten grandstanding. Although Curtis started off singing standards, his muse sprouted unstoppable wings as his songwriting matured, speaking to America's besieged ghettos and oppressed millions relentlessly being ground into the dirt. 'Keep On Pushing', 'It's Alright', 'We're A Winner', 'Choice Of Colours', 'This Is My Country' and era-peaking 'People Get Ready' established this 'gentle genius' as the movement's most inspirational voice, spreading evocatively poetic messages of hope and equality with dignity and controlled power. Then there was his heart-melting way with a love song. Drawing from his deep gospel roots, Curtis intuitively navigated street tides and nationwide movements, taking black pride into the charts as a devotional young dude who carried the news in songs with headlines for titles. If JB, Sly and Hendrix screamed black power through the electric shock of their very existence, Curtis provided its calmer, doggedly-romantic social conscience.

Curtis was born in Chicago's impoverished Southside ghetto, where a quarter of a million struggling souls crammed into a seven-mile ribbon of rotten tenements. With an absentee father, he was man of the house by five years old, fending for three siblings and mother Marion. He never lost childhood memories of starving in fleabag hotels populated by junkies and hookers, worthlessness rammed at him by school bullies for his slight build and buck teeth, underpinned by racism that gripped Chicago as much as the south. Robbed of a happy childhood, Curtis was driven into his own private world gripped by music, prone for life to shut himself in his room. His mother taught him songs at the piano and read him pioneering African-American poet Paul Laurence Dunbar. Gospel and the church were vital survival lifelines and Curtis was deeply inspired by the devotional music he heard at his grandmother Annie Bell's storefront Traveling Souls Spiritualists Church, countered by the gutbucket blues he heard being whipped up in nearby clubs by Muddy Waters, John Lee Hooker and other giants.

The Mayfields were early occupants in the vast Cabrini-Green housing project on Chicago's Near North Side. Although it would degenerate into a notorious crime hotbed, this was untold luxury for the family, especially their first single occupancy bathroom. By seven, Curtis was singing in the Northern Jubilee Gospel Singers quintet alongside friend Jerry Butler, performing in Chicago's churches before hitting the gospel touring highway. Although influenced by cathartic Swan Silvertones vocalist Claude Jeter, the Five Blind Boys of Mississippi's apocalyptic Archie Brownlee and Cabrini-Green neighbours the Staple Singers, it was Sam Cooke, black music's first crossover superstar, who remained Curtis's biggest inspiration. Sophisticated, urbane and politically aware, Cooke owned his publishing and SAR record label.

Armed with his unearthly voice and unique guitar style he taught himself with his instrument tuned to black notes on the piano, Curtis formed the Alphatones before joining Butler in The Roosters, whose Sam Gooden and Brooks brothers Arthur and Richard had come in from Chattanooga. Naming themselves the Impressions in '58, the group scored a top 20 smash on Vee-Jay subsidiary Abner with celestial ballad 'For Your Precious Love'. Soon no strangers to America's gruelling black gig circuit, Curtis turned 16 onstage at Harlem Apollo, one of many venues that swooned to the song's sonorous magic as the Impressions broke its box office record. Unsuccessful singles followed until Butler departed to pursue a solo career, joined by Curtis, who co-wrote hits, played guitar and learned business ropes. Although being dropped by Vee-Jay in 1960 put the Impressions on hold, Curtis saved enough to relaunch them the following year, ex-Roosters baritone Fred Cash replacing Butler. Following Sam Cooke's example, Curtis set up his own publishing company to save his blossoming songs from music industry predators. The Impressions signed to ABC Paramount in autumn '61 and released the exotic 'Gypsy Woman', making the top 20 and allowing the Impressions' self-titled '62 debut album. Recorded in August '63, the insidiously simple optimism of 'It's Alright' created an early freedom movement anthem and made the top five. After Brooks brothers departed, the Impressions arrived at their classic lineup of Mayfield, Cash and Gooden, a vital future collaborator arriving when jazz veteran Johnny Pate came in as arranger. The seminal Chicago sound was born, distinguished by heavenly three-part harmonies, flying strings and beefy brass. 1964's *The Never Ending Impressions* was the trio's first complete work, showing further advances in Mayfield's song-writing on gloriously defiant love ballad 'I'm So Proud' and 'I Gotta Keep On Moving'; a fugitive chase song said to have influenced Bob Marley's 'I Shot The Sheriff'.

The civil rights movement gained its leading icon after eloquently charismatic Baptist minister Dr Martin Luther King emerged triumphant from 1955's Montgomery Bus Boycott, conducted after Rosa Parks refused to give up her seat for a white passenger. King formed the Southern Christian Leadership Conference with other church leaders to provide direction fighting racism and segregation non-violently. In February 1960, four students from the all-black North Carolina Agricultural and Technical College sat at the segregated lunch counter at Greensboro's Woolworth's to protest being refused service, sparking sit-ins through Virginia, Tennessee and Georgia, spreading to Northern states. The Student Nonviolent Co-Ordinating Committee and Congress of Racial Equality (C.O.R.E.) began Freedom Rides; long bus journeys whose passengers faced jail and firebombing as they tried to use bathrooms and water fountains at terminals. Public outrage at abuse inflicted on the riders led to Kennedy's administration ordering a desegregation order, which took effect that November and allowed people of any colour to use all facilities. Although the 60s saw giant steps in removing barbaric restrictions on African-Americans, murderous racists in the pig-ignorant south continued their neo-Nazi terror tactics, including unleashing firehoses and dogs on peaceful demonstrations. Led by King on August 28, 1963, the March On Washington drew thousands, who heard Dylan, Joan Baez, Odetta and Harry Belafonte. Prompted by Mahalia Jackson, King gave his era-defining 'I have a dream' speech, but nightmares continued, such as bombing the 16th Baptist Church in Birmingham, Alabama, killing four young black girls. After President Kennedy was assassinated that November, his successor Lyndon Johnson brought home 1964's Civil Rights and Voting Rights bill banning discrimination based on race, colour or religion regarding jobs, accommodation or public facilities. Two weeks later, 15-year-old black teenager James Powell was shot dead outside a Harlem summer school by a white policeman for allegedly brandishing a knife. A protest rally turned into rioting and looting that raged that July.

Hottest record in New York that week was the Impressions' 'Keep On Pushing', Curtis's first outright message song and title track of their latest album. The freedom movement adopted his call-to-arms sermon of hope as it rose to number ten in R&B and pop charts. The album saw the group more socially relevant while its love songs were Curtis's deepest yet, including stunningly-perfect 'I've Been Trying'. The production of the Wings Over Jordan's 1949 gospel tune 'Amen', which Curtis heard in Sidney Poitier's *Lilies Of The Field* movie, was built on military drums and used as civil rights marching music. The album made the top ten (There it is next to Ravi Shankar and Robert Johnson on the sleeve of Dylan's *Bringing It All Back Home*).

With the 1964 Civil Rights Act considered too little too late or not adhered to, black communities started favouring direct action over King's peaceful approach. Enlightened former gangster Malcolm X was a ferociously-compelling speaker who incited militant passion by declaring African-Americans had to achieve freedom 'by any means necessary'. Malcolm was blasted with a shotgun while speaking at Detroit's Audubon Ballroom on February 21, 1965. Grief was widespread and Malcolm became a martyr-like figure. In December '64, Sam Cooke, a friend of Malcolm's who supported King, southern student protests and desegregation at his shows, was so riled at racism he encountered on tour and moved by Bob Dylan's 'Blowin' in The Wind' - itself modelled on the melody of 'No More Auction Block For Me' as performed by Odetta and Paul Robeson - that he wrote 'A Change Is Gonna Come', the impossibly moving ballad that became another defining song of the freedom movement (sadly released after he was mysteriously gunned down in a seedy LA motel).

Curtis composed his own great movement anthem, 'People Get Ready' inviting all to join the freedom train using sensitive seduction rather than soap-box bellowing. The train imagery relates to the metaphysical Underground Railroad escape route for slaves before the Civil War or that decade's Great Migration that saw African-Americans swarm to northern ghettos that became cities within cities and tinderboxes for 'civil disobedience'. In *Party Music*, Rickey Vincent observed that 'At its height, soul music was the living pulse of the black community, the conscience of the movement, and a daily inspiration to keep on pushing. When Curtis Mayfield wrote 'People Get Ready' in

1965, he was tapping into a collective sense of anticipation of an oncoming social transformation.'

The song reached number three R&B and fourteen pop. By the time it became a set staple for Black Power house band The Lumpen later in the decade, times had got darker and militant, Curtis's timeless message translated into an uprising anthem calling to get ready for radical change ('People get ready, revolution's come/ Your only ticket is a loaded gun'). As 'People Get Ready' led the Impressions' same-titled album to number one in the soul charts, the Impressions continued gigging relentlessly, including the Chitlin Circuit where they were sometimes backed by scuffling guitarist Jimmy James. As George Clinton said, 'You can hear a lot of Curtis in Jimi Hendrix. Every guitar player wanted to play like Curtis.'

After three albums that held back on movement anthems and comment, Curtis knew he needed to push the Impressions into modern times and firm up their message. Breakthrough arrived with 'We're A Winner', an instant black pride anthem and R&B chart topper when released as a single in January '68, busting his message out of the church and into mainstream racial politics. It directly influenced James Brown's 'Say It Loud – I'm Black And I'm Proud' and led 1968's same-named Impressions album. Curtis started Curtom Records, 'We're a winner' its motto. The label personified Black Power and economic self-determination, its first Impressions single the tautly-dramatic blues of 'Fool For You', whose swooning chorus took it to number two R&B. The group immediately sounded more vividly mature than the ABC years, Curtis and Pate's telepathic relationship bolstered by Donny Hathaway's arrangements and keyboards.

The sessions were conducted under the huge shadow cast by King's devastating April assassination. In a year that saw worldwide protests in Paris, Chicago and Prague, the civil rights movement had lost its peaceful leader, grieving panic manifesting as angry rioting, including in Chicago. The cause lost another vital ally two months later when Democratic Presidential candidate Robert Kennedy, who praised King and promoted equality, was also murdered. The mood turned confrontational that August in the riots around Chicago's Democratic National Convention. When corrupt racist Nixon claimed the Presidency that November, he cut spending in poorer areas and demolished positive steps achieved in recent years.

Curtis responded with that November's remarkable *This Is My Country*; the cover depicting the Impressions looking cool against a burnt-out tenement heralded songs that beamed like a beacon in the despair that spilled into '69. 'They Don't Know' declared 'We have lost another leader' and 'We cannot let our people be until we're all out of poverty'. If the desolately self-blaming 'Gone Away' (co-written with Curtom genius Donny Hathaway) was a song of loss, the album also featured some of Curtis's most gorgeously-melodic ballads, including 'I'm Loving Nothing' and 'Love's Happening'. The title track laid claim to a place in society, referencing 300 years of slavery and lost activists and leaders; 'Too many have died in protecting my pride for me to go second class' sang Curtis with barely-restrained emotion. Released as a single, it went to number three R&B and 25 pop. Stark and soulful with a southern Stax twist, *This Is My Country* was a transitional milestone that reflected the cusp of this new year.

May '69's *The Young Mod's Forgotten Story* reflects the nationwide grief over Bobby Kennedy's hopes-dashing removal, starting with the gripping title track and 'Choice of Colors'; another protest landmark. The song eschews cliched sloganeering as Curtis addresses his community with stately grace and without histrionics, declaring back-biting and fuss no answer, nor aggression or desperation. Its B-side is the album's upfront closer, 'Mighty Mighty (Spade and Whitey)'; another hard-hitting post-assassination reflection ('We're killing off our leaders…It don't matter none black or white/We all know it's wrong and we're gonna fight to make it right'), Curtis suggesting uniting to face a common malaise that hit all colours, not just the ghetto, pointing to his future as he presented messages as concepts. Another *Young Mods* track (and single), 'Seven Years' uses Hathaway's gospel expertise and breezy vibe to cloak another sad tale about the end of a love affair and 'My Deceiving Heart' addresses Curtis's own infidelities, although there are still billowing love ballads such as Stax-like 'Love's Miracle', 'Soulful Love' and exquisite 'The Girl I Find'.

Curtis continued this period of supernova creativity by giving Curtom's roster songs and productions, including Donny Hathaway and June Conquest's 'I Thank You Baby', the remarkable Baby Huey, Five Stairsteps' *Love's Happening* album and Major Lance plus several Impression singles. He was especially excited about the debut album he was working on with Baby Huey. The 350lb James Ramey, who had come to Chicago from his native Indiana in '69 and called himself after the 50s cartoon duck, impressed Curtis enough with his supercharged, larger-than-life stage act to sign him. Produced by Curtis, his album included three Mayfield compositions; 'Hard Times' examining the harsh reality of trying to pursue a good life in the corrupted ghetto jungle, 'Mighty Mighty' and 'Running'. Curtis's great optimism was shattered when Huey suffered a drug-related heart attack in October 1970, leaving Curtom to put together the posthumous set that also included his epic rendition of Sam Cooke's 'A Change Is Going To Come' and the Mamas and The Papas' 'California Dreamin'. Another soul tragedy, Huey went on to become a cult fave with the next generation's hiphop community.

At least Donny Hathaway would find success and realise enough of his precocious potential to became a major force in soul, albeit briefly. Born in Chicago and raised by his grandmother in St Louis, he won a scholarship to study music at Washington DC's Howard University, where he befriended classmate Roberta Flack and sketched out seminal future hit street-scape 'The Ghetto' with Chicago homeboy Leroy Hutson. Donny dropped out of university to join Curtom. By '69, Roberta had signed to Atlantic and released her *First Take* debut (which included Donny's seething 'Tryin' Times'). After falling out with Curtis, Hathaway followed her after being spotted by King Curtis. In 1970, 'The Ghetto' was unleashed to introduce jazzy groove and social conscience into soul, appearing on that year's *Everything is Everything* debut. Although Hathaway's promising career enjoyed a fabulous start through further albums, including '72's sizzling *Live*, he suffered crippling paranoid schizophrenia, jumping out of a Central Park hotel room window in '79.

Curtis now knew he had to continue his own mission solo and, as he created his first album under his own name, recorded one last Impressions album with veteran arrangers Riley Hampton and Gary Slabo. *Check Out Your Mind* is a noble swan-song. The solo career that swept through the 70s but struggled in the 80s (when I got to see him mesmerise the Glastonbury festival in the afternoon sun) included *Superfly* and hard-hitting masterpieces *Back To The World* and *There's No Place Like America Today*, dealing with the unjust problems that faced black servicemen returning from the Vietnam war.

Curtis had singlehandedly built an empire that proved too exhausting to maintain. It could only come tumbling down, exacerbated by changing trends like disco, but his remarkable voice and songwriting continued to resonate until the freak onstage accident that rendered him paralysed from the neck down for nine years, before he passed away in 1999. Now he stands as one of soul's all-time greats, its most fearless fighter as he battled poverty, racism, music business, passing trends and, finally, total paralysis. One of the greatest compliments I've ever been paid happened when Curtis's widow Altheida read a piece I'd written about her late husband for *Shindig!* in 2016 and contacted me to say how much it had touched her. She asked if I'd write the definitive biography he's never enjoyed with her; sadly, no major publishers were interested.

Alchemy in the UK

I'm smitten by an underground magazine called *Gandalf's Garden* which, amidst its mystical expounding, presents spectacular psychedelic artwork that heavily influences my own efforts. Issue four includes a piece on the mysterious Third Ear Band who, after hearing them on Peel, have sparked an unusual curiosity with their hypnotically-pulsing Druid ritual music, eerie drones and suggestion of arcane magical forces. This month sees *Alchemy*, their first album, released among the initial batch from Harvest, EMI's new progressive rock label. Titles like 'Ghetto Raga', 'Stone Circle' and 'Egyptian Book Of The Dead' follow a pattern in which Paul Minns's oboe hails the dawn followed by Mel Davis's low-slung cello moan, leader Glen Sweeney's metronomic hand-drum and Richard Coff's violin sawing or soaring, depending at which point of the ever-building hypno-trance they're at. Third Ear Band referenced barely any western sounds, except maybe medieval early music; pagan, unspoiled and ancient as a hundreds-of-years-old tree. Truly weird shit and I loved it.

Somewhat incredibly, it's taken 50 years for TEB to receive any due attention. Luca Ferrari, the guy behind the Mike Taylor book, runs a website devoted to them and produced their first biography, *Necromancers of the Drifting West*. Sweeney has departed this world, removing any chance of a reunion. Former Taylor band-mate TEB co-founder Dave Tomlin's fabulous memoir *Tales from The Embassy* (about the years the London Free School pioneer and pals squatted in the Cambodian Embassy) gives a vivid account of the group's formative antics, as outlined by Sweeney in *Gandalf's Garden* when he recalls, 'Dave Tomlin was the first guy I had ever met who used his music to influence people, to turn them on, or freak them out…I had never seen music used like that before.' While improvising at the Free School, Sweeney and Tomlin were joined by floating figures such as trombonist Dick Dadem and bassist Roger Bunn. Always underpinned by Sweeney's unrelenting hand drum pulses and heavily influenced by Ayler and Coleman-style free jazz, they played guerrilla sets on bandstands at Kensington Gardens or Hyde Park until police pulled them off. Every week from late '66, they took the stage at the UFO club around four in the morning to provide a soothing chill-out soundtrack when knackered psychedelic revellers were crashing. Sometimes Mike Taylor joined in on his hand-drum, although at the Festival Of Love event he lay in the middle of the dancefloor while dancers hot-footed around his prone form.

Calling themselves Giant Sun Trolley, they appeared at the 14 Hour Technicolour Dream and played UFO until July, when Tomlin took off on Mark Palmer's hippie caravan around the UK. Sweeney (who Tomlin describes as a former cat burglar) hooked up with a band called Hydrogen Jukebox, who split amidst *The News of The World*-stoked media furore after Dadem cut off his girlfriend's dress with scissors onstage at the Roundhouse, leaving Sweeney forming the Third Ear Band. In a *Zigzag* piece he wrote about TEB, Sweeney recalled the prototype TEB playing ' 'electric acid raga' – which was terribly pretentious, and in fact was the most diabolical thing you ever heard in your life', with a guitarist on acid 'until he eventually flipped…and ended up in a nut-house.' According to Sweeney, the Third Ear Band arose from the band having their electric gear stolen, leaving him playing hand drums with classically-schooled Paul Minns on oboe, violinist Richard Coff and cellist Mel Davis, exploring extended ragas laced with European folk and medieval melodies over unerring drum pulses. After appearing at All Saint's Hall, Powis Gardens in August '67 with Fleetwood Mac and Quintessence (and Middle Earth the following month with the Graham Bond Organisation), the band built a following through its residency at Jim Haynes' Arts Lab in Drury Lane, incubating in public through chance and instinct.

TEB played underground hot-spots through to '68. 'I called the music 'alchemical' because it was produced by repetition,' explained Glen. 'Each tune would change every time we played it. On the drums, the beat reduced itself to minimalism to the point of almost microtonality. It was listening to each beat as if it was a symphony.' TEB's biggest appearance yet was at the Alchemical Wedding at the Royal Albert Hall where John and Yoko introduced their 'bagism' concept. They first recorded with Ron Geesin, tracks released as the contract-swerving National Balkan Orchestra on one side of a Standard Music Library Disc.

After impressing Peter Jenner at All Saint's, TEB fell under the wing of Blackhill Enterprises and got signed to Harvest. January saw their first appearance on *Peel's Night Ride*, sending their ethereal magic out of my transistor radio with two future LP tracks plus 'The Grove' and 'Pierrot'. In March they recorded Alchemy. Peel played jews harp on 'Area 3' and Tomlin contributed 'Lark Rise', composed while riding the hippie caravan around the UK. Arriving in London, he visited the studio, donated the track, played violin then left for India. The following month, Third Ear Band will open for Blind Faith in front of 150,000 punters at Blackhill's Hyde Park free concert. They are high in my fantasy gig list, along with Graham Bond.

Crosstown Traffic

Sitting in a friend's bedroom, soaking up their heady *Mr Fantasy* debut album, Traffic seemed to have landed on a magic carpet from a faraway place, born from a rare alchemy that can spark up between likeminded musicians. Unlike Cream (although they were to temporarily break up in 1969), Traffic transcended their brilliant initial supernova to continue into the mid-70s, but for a few idyllic months in '67 embraced a lifestyle so unusual in Britain at that time a mysterious legend and huge press buzz erupted around them. No band had 'got it together in the country' before.

Such earthly concerns were furthest from their minds when 18-year-old Steve Winwood and fellow midlands music scene musicians Dave Mason, Chris Wood and Jim Capaldi moved to a 19th century Berkshire farm that April. Winwood was the teenage prodigy who'd brought his love of Ray Charles into the top ten with the Spencer Davis Group then abruptly left, explaining 'I feel like I've done all I can with this group.' Capaldi was the charismatic drumming dynamo who wrote lyrics, jazz group veteran Chris Wood the sweet magician who used his flute like a paintbrush, daubing the music with pastoral tones, or invoked the roar of King Curtis on tenor sax. Mason was a 19-year-old pop-fixated loner trying to nurture his songwriting against the bucolic frolics erupting in The Cottage. Away from the hyperactive swirl of swinging London, the four wanted to make music that could venture deeper by letting the spirits take over.

Half a century later on a rainy winter afternoon, I'm sitting in our own ancient cottage in Thaxted with the sitar-caressing figure I first saw singing 'Hole In My Shoe' on *Top Of The Pops* on the other end of the phone from his tour bus outside his Carson City, Nevada homestead. Soon the jaw-dropping anecdotes are flowing from a musician who was definitely in the right place at the right time, starting with Traffic hitting it off with the Stones and Hendrix at Olympic and playing on their landmark albums. Dave had once been the square peg in Traffic's round hole, literally seeing his muse and latent songwriting talent growing in public after he joined the band. He was about to bring his Traffic Jam show to the UK, ironically as the band's main surviving ambassador.

'Jim Capaldi and I grew up ten miles apart and had some bands together,' he remembers. 'Obviously we were fans of the Spencer Davis Group and got to meet Steve in Birmingham at a place called the Elbow Room. The four of us would just play music and it developed into Traffic. I was nineteen years old. It was a time for me to find out what I could do. I didn't start writing until Traffic.'

Winwood had been staying at a mate's Harrow Road basement flat where Wood, Capaldi and Mason were regular visitors, Traffic coming out of all-night discussions about music that fanned the flame ignited at Elbow Room jam sessions. They had a deal with Island Records, the UK's first hip independent record label that Chris Blackwell had started in '62 to release reggae music he loved from growing up in Jamaica. They knew they had to get out of London to do this. Blackwell's high society sorties had spawned his friendship with Sir William Pigott-Brown, a former champion jockey who had inherited £750,000 on his 21st birthday and owned 1800 acres of Berkshire Downs surrounding Sheepcot Farm cottage, which he agreed to rent for a nominal fiver a week. Bands like the Beatles had been linked with cities before but never a house. Located at the foot of the Berkshire Downs near Aston Tirrold, Sheepcot Farm had been built in the mid-19th century and was still only reachable by a rutted dirt track. Its mystique was further enhanced by surrounding ancient countryside including hill forts, chalk carvings and mysterious stones.

The Cottage was a two-storey stucco building hidden by trees and bushes, boasting low Tudor ceilings, oak-beam floors, thick plaster walls and big fireplace with real log fire. A large cement platform in front served as a stage on which the band could jam through the summer night, illuminated by the vivid light show projected onto the building. The main room was crammed with guitars, keyboards, drums, horns and Marshall speakers. The jams that produced songs, wreathed in marijuana smoke and sometimes driven by liquid LSD, could last for days.

'It was a great time,' recalled Dave. 'Obviously anyone who was making it would gravitate to London, whereas we went against the grain and placed ourselves in the middle of nowhere. It wasn't too much of a stretch for me as I grew up roaming around farmland as a kid. It was an innocent time; we were young. The thing about Traffic I always thought was so great was the different musical interests of each person. We had very diverse tastes musically and also a lot in common that we loved. I look back now and think of Traffic as one of the first real alternative bands.'

The band explored the energy that sparked between them like a molten ball ready to be harnessed, between round-the-clock excursions into the surrounding countryside in their World War Two army jeep. But a subliminal rift formed as Winwood, Capaldi and Wood worked together while Mason struggled to master songwriting alone in his room with his guitar. 'It was a situation where I didn't know what I could do, so I started writing. I didn't know if I could or couldn't so it was a personal exploration. Jim and Steve became a writing duo. All those Winwood-Capaldi songs are Jim's lyrics, from 'Mr Fantasy' to 'Paper Sun'.'

The latter became Traffic's first single after they started recording at Olympic, their second home until November at the same time as the Stones were recording *Their Satanic Majesties* and Hendrix sculpting *Axis:Bold As Love*. Olympic's hotshot engineers, including Eddie Kramer, Andy Johns, George Chkiantz, Chris Kimsey and Phill Brown, worked with Traffic too. Having been brought over from his native America to produce the Spencer Davis Group at the suggestion of his mentor Stanley Borden (the RKO studio legend who was Island's original backer), Jimmy Miller was a logical choice of producer.

The exotic 'Paper Sun' came cascading out of my little transistor radio tuned into Radio London in May as it rose to number four. 'I used the sitar on 'Paper Sun' and 'Hole In My Shoe' (plus 'Utterly Simple' on the first album),' says Mason. 'It was basically just my exploration of musical genres. I was always listening to all kinds of blues, jazz and pop. I was listening to Bulgarian music then got into Indian music. At the time I was just fooling around playing various different instruments, not very proficient on anything apart from guitar really. George Harrison gave me my first sitar. It was actually the first sitar that he had gotten and I wish I still had it!'

Traffic found their inspiration slowed to a stoned trickle by August, until friends from London visited The Cottage bearing the liquid LSD that inspired a creative breakthrough. After a day's cavorting around the countryside, the band worked up a sensational version of 'Feelin' Good' from Anthony Newley and Leslie Bricusse's 1964 musical *The Roar Of The Greasepaint…The Smell Of The Crowd* that they had heard on Nina Simone's *I Put A Spell On You* album. As early morning dawned and acid tapered down, Capaldi sat in front of the roaring fire sketching a figure in a spiked hat hanging on puppet strings. Under it he scrawled 'Dear Mr Fantasy, play us a tune, something to make us all happy.' When Wood found the discarded sketch he started playing a bass line that the others locked into after returning from an early hours drive. Traffic had found their album's title and centre-piece song. That evening they drove to Olympic and recorded it live.

'Jimmy was a great producer,' says Mason. 'He created a great atmosphere in the studio; very up, very positive. That was his biggest strength; he was a great inspiration and driving force.'

In July, Mason announced he had written his first proper song so the band recorded 'Hole In My Shoe'. Island MD David Betteridge knew it was a hit and insisted it become next single. Draped in Mason's sitar and inspired by a dream, the song set a psychedelic fantasy benchmark as it told the story of a girl waking up from a dream to discover a seagull stealing the ring from her hand. Her famous breathless spoken interlude about climbing on the back of a giant albatross came from Blackwell's six-year-old step daughter Francine Heimann. 'Hole In My Shoe' reached number two, resulting in the unforgettable sight of Mason sitting on a cushion cradling his sitar on *Top Of The Pops*.

Traffic made a low-level live debut in Oslo before appearing at the Saville Theatre in September before an audience including Jimi Hendrix, Brian Jones and the Hollies, Paul McCartney watching in the wings. Their third top tenner came two months later with 'Here We Go Round the Mulberry Bush', the theme for Clive Donner's movie adaptation of Hunter Davies' coming-of-age novel. *Mr Fantasy* followed in December as Traffic's motherlode incantation from the mysterious Cottage, endowed with strongly evocative songs, musical fireworks and epic title track that sent it to number 16. February '68's single was the haunted 'No Face No Name No Number', an overlooked work of stunning beauty. Winwood never sounded so desolate against Wood's mournful flute. This may sound strange but, for me, the song will always be linked to my sadness over losing Fluff, my pet rabbit. I've kept these furry friends since I was eight years old but Fluff was my first character rabbit, prone to nibbling my dad's prized greens. The melancholy mood of Winwood's lost lament somehow said it all.

By the time *Mr Fantasy* was released Mason had left Traffic for the first time. 'The success came so fast, I was so young I just couldn't handle it. There were major pieces in the *News Of The World* and Sunday papers about me just walking out but it wasn't to do with any bad blood or anything. It was just literally too much for me so I decided to back out of it. That's when I developed a relationship with Hendrix and produced *Music In A Doll's House* for Family.' A one-off 45 for Island thrust Dave's name solo for the first time, although 'Just For You's heady pop-psych and eastern-tinged 'Little Woman' both featured Traffic. Hanging and playing with Hendrix and the Stones at Olympic boosted his confidence. At that time, they'd often pop their heads around the door to see how their supposed 'rivals' were doing, sometimes chipping in. While Traffic were recording *Mr Fantasy*, Hendrix was embarking on *Electric Ladyland* and the Stones sharing Jimmy Miller to start *Beggars Banquet*.

'It was all happening at Olympic because that's where everybody was recording. Jimmy Miller ended up producing the Rolling Stones and the Stones, Hendrix and Traffic used the same engineer. They'd be around when we were coming in, or they were going out. There was a lot of cross pollination. I played on 'Street Fighting Man'; some of the drums and that weird little shehnai at the end.

'The Speakeasy and Bag O' Nails were these semi private clubs that artists could go to late at night without being bothered,' recalled

Dave. 'There'd be Hendrix, a couple of Traffic, McCartney and Lennon; it was very easy to get to know somebody back then. I'm very fortunate that I got to spend time at some significant recordings of Jimi's. During that period when I had left Traffic I was seriously talking to him about joining him on bass but his management put a stop to it. Hendrix played all the bass on his records anyway. Basically, he was a very quiet guy. I figured he was probably born with a guitar in his hand! In the studio he was all about work and getting things done. With Clapton being our British guitar hero, you mastered every blues lick known to man, but Hendrix was taking things further. He was so creative in the studio and there were so many different things that he was doing. I've been fortunate and played on a lot of very famous artists' stuff but Jimi has to stand out most.'

After Mason and Hendrix heard a pre-release recording of Dylan's *John Wesley Harding* at a friend's flat, the pair went into Olympic and Dave played acoustic guitar on Jimi's incendiary version of 'All Along The Watchtower' (and sang backing vocals on 'Crosstown Traffic').

Now a multi-instrumentalist trio, Traffic were touring the US. In New York, Chris Wood got a call from Hendrix, who suggested the band book into the Lincoln Square Motor Inn where he was staying. Hendrix was at the Record Plant recording *Electric Ladyland* so Wood supplied ethereal flute to '1983 (A Merman I Should Turn to Be)'. Two days later, Winwood and his Hammond joined Jimi, Mitch Mitchell and Jefferson Airplane's Jack Casady on the epic 'Voodoo Chile' (I've got the astounding 30-minute original of which the album version is just a snippet).

Traffic found they didn't have enough songs when they started recording their second album at the Record Plant. Mason turned up, having spent time on the west coast and ten days on a Greek island writing songs, including 'Feelin' Alright' and 'You Can All Join In'. He was back in the band. 'That came about because I went over to the studio and they only had five songs. 'I've got five songs here if you want 'em'. It was like, 'okay, you're back in'! So I did the second album. For me, things really started to gel writing-wise and musically on the second Traffic album. Once again, my songs were picked for the singles.'

Back home, The Cottage had become the proverbial house for everyone, relentlessly invaded by friends, hangers-on and musicians hoping some of its magic would rub off, including Pete Townshend,

Keith Moon, Jeff Beck, Tim Hardin, Christine Perfect, Steven Stills, Eric Burdon, Eric Clapton and Ginger Baker. The latter two became close to Winwood while African percussionists Remi Kabaka and Rebop Kwaku Baah clicked with the others during jam sessions.

Traffic's album was finished by May, Mason's five tracks including country-flavoured hoedown 'You Can All Join In' and 'Feelin' Alright', defining that time when psychedelic fantasy gave way to an earthier funky honk continued on the other three's 'Pearly Queen', 'No Time To Live' and '(Roamin' Thru The Gloamin' With) 40,000 Headmen'. *Traffic* became their second classic of the era, 'You Can All Join In' providing the title track on a compilation album that, at 14/6d (75p), was among the first budget sets; a gift for impoverished school-kids boasting hot new tracks from Jethro Tull, Spooky Tooth, Free, Fairport Convention and John Martyn.

July saw Traffic headline the second Hyde Park free concert over the Nice and Junior's Eyes. They toured Europe and America while *Traffic* was released in October, hitting number nine in the UK. Mason freaked out in New York and left again. Even The Cottage's benevolent energy seemed to have turned negative. Winwood walked out in Amsterdam, leaving Blackwell faced with telling the band.

'The problem was that the songs that were picked as singles were mostly my songs,' Dave told me. 'That's what created a problem for the other guys and, basically, that's why it broke apart.'

Dave reveals he nearly formed a band with Ginger Baker when the drummer left Cream in late '68. 'We had a few rehearsals with myself, Ginger and Bobby Gass (later Bob Tench) on bass. We were going to form a group called Salt but my guitar chops were only adequate. I was like, 'No no no, this is another trio, it's gonna try and be another Cream and I ain't trying to be another Eric Clapton!' I decided to go (to America) and see what happened. Plus, the taxes in England were enormous.' Mason headed for California in '69 with only Gram Parsons, who he'd met at the *Beggars Banquet* sessions, in his address book. 'Gram was the only person I really knew musically over there. He was a good guy, just real nice and a pleasure to be around. I slept on his couch for two or three weeks and he introduced me to Delaney and Bonnie, who were an awesome live band.'

Winwood formed Blind Faith with Clapton, Ginger and Family bassist Ric Grech. Seeing his flagship band Traffic disintegrating (and Blind Faith recording their album with Jimmy Miller for Polydor),

Chris Blackwell 'leased out' Winwood from Island, summoned Mason back to the UK and suggested forming a band with Wood and Capaldi plus organist Mick Weaver, aka Wynder K. Frog, who'd recorded an album with Miller entitled *Sunshine Super Frog*. Within weeks, Mason, Capaldi, Wood And Frog were debuting at Mothers with a loose set featuring Mason's Traffic highlights, new songs including the lovely 'World in Changes' and 'Waiting On You', plus covers of Albert King's 'Born Under A Bad Sign' and traditional 'Long Black Veil'. The band recorded Peel sessions and tracks at Morgan Studios with Miller but, ultimately, without Winwood this was a jam band with a few good songs. It lasted 60 days.

That was what I thought when I witnessed MCWAF's most momentous gig, opening for Hendrix at the Albert Hall in February. Great to groove to but not much more. Dave can't remember being spotted in the pub around the corner with Jimi before the show but can reflect, 'That band didn't last long because, for a start, you can't replace Steve Winwood. I was like, 'This is cool' but it was trying to emulate what we'd been doing. You can't go in there and replace Steve; he's just too talented. It was like trying to replace Hendrix. I was like, 'Nah, it's not gonna work for me'.'

As MCWAF dissolved, Winwood started recording with Blind Faith, who would debut at Hyde Park followed by the seven week US jaunt that broke the band after one album. Even though Blind Faith had formed out of informal jamming between Winwood and Clapton, once Baker was in and front pages screamed 'Supergroup', Eric found himself paddling pretty much the same boat as in Cream, facing the same crowds craving what they knew instead of allowing the band to move on and do what they liked.

Without any band at all, Island released Traffic's *Last Exit*, consisting of singles including Mason's 'Just For You', both sides of the previous December's 45 - the mystic southern gumbo of 'Medicated Goo' and exotic baroque-soul vehicle 'Shanghai Noodle Factory'. Soul vamping instrumental 'Something's Got A Hold Of My Toe' was an out-take, obscure Cottage gem 'Withering Tree' had flipped 'Feelin' Alright'.

On the live side two, 'Feelin' Good' is the showtune that sprang to life during August '67's acid trip then became a set staple, the trio slithering through freewheeling solos and baroque riffs until

Winwood's Hammond takes it out on a Bach-like fugue. 'Blind Man' was a bluesy chug. At least it was better than Cream's *Goodbye*.

Traffic had driven off – for now.

Air Lift

There's a weird band on *How It Is* calling itself Thunderclap Newman. The drummer sings in a falsetto suggesting his stool is exacting something terrible on his tackle, but no mistaking his message; 'The revolution's here' and 'We have got to get it together.' The guitarist looks my age, which is reassuring, but the guy on the piano looks like my dad. Portly, bespectacled, balding and respectably dressed, this is Andy 'Thunderclap' Newman himself, plinking the keys and smiling benignly through a call-to-arms anthem called 'Something In The Air'. It isn't the last time this unlikely band appears on TV as, by July, the single is at number one, where it spends three weeks.

Thunderclap Newman was dreamed up by Pete Townshend as a vehicle for his former flat-mate and chauffeur-songwriter John 'Speedy' Keen, who wrote 'Armenia City in The Sky' on *The Who Sell Out* (as Speedy pointed out, that should have been 'I'm An Ear Sitting In The Sky'). Townshend recruited old art school jazz pianist mate Newman and 15-year-old Glaswegian guitarist Jimmy McCulloch, producing 'Something In The Air' as their first single. 'I wanted 'Something In The Air' to be like a quiet revolution song like a whisper, rather than a big shout,' Speedy told Pete Frame the following year. Flop follow-up 'Accidents' and LP *Hollywood Dream* consigned the band to one hit wonder status, but that hit almost defined that year.

Speedy stuck around Track, a cheery husk by the time I met him producing Johnny Thunders and the Heartbreakers and Motorhead's debuts in 1977. That year sometimes found me hanging out at Track's offices near Carnaby Street. There was Speedy and even Andy Newman, smiling like a genial piece of office furniture. By that time, McCulloch had left Macca's Wings; he died of a smack overdose two years later, aged 26. Speedy bowed out in 2002.

RECORDS

Tyrannosaurus Rex: *Unicorn* **(Regal Zonophone)**
During the school holidays, I'm going out with a nice but rather conniving girl called Elizabeth. She's best friends with Vivian, the one who dumped me. Liz lives with posh parents in a large house and we'd sit in the dining room playing records. I still only have two albums; Beefheart (too much for her) and the more acceptable *Donovan In Concert* as a souvenir of my RAH gig. One day I come round clutching the third Tyrannosaurs Rex LP and we hammer it, intently hearing Bolan and Took's bleat-and-bongos pitter-patter expanded by producer Tony Visconti with piano, organ, bass, even drums on mini-watercolours like 'Chariots of Silk', 'The Seal of Seasons', 'Cat Black (The Wizard's Hat)' and Spector-with-fairydust 'She Was Born To Be My Unicorn'. Peel reads a Bolan short story during 'Romany Soup'. Soon Liz dumps me too. I couldn't give a shit, there's too much great music going on for my young brain to cope with woman trouble. If I hear *Unicorn* now, I'm right back in that bland dining room - which is why it usually stays in its sleeve - but I know every note and goat-like twitter. Next Bolan will go electric and sack Took for drug over-indulgence or whatever. 'When we did the LP it was very obvious to me that it was going to be the last one I did with Steve - in fact we both knew that at the time,' Bolan told Frame the following year. 'We were living in Cornwall and Wales, and I was very close to the earth...It was a period of clarity and purity - and Unicorn was very much into my soul.'

Richie Havens: *Richard P. Havens, 1983* **(Verve)**
When Richie was making his third album follow-up to *Something Else Again* during apocalyptic '68 he was filled with Orwellian dread, 'as if the next year was going to be 1984.' He decides to call it 1983 and make it a double-disc monument for the times, mixing eloquently conscious statements on his country at war, with itself and Vietnam, along with the covers his rich soul unflinchingly claims as his own. It will be his breakthrough, critically and commercially, presaging future fusions of folk, rock and world music. Partly recorded at a July '68 Santa Monica concert, *1983* captured each facet of Havens' towering quiet strength and liberated stage magic, driven by his distinctive open-tuned guitar scrabble. Richie's originals included 'Indian Rope Man', 'For Haven's

Sake', 'What More Can I Say John?', 'Just Above My Hobby Horse's Head' and bleakly resonant civil rights narrative 'The Parable Of Ramon'. His supernatural interpretative powers coax new depth and resonance out of Dylan's 'I Pity The Poor Immigrant', Donovan's 'Wear Your Love Like Heaven', turn Leonard Cohen's 'Priests' into a sepulchral reverie and makes 'Strawberry Fields Forever' sound like it was written for the March on Washington. Richie never made bones about loving the Beatles, also covering 'With A Little Help From My Friends', 'She's Leaving Home' and 'Lady Madonna'. His humble dignity came from coming up in Bedford-Stuyvesant as a poet, painter and singer who visited the Village after some kids called him a beatnik, then created a reputation in the coffeehouses that saw him recording by '66. It's taken just three years for Richie to paint his masterpiece and be recognised as embodying everything this counterculture should. Richie's huge heart stopped beating in 2013, leaving *1983* a consummate document of the irrepressible, charismatic spirit that will soon be riveting half a million at Woodstock, where his ashes are scattered.

Pharoah Sanders: *Karma* (Impulse!)

When tenor sax colossus Farrell Sanders pitched up in New York from Little Rock, Arkansas he didn't know a soul, sleeping rough until Sun Ra took him in, insisted he use his grandmother's nickname of Pharoah and inducted him into the Arkestra. Pharoah played with Ra as part of the Jazz Composers Guild's Four Days In December event at New York's Judson Hall and recorded his self-titled debut album for ESP-Disk in September '64, his animated growls, howls and ricochets sounding too big for the band. After distinguishing himself on the monumental *Ascension*, he was asked to join John Coltrane's group, appearing on *Om and Meditations*. He carried on until Coltrane's death in July '67, already striking out on his own with '66's *Tauhid*, backed by Henry Grimes and guitarist Sonny Sharrock, dominated by the 16-minute 'Upper Egypt & Lower Egypt'. *Karma* unleashes Pharoah's mellifluous soaring melodies and searing skronk over dense African percussion and Leon Thomas's yodelling throat singing on 32 minutes of 'The Creator Has A Master Plan'; all riding on Richard Davis's insidious bass-line (Davis had recently made a monstrous showing on Van Morrison's *Astral Weeks*). December's *Jewels of Thought* boasts another epic in 'Sun In Aquarius' with its rumbling Lonnie Liston

Smith piano fusillade, percussive heaves and that memorable point where Pharoah enters full-bore around twenty minutes in.

Pharoah also appeared on Leon Thomas's solo debut *Spirits Known And Unknown* for Flying Dutchman. Bookended by the groundbreaking throat-singer's take on 'The Creator Has A Master Plan', it's a period classic, backed by the tenor titan's band. 'Malcolm's Gone' and 'Damn Nam (Ain't Goin' To Vietnam)' are searing comments on the assassinated figurehead and murdered multitudes, the latter pulling no punches as, over cocktail jazz, Leon implores, 'How can a man get a thrill, if he's got to drop some napalm and never see the guy he's gotta kill?' Jazz's transcendental new alien hailed from East St Louis, sang in Count Basie's band and was inspired to yodel after hearing Leadbelly, along with pygmies.

John Lennon & Yoko One: *Unfinished Music No. 2; Life With The Lions*
George Harrison: *Electronic Sound* (Both Zapple)

In Beatles-world, it's good fun watching them shoot themselves in the foot for diehard Fabs purists simply by indulging the artistic whims their success allows. As the band splinter and Apple goes wrong, John and Yoko continue flying their togetherness flag even higher since their March wedding, releasing *Unfinished Music No. 2: Life With The Lions* - one side Yoko screaming and John feeding back his guitar at Cambridge University (joined by experimental duo John Tchikai on sax and percussionist John Stevens), the other recorded on cassette when Yoko was suffering a miscarriage at London's Queen Charlotte's Hospital, with the pair reading their press cuttings. To make the going easier on 45, John hooks up with Macca for 'The Ballad of John and Yoko', howling about the relentless, often racist persecution the couple are getting for their marriage and artistic explorations. Like an aural bulletin, it made sure the couple continued living their life in public but made number one as a catchy toe-tapper. After recording 'Give Peace A Chance' as a 'We Shall Overcome'-style singalong during this month's Montreal bed-in, it'll be back to avant-love business with *Wedding Album*.

Also released on the short-lived Zapple imprint, George's *Electronic Sound* arrives like a statement of solidarity in the noise indulgence stakes. Basically, it's Harrison pissing about on his new toy, the Moog Synthesiser. Elektra engineer Bruce Botnick recalls spending an afternoon showing George the ropes on Sunset Sounds' new Moog around that time, although synth-boffin Bernie Krause has reason for being pissed off when his demonstration of the new gadget shows up on *Electronic Sound* during 'No Time Or Space'. 'Under The Mersey Wall' catches George producing synthesised flatulence at his Surrey home. Soon everybody will be doing this so fair play for a bold move.

The Meters: *The Meters* (Josie)

The creeping gumbo of New Orleans funk is minted on the first of eight albums released over the next few years by keyboardist Art Neville, guitarist Leo Nocentilli, bassist George Porter and drummer Ziggy Modeliste, aka The Meters. Whereas this same month sees Booker T. & The M.G.'s uncork *The Booker T. Set*'s collection of popular hits given the Stax studio treatment, Nite Cap house band the Meters are more concerned with what's going on at ground and groin level, leading with 'Cissy Strut', a massive jukebox hit that led the homophobic 'cissy' dance craze (compounded on the set by 'Sophisticated Cissy'). Fortunately, gay crowds love to revel in themselves and the track's a hit in Harlem's clubs. Elsewhere, the Meters unleash a skin-tight funk in which nothing seems like hard work; effortless grooves that swung with intimate syncopation. They will repeat the exercise in December with *Look-Ka Py Py*. By '76, the Stones will ask them to support on the flower stage tour (unfortunately muddied by appalling sound when I see them at Earls Court).

Joni Mitchell: *Clouds* (Reprise)

As Ben Fong-Torres points out in Joni's *Rolling Stone* cover feature, folk-based music had ditched message songs in favour of the personal and poetic, as pioneered by Leonard Cohen. *Clouds* shows Joni leading this new field and good at more than writing hits for other singers, as she had with Judy Collins and 'Both Sides Now' or Tom Rush with 'The Circle Game'. Now finding her feet, the singer from Alberta, Canada will be a force in her own right, shacked up with Graham Nash (himself releasing an album with his new supergroup that fails to find a home in my young brain; so clean and squeaky I find it impossible to connect with their canyon carol singing). Although ashamed to admit I have a bit of trouble getting past Joni's voice too (a tad Baezy), there are great songs afoot, including 'Tin Angel', 'Chelsea Morning', 'Songs To Aging Children Come' and 'Both Sides Now' (written after reading

Saul Bellow's '59 novel *Henderson the Rain King* on a plane, appreciating its reference to looking down at clouds out the window, realising she'd looked up at them as kid; like life and death). It's her lyrics that hit home, touching on the occult, Vietnam warmongering, going much deeper than the usual folk trill. The greatness to come was all there.

CHAPTER SIX

JUNE

FRIARS OPENING NIGHT; THE STONES SACK BRIAN; SPILLING BIG-EYED BEANS ON BEEFHEART; GETTING STRAIGHT WITH ALICE COOPER, THE G.T.O.S & JUDY HENSKE; NEW YORK DISCO RIOT; IBIZA FLOYD; THE IMMORTAL OTIS

June 2 1969 is the opening night of Friars Aylesbury. In many ways - some I don't know yet, others I'd never have dreamed of - my life starts cranking on to its future path here, as bands I've only heard on Peel become real live beings blasting from that little stage. And that's just the start as, on so many levels, the gate swings open to reveal a whole new world beyond my Aylesbury bedroom.

Among the first ten punters in the queue, I receive the membership card I designed making me member number 6 (same number as Patrick McGoohan in *The Prisoner* - yes!). The anonymous mid-50s-style hall is small, low-ceilinged and wide; an extension of the Ex-Servicemen's Club main bar next door where ex-military codgers huddle over pints telling their war stories. A couple of hundred punters could pack this place to the low rafters, and soon will.

Walking into the foyer marks the first time I clap eyes on a copy of *Zigzag* - on the United Frog merchandise table along with underground publications including *OZ*, *International Times* and *Gandalf's Garden* (all procured by Robin Pike on sorties to a London distributor). Then it's time to brave the hall. As my only previous gig experiences have been the Albert Hall and Wembley's Empire Pool, these are my first timid steps into a real club, that mythical wonderland I've only read about. First impressions are always the most lasting and I still get a mild euphoric shiver when I recall encountering my first psychedelic light show and being instantly transfixed by the technicolour globules eating each other on the walls courtesy of Optic Nerve, two guys with big afros manning projectors and oil wheels (They're christened the Gollies - those were different times!).

There's already music playing - the first time I've heard records pumped LOUD through a PA system. I can pinpoint that moment as being when my brain slotted irrevocably into its lifelong default position. The song is Creedence Clearwater Revival's 'Bad Moon Rising', John Fogerty's warning that you can protest and even get things changed all you like but nothing will stop nature and the elements when they feel like wreaking havoc. The line 'Hope you've got your thing together' sticks and I still smile every time I remember it. I would get my thing together and no schoolyard bullies, domestic restrictions or military-minded megalomaniac teacher was gonna stop that happening, even if it will involve braving my own elemental storms along the way (How those Victorian Nazis would've loved today's conservative haircuts!).

Behind the first double record decks I've ever clamped eyes on, a long-haired bespectacled hippie in Ken Market hoop-necked finery and velvet trousers is jiggling and smiling. He's Andy Dunkley, the London-based DJ who will become a much-loved fixture at the club in its first year, responsible for instilling my love of elusive shrink-wrapped imported LPs and the art of stoking a crowd for the main event with astute programming. One of the 'Big Three' hip DJs with Peel and Jeff Dexter, Dunkley is everything the club's about distilled into human form and seems impossibly cool. From that night, I want to do what he does: play records I love to get people going. To make a living out of it is beyond comprehension then, but how to spend the minimum amount of time doing something I didn't want to do was in the bag and sticks with me now. You create your own excitement and not once in my life have I ever been bored in my own time.

My two friends and I perch in the second of three rows of chairs facing the stage, itself only about eighteen inches high. Wide-eyed and curious, I watch roadies testing the gear before the first band take the stage. I'd already heard Mandrake Paddle Steamer on their recent Peel session, then when he played sole Polydor 45 'Strange Walking Man', which joins other proto-prog titles like 'The Ivory Castle of Solitaire Husk', 'Couger and Dark' and 'Janus Suite'. At this point, the sheer novelty of witnessing a band up close beats their workmanlike prog tropes.

Thankfully, Dunkley comes on again. Taking my heart in my mouth, I timidly approach his decks to the left of the stage and ask who's playing that ecstatic guitar riot going on. It's American jazz guitarist Larry Coryell and the tune's 'The Jam With Albert'. Andy shows me the thick cardboard import gatefold sleeve and smiles, knowing he's getting through to at least one audience member. As I will later find out, that can make a DJ's night.

A chair and two microphones are placed on the stage for tonight's headliner Mike Cooper, one of the many lone singer-guitarists then treading the circuit. In his specs and blond comb-over, he seems pleasant and humble as he adjusts the microphone and strums his National Steel guitar before playing blues tunes off his recent debut album *Oh Really?*, arcane nuggets such as 'Crow Jane' and 'Death Letter'. It's great watching this devoted master at work, especially when he reminds me of my beloved John Fahey on the extended raga-like improvisations that point to where Cooper heads on his next album, *Trout Steel*. Sometimes he sings, an attractive crack allowed to appear in his grainy voice. There's no shouting from either of the tools Cooper uses to create his music but it's enough to hold those in the front rows in rapt hush.

Later it turns out I caught Cooper during the transformation that will see him playing with British jazz warriors from Mike Gibbs' band and forming the Recedents with our own Lol Coxhill in '82. I learn he hails from Reading, stoking its folk scene with his club The Shades, where he opened for the likes of Bert Jansch, John Renbourn, Davey Graham and Al Stewart. Living with his family in Australia during the 50s broadened his world-view and love of exotica when the boat voyage stopped off in Asia, taking him on several musical paths, including his lifelong fascination with Hawaiian music and the Pacific islands. No doubt, sporting one of his famous collection of Hawaiian shirts, Cooper is still making his 'post post-modern exotica.'

I ride home on a bright new cloud but my euphoria has plunged back to earth by the following Monday's Pretty Things gig after school and parents decide Friars is a den of drug-crazed hippies and no place for this 14-year-old. Having tasted the magic, it's agony sitting out that summer knowing Free, Blossom Toes, Edgar Broughton (who sprays 'Out Demons Out' on the nearby council offices afterwards), King Crimson, Mighty Baby, Principal Edward's Magic Theatre, Quintessence, Van der Graaf Generator, even Peel himself are a short walk away. But I'm not giving up that easily.

Thinking about it now, this cruel twist can be seen as the crossroads where I was forced to pick from two distinctive life paths; one the route being thrust upon me that would have meant buckling down, getting O and A levels in subjects I'd never need that bored the pants off me (maths, physics, etc) and getting into sweaty sport rituals and dull school activities (I'd already tried cello lessons and the chess club). All this mundanity proved impossible to channel energy into when there was a new Captain Beefheart album to get to grips with and, most frighteningly, could only lead to the afore-mentioned pre-ordained horror of a life spent wasted in drudgery looking at the clock on the wall in a dead end job. I'd already had enough of willing the tickers of classroom clocks. Things were boiling to a head inside my restless teenage brain. By now, I hated games even more (and still have a major aversion to 'team' anything, the phrase 'work out' and anyone in comedy shorts shrieking 'bring it on', grunting 'let's do this' and, while we're at it, passing the sentence 'You smashed it'). Loud music, long hair, girls and gigs were winning every time, joined by a fervent desire not to end up (or look) like everybody else. Despite ending up in some less-than-pleasant situations, they'd be outweighed by countless, once-in-a-lifetime great ones. It would all be worth it. As Lou Reed so beautifully put it in 1975 when it was starting to mean something, 'My week beats your year.'

Stone Alone

When being imprisoned from going to Friars was igniting my nascent rebel spirit, like countless times over coming decades I fell back on the Stones, playing the few records I had while sifting through the files of cuttings and memorabilia I'd been building into the (still-ongoing) archive since '63. In December '68, *Beggars Banquet* had compounded what was stirring in their camp when they roared back after '67's troubles with 'Jumpin' Jack Flash', witnessing that NME Pollwinners Concert still ringing loudly in my psyche. The changes charging the band's resolve could have been embodied in Keith's black leather jacket standing out in a field of frilly paisley shirts. The Stones knew they had to reclaim ground lost to psychedelic whimsy with a killer album, so revisited the music at the root of their inception in a crossfire hurricane of attitude, sex and potent socially-loaded vignettes that consolidated the single's raw promise.

Beggars Banquet opened the door to the golden run that would establish the Stones as unchallenged greatest rock 'n' roll band in the world, rewriting their own rulebook and bringing the music into the new age. That transformation was caught by Jean-Luc Godard's camera as 'Sympathy For The Devil' swelled from folky strummer inspired by Marianne Faithfull's reading list into the epic incantation unveiled on David Frost's TV show one Saturday night. The Devil was now Jagger's name (until Altamont made that look rather silly, anyway). Meanwhile, Brian had made his last significant contribution to the band he formed after the exquisite 'No Expectations' started life when the group sat in a circle around a microphone and he sculpted its sweeping slide guitar solo.

By June '69, the Stones had pretty much moved into Olympic, still grafting with Jimmy Miller on the album that would become *Let It Bleed*. 'Jimmy Miller is a great producer,' said Nicky Hopkins, the ubiquitous session maestro whose piano was a key element in the band's evolving sound. 'He's got the ability to keep them there and keep them at it. I don't think anybody else could produce their records. He's going along with what they want to do. He doesn't have this ego that it's got to be how he wants wants it.'

We know the album's going to be called *Let It Bleed*; often assumed to be a play on the recently-recorded Beatles single 'Let It Be', even though that won't be released until the following year. Keith calls it 'just a coincidence', although Macca's tune had been kicking around for a few months. With the close friendship between the two bands, there's no way the Stones couldn't have known, although the song was embedded in the patent Stones creative process from its beginnings as 'If You Need Someone'.

Songs at work-in-progress stage, from sketchy jam to almost fully-formed, include 'Live With Me' (its lascivious vamp clinched by Bobby Keys's searing sax), 'Monkey Man' (mutated from Italian holiday creation 'Positano Grande' into a satanic junk-barb riposte), rollicking 'I'm Going Down', strutting 'Jiving Sister Fanny' and 'And I Was A Country Boy' (which would both have to wait until '75's *Metamorphosis* out-takes cobble-up to see the light of day). They laid down an acoustic try-out of a new one called 'All Down The Line' which, like sepulchral gospel ballad 'Get A Line On You' and swaggering romp 'Give Me A Drink' (the nascent 'Loving Cup'), will wait until *Exile On Main Street* two years later before considered sufficiently marinated. Interestingly (to this Stones geek anyway), a *Let It Bleed* acetate is cut featuring 'Midnight Rambler', 'Love In Vain', 'Let It Bleed' and 'Monkey Man' on side one and 'Gimme Shelter', 'You Got The Silver', 'Sister Morphine' and 'Loving Cup' on side two. Jagger told the following month's press conference the Stones were planning to release two albums, starting with the first in September. Must've been one of 'em.

On June 5, Jagger (who'd been busted for hash the previous month) went to the huge free concert in Hyde Park staged to introduce new 'supergroup' Blind Faith to the world. Much to my grumbling disappointment, I wasn't allowed to go but, by all accounts, the event itself dwarfed the band that started as Steve Winwood, Eric Clapton, Ginger Baker and Ric Grech getting together to play some rootsy anti-Cream music and ended with Eric cast back on a world stage he didn't want. Pete Frame's account in *Zigzag* mentioned flower power's 'florid kaftans' giving way to 'a reversion to the denim/gypsy/beat, generally drab apparel that preceded the flower era' and the 'mellow harmony' of the Third Ear Band starting proceedings. That was before the Edgar Broughton Band got fists pumping the air bellowing 'Out demons out', the magnificent Richie Havens 'inspired gentle amazement' with his giant charismatic passion and Donovan invited himself up for a surprise guest spot, two new songs falling short before 'Colours' tweaked the familiarity buds.

If the 150,00 present expect the heavens to shimmer when Blind Faith take the stage, instead they get a low-key set that will grace their only album later in the year, starting with Buddy Holly's obscure 'Well Alright' and including Winwood's wailing 'Can't Find My Way Home', Clapton's magisterial 'Presence Of The Lord', along with the Stones' 'Under My Thumb', before Ginger ignites his double bass drums on extended jam 'Do What You Like'. Of course, those craving the always-annoying 'something we know' mutter and maybe the whole thing's summed up by the *Evening Standard* describing the gig as Cream's farewell concert.

The event's magnitude spurs Jagger into agreeing that the Stones will headline the next one on July 5. With a US tour projected for later in the year, the sad conclusion comes that something has to be done about Brian, whose drug convictions prevent any hope of him getting a visa. His barbs and booze intake have rendered his contributions to the ongoing album minimal at best, so a gruelling tour would be out of the question anyway. The band know it, and Brian knows it. They just have to tell him.

Now we're back on that ancient over-saturated ground covered endlessly in whole books but, on June 8, Mick, Keith and Charlie drove to Cotchford Farm, the idyllic abode near Hartfield, Sussex where Brian moved the previous November. It had previously belonged to A.A. Milne, author of *Winnie The Pooh*, who erected a statue of his son Christopher Robin in the garden and installed a heated outdoor swimming pool. Keith described the three telling Brian what he knew was coming as 'a bit like going to a funeral, really.' Brian's inevitably damaged pride kept him talking about plans he had for life beyond the Stones - recording with Alexis Korner and John Mayall, even a supergroup with Hendrix and Lennon, although he had already been to Morocco recording Jajouka musicians. After the three Stones left to carry on the band he had formed, Brian sat alone and cried.

The following day, Stones publicist Les Perrin issued a statement, supposedly from Brian, declaring, 'I no longer see eye to eye with the others over the discs we are cutting. The Rolling Stones' music is not to my taste any more...I have a desire to play my own brand of music, rather than that of the others. We had a friendly meeting. I love those fellows.' Waiting in the wings since auditioning the previous month was twenty-year-old blues virtuoso Mick Taylor, who had been through the John Mayall finishing school after replacing Peter Green in the Bluesbreakers. Taylor's stinging fluid tone graced *Crusade*, *Bare Wires* and *Blues From Laurel Canyon* before the ever-restless Mayall deciding to go acoustic in early '69 brought his departure.

On Mayall's recommendation, Jagger invited Taylor to a Stones session, where he won them over by revamping 'Honky Tonk Women' into a grinding barroom hump, along with playing along to 'Gimme Shelter', 'Live With Me' and 'Give Me A Little Drink'. 'I just assumed I was the best guitarist available at the time,' said Taylor. He was probably right as first choices had been Eric Clapton - too busy - and Ronnie Wood, who never got the message after Ronnie Lane answered the phone at the Stones' Deptford rehearsal room where the nascent Faces were finding their mutual feet. Another angelic-looking blond, Taylor was quiet and studiously dexterous as he unleashed quicksilver runs and pin-sharp blues with that clear, mercurial complement to Keith's dirty grind, even if the 'ancient art of weaving' was put on hold. Keith had been playing all the guitars for years anyway after Brian

211

started exploring other instruments then became too fucked up. It was at this point Keith the Rhythm King emerged (It should be remembered the 'old-timer' was still only 25 at the time).

Taylor was introduced at a photo-call in Hyde Park on the thirteenth, when July's free concert was announced. 'He doesn't play like Brian, he's a blues player,' quoth Jagger, somewhat clashing with Jones's asserting he wanted to return to blues roots. Talking to *Melody Maker*'s Chris Welch, Jagger stressed how well Taylor was settling in and getting on with Keith; 'The new band isn't going to be like early Stones. The thing is to go on, on, doing something new.' And Brian? 'I can tell you very little - it's better you ask him yourself. I guess he just wanted to do something different and he has done for a long time.'

Fast and Bulbous

Happily assured the Stones are in action (with no idea of tragedy to come), I wait out my Friars ban through June then the summer holidays. Liz is a fairly dull distraction compared to the records requiring deep investigation as I crouch over my dad's drawing board channeling my gig-bereft frustrations into darker hues and tortured figures on my psychedelic posters. Suddenly, towering above everything comes Captain Beefheart's *Trout Mask Replica*, unveiled by an awe-struck Peel one Sunday afternoon. Even if he goes for more 'normal'-sounding tracks like 'Ella Guru' and 'Moonlight In Vermont', it knocks me for a loop. I particularly remember the effect the Captain wrapping his fearsome voice around the phrase 'jack rabbit' in unaccompanied field holler 'Orange Claw Hammer' on my bunny-fixated brain, and the immensity of 'the bubble popped big' on 'The Dust Blows Forward 'n' The Dust Blows Back', also a capella. *Trout Mask* is undoubtedly a work of mad genius, a monster that will devour normal music like Godzilla standing on his hind legs with a six foot boner playing tenor sax during a planetary collision between Venus and Saturn; how I hope Sun Ra will sound when his spaceship crash-lands in my back garden.

Bear in mind this was way before the album was routinely singled out as the furthest-out statement of the last century, a shape-shifting masterpiece shrouded in weird mythology that portrayed Beefheart as the deranged monster genius who imprisoned his band, subjecting them to cult-like pressures and abuse as they translated his commands into its alien barrage. But, for a few weeks, as Peel continued to play what he declared his favourite LP of all time then after I splashed out on the import, *Trout Mask* just seemed like it'd beamed in from a parallel universe or distant planet. Wandering around school, it was fun to walk up to random pupils, adopt a deep American growl and exclaim 'A squid eating dowel in a polyethylene bag is fast and bulbous, got me?' *Trout Mask* clinched my love of wild free jazz, the sax-charged intro of 'Hair Pie Bake 1' alone enough to spark Ayler or Coltrane investigations. Guitar-wise, 'Pachuco Cadaver' swung like an extra-terrestrial todger at a Martian barn-dance. Beefheart used his full-throated blues roar or babbling vocal incantations like an instrument and his words were beyond surreal, more like a new strain of the English language. Take 'Old Fart At Play' (whose title bequeathed a punk rocker catch-phrase): 'Pappy with the Khaki sweatband/Bowed goat potbellied barn-yard/The old fart was smart/The old gold cloth madonna/Dancin' t' the fiddle 'n' saw.' There were 28 like that; all shapes, sizes and dimensions.

Craving info, it's *Zigzag* that carries first hints of the coming colossus, starting with Frame's Zappa interview in which Frank talks about what's coming on the Straight label he's started with manager Herb Cohen (though Beefheart has already stressed no desire to be lumped in with the label's other 'freaks and animal crackers'). 'I think they're in for a very big surprise as to what Captain Beefheart is into and where he's at,' reveals Frank when Frame mentions the UK cult around the Captain. 'The new album that he's just made is a two record set and the roots of that record are in Delta Blues and avant-garde jazz - like Cecil Taylor, Thelonious Monk and John Coltrane and a lot of other things...It's perfectly blended into a new musical language. It's all him. And it bears no resemblance to anything anybody else is doing.'

My Beefheart fixation had started in '67 with Peel caning period piece debut *Safe As Milk* (named after radiation) on his Radio One show, breaking the bottle on the Captain's cult before it sailed into the turbulent, unpredictable waters navigated over the next 15 years. As I've said, my inner trainspotter wrote everything Peel played in an exercise book so I can report that, on his maiden *Top Gear* show, going out on the Sunday afternoon of October 1, the first Beefheart track spun on the BBC was the jaunty 'Yellow Brick Road', followed the next week by the eerie Theremin howl of 'Electricity'.

Along with a young Ry Cooder, the Magic Band featured 18-year-old drummer John 'Drumbo' French, thrown in at the deep end before spending the next 13 years going and coming as Beefheart's musical director, cosmic foil and often punch-bag. Talking to French in 2008 proved an eye-opening experience, revealing how beneath the Captain's lovable-eccentric persona propagated by myths and amazing records lay a talent so precociously volcanic and an ego so huge it often sent those under his control to the outer limits of physical and mental endurance.

As with many characters in this book that I later encountered, if you'd told me then that 30 years hence I'd be getting major insights into Beefheart's surreal story from a key member of the Magic Band I'd have fallen off my chair and learned the trombone (and sailed to the moon on a cloud of disbelief if you'd added the afternoon I will get to spend with the Captain himself). French experienced every aspect of the man who called himself Don Van Vliet after his dad's Dutch ancestry, including tours, triumphs and trauma. He's also the fellow who translated Vliet's random piano poundings and whistling into the album that became *Trout Mask Replica*, rehearsing the band for the Captain's approval at a Hollywood Hills prison house where food was a luxury - then never getting credited on the sleeve.

Before such revelations, this is a good place to see what spawned this being called Captain Beefheart. Born in Glendale, California, in 1941, Don Vliet was relocated to suburban Lancaster, on the edge of California's Mojave Desert, at an early age as his parents tried to discourage his prodigious artistic leanings. Attending Antelope Valley High School he befriended fellow pupil Zappa, discovering a mutual love of Chicago blues and doo-wop. Around '58, they were planning a band called the Soots and a film called *Captain Beefheart Meets The Grunt People*. When nothing came of either, Zappa formed the Mothers Of Invention while Don took the Captain Beefheart name and joined the original Magic Band already formed by guitarist Alex St Clair Snouffer with bassist Jerry Handley, guitarist Doug Moon and drummer Vic Mortensen (later replaced by Paul Blakeley). In spring '65, Captain Beefheart and His Magic Band signed with A&M Records, releasing two singles: a cover of Bo Diddley's 'Diddy Wah Diddy' and 'Moonchild' (which I was lucky to find for ten pence in the local Oxfam shop five years later). In early '66 the band cut demos for an album, working with local producer Gary Marker on grittier self-written R&B-

psych outings that failed to impress A&M boss Jerry Moss and they were dropped.

Peel became Beefheart's first and greatest champion after stumbling across a single in the reject bin while working at a San Bernadino radio station in April '66. Witnessing the band supporting Them at LA's Whiskey A-Go-Go, he said it was, 'like hearing Elvis for the first time. I reeled out into the Hollywood night knowing that nothing would ever be the same again.' John French replaced Blakeley in October '66. Growing up in Lancaster, he'd learned to read music before hearing Sandy Nelson turned him to drums. When his parents bought him a cheap kit it had no snare or cymbals, explaining his distinctive tom tom-hihat combinations. French had played with local bands the Intruders and Allusions alongside guitarists Jeff Cotton (future Antennae Jimmy Semens), the pair hitching up with bassist Mark Boston (Rockette Morton), and later Bill Harkleroad (Zoot Horn Rollo) in Blues In A Bottle (somewhat debagging Beefheart's claim he taught them all they knew).

French became Beefheart's musical rock, revolutionising rock drumming by playing his kit as lyrical equal rather than straight timekeeping. 'My first impression was that Don was very opinionated and made people feel uncomfortable because he forced his opinions on them,' he told me. 'However, he could also be quite charming. I asked him about his voice, and he told me that he'd been influenced by Howlin' Wolf. I noticed that Don and the entire band seemed to have a certain 'air', a similar subset of personality traits that seemed to stem from Don. The way people spoke, certain phrases that were used led me to believe that Don was a very strong influence on them all.'

Bob Krasnow, of Kama Sutra offshoot Buddah, loved the Magic Band and signed them. In spring '67, before recording their first album, Gary Marker brought in his former Rising Sons bandmate Ry Cooder. Recording took less than a month, Cooder fulfilling the musical foil role Vliet would always need and French would assume; in other words, someone who could arrange the deluge of ideas gushing out of his virulently-creative brain.

'We recorded *Safe As Milk* in the spring of 1967, so I had time to learn most of the stuff,' recalled French. 'However, Don wasn't good at utilising time, so many things were put off or completely overlooked. I tried to catch as much of it as I could, but was not an assertive person, so many questions were still in my mind. 'Abba Zaba's bass solo section was taught to me the night before we recorded it. The 'Sure 'Nuff' drum part was completely re-arranged, as was the entire piece, by Ry Cooder. He was very specific about what the drums should do and I had to practise alone to master the requested pattern. 'Electricity' had a completely different, much more boring beat before Don came up to me at the demo session and re-wrote it by 'singing' parts to me. Don encouraged me to step out and not be afraid to try anything new. He made me believe that I could do anything on which I set my sights.'

After a disastrous warmup for the Monterey Festival dissolved into knockabout farce, Cooder left between the album's recording and its release that September, replaced by French's old band-mate Jeff Cotton, whose spidery style suited the uncharted musical directions burgeoning by the time they entered T.T.G. studios in November '67 to work on a double album titled *It Comes To You In A Plain Brown Wrapper*. French recalls half the album planned as Magic Band songs, the other 'a kind of psychedelic blues-jam group' called the 25th Century Quaker. Various reasons were given for the project stalling, including Buddah balking at the strange new sound (although they released four lengthy excursions as *Mirror Man* in 1971, claiming they'd been recorded in '65!) The tracks display a stunning progression into stretched-out blues mantras, avant-freeform and psychedelic blues blowouts, the haunted sea-shanty ectoplasm of 'Korn Ring Finger' presaging *Trout Mask*'s mutant blues.

Peel's relentless campaigning resulted in *Safe As Milk* being released in the UK by Pye International in February '68, promoted by the Magic Band visiting the UK and recording a *Top Gear* session. The DJ acted as guide and driver as they played colleges and underground clubs like Middle Earth. 'I knew he was a great guy when I saw him break into tears while introducing us onstage,' says French. 'He wasn't afraid to be emotional.'

After the tour the group re-recorded *Brown Wrapper* songs and disillusioned Alex Snouffer left, eventually replaced by Bill Harkleroad after a second UK tour that year. While the band were away, an allegedly acid-fried Krasnow mixed *Strictly Personal*, splashing on studio effects like phasing, releasing it on his new Blue Thumb label that December. 'Can you believe some of the mixes those monsters pulled on me, like the alka seltzer fizz they put on *Strictly Personal*?', Beefheart told me in '77. But it was the first LP I bought after I got a record player and, coming to know every nuance from the gutbucket

'Ah Feel like Ahcid' to last resonating shock-wave of 'Kandykorn', will always have a special place in my cerebral pleasure library.

After the album bombed, Beefheart found himself without a label but conveniently Zappa was launching Straight and signed his old school mate (and nemesis). The new Magic Band, completed by Mark Boston replacing Handley, entered Sunset Sound to record with Zappa producing, laying down 'Veteran's Day Poppy' and 'Moonlight In Vermont'. After the pair's rivalry reignited, Vliet took control and shut the band in a house on Ensenada Drive, Woodland Hills to commence seven months rehearsing in grim, deprived conditions, often spiked with acid. Zappa planned 'field recordings' at the house, and links survived but *Trout Mask* ended up recorded at a Glendale gospel studio called Whitney. The band were so well-drilled they careered through the set in one take, done after four hours. Vliet recorded his vocals without headphones, going on leakage from the control room. The double album was complete in four days.

Trout Mask was released in the US with its famous fish-head cover (actually a carp's head stuffed with tissue that Vliet said 'really stank, man'). Incredibly, French isn't credited while the Mascara Snake replaces him on the inside jacket cover shot. Vliet declared his mission was 'trying to mash up the mind in many different directions', completely winning over Lester Bangs, who described it as 'the most outrageous and adventurous album of the year.' Released in the UK the following November, it made number 21.

The first the world heard about *Trout Mask*'s fraught conception was when *Zigzag* fielded a report from Barry Miles sitting down with the man himself in LA. This is where the album's mythology first emerges (through Beefheart's eyes and self-hype). Miles describes his host as 'a big man, a prickly presence, a warm humanity, a large smiling hedgehog, a friendly Dickensian uncle, eyes that sparkle and dart - quick as humming birds - seeing everything, missing no details at all. His grey top hat and overcoat a little incongruous in the warm Southern Californian night. A man just too creative, too human for the 20th century, so interested in people that he surprises them: ending each sentence with 'You understand?' and waiting for the affirmative before continuing. A person you know instinctively you can trust.'

Details about recording are revealed; band locked up for weeks, deprived of food or outside world contact, one wandering off into the desert wearing a dress and a helmet; album recorded in eight hours,

Beefheart taking up sax for the occasion, claiming to have taught the band (all seasoned musicians except for bass clarinetist cousin the Mascara Snake). Nearly 30 years later, French told me what went down in that stinking house in the hills (his account given full rein in his astonishing memoir *Through the Eyes Of Magic*, which I was honoured to be asked to write jacket notes for). No wonder the Magic Band's intricately-tooled chamber combustion sounded so wired, Beefheart's colossal persona rearing throughout like Poseidon keeping the clashing rocks at bay in *Jason And The Argonauts*.

'That experience was both fascinating and dreadful for me,' he begins. 'Don had hooked up with Frank Zappa after the *Strictly Personal* mess. They hadn't been on speaking terms, and I could see that Don was very competitive with Frank. Zappa used piano on which to compose, so Don decided he needed a piano also. Of course, he knew nothing about music, and little about reel to reel tape recorders. He expected me to record hours of his noodling about on the keys. I immediately saw this was going to be a disaster. Trying to explain anything technical to Don was nearly impossible, I finally told him the recorder was broken. He bought it. Shortly after this, I succeeded in transcribing on music manuscript paper something that he had played. He asked me later, 'Can this be played?' I stated, 'Yes,' and succeeded in convincing him by playing it back. So, each time Don would create, I sat next to him and transcribed. I soon had skeins of little one and two-bar musical phrases jotted down in a spiral-bound work-book, often with no title, so I started forcing Van Vliet to give me working titles so we would know when one creative session ended and another began. I then questioned Don on who plays what and he said, 'Oh, you know…', leaving this responsibility to me. Eventually, I bought a bunch of small notebooks like kids use in school and carefully rewrote the stuff in the order I had decided it should be in. Since deciding the order was up to me, I usually spent time alone at the piano and would just play through everything, writing numbers and letters for parts and names. This would then get taught in the order I had decided. I also started jotting down how many times each person would repeat each part.

'After a short while, it became apparent that this was going to be a monumental task and take months. Also, there were seldom any drum parts written, so what was I supposed to play? I began writing my own drum parts in the same style. Often, the guys were playing different time signatures, so I tried to capture the essence of what they were doing,

218

often combining two and three rhythms in the same beat. The work became a daily routine of me sitting for hours on a piano bench playing parts to the guys. They would come in for each section of the song. This took weeks but, once it was done, I was able to find anyone's part immediately. I don't think anyone except Bill actually read music, and he chose to learn by ear, but had a more logical manner of learning than the others, who would have to hear it played perfectly before trying it. I wasn't a trained keyboardist and had barely enough ability at first to play anything twice correctly. I learned soon enough.

'During this whole period of time, Van Vliet established a 'cult' atmosphere established upon his own paranoid-schizophrenic fears that 'behind the scenes' there were a series of imaginary plots and sub-plots being crafted to overthrow his dictatorship. Being older, bigger and louder, he managed to intimidate us into behaving in a manner which we all later regretted; the key word being 'betrayal'. We had all been friends, but now we were forced to undergo gruelling interrogation sessions, sometimes lasting for days with no sleep, in which our so-called 'problem' was investigated. The only one with a problem was Don himself. We all knew this subconsciously but were in denial, partially because of being intimidated, and partially because we wanted to finish what we started, which we did, but not without a lot of regret for our actions during these meetings.

'I would say that I would have liked to have had 'arrangement' credits, as it's a lie that Don 'arranged' most of this. In many ways, all Van Vliet's compositions are collaborations, to varying degrees according to the song. To the public he became a genius; the guy who took 'untrained' musicians and taught them all this music that he wrote in eight hours on piano. Of course, the man talked incessantly and was constantly dictating lyrics or prose. He also had great musical ideas, but needed help most of the time putting them into any kind of playable arrangement.'

Talk about bubbles popped BIG. For 40 years, I'd been in awe of *Trout Mask* and it turns out Beefheart only hummed it while John French played it, or rather made it playable for the confused, tortured musicians who, to their credit, brought it home so spectacularly. French was only 21; the real genius at work. As his later Magic Band-mate Gary Lucas (now a highly-regarded guitarist in his own right) told me, 'John French is one of the greatest drummers in the world. Beefheart's music would have sounded pretty lacklustre without his input.'

219

Although there's no disputing Beefheart's immense voice and charisma, or torrential grasp of surreally-juxtaposed words, his claims to have taught the band every note make him an expert con man too. I experienced it myself in '77 when I spent an afternoon with the Captain, never dreaming I was being charmed the way he'd played Miles, Ben Edmonds and countless others. I've got over that now and, if not the benign smiling hedgehog I went for before, prefer to remember Beefheart as a thoroughly nice man, a remarkable entity whose like we'll never see again (despite many wannabes still believing a bit of wackiness will get them half the way).

After *Trout Mask* came further milestones, including 1970's equally extreme *Lick My Decals Off, Baby* ('I don't consider *Decals* to be superior, just different, and more concentrated,' says French. 'I think it's better than *Trout Mask* in some ways, but I prefer the lyrics on *Trout Mask*'). January '72's *The Spotlight Kid* revisited a more accessible blues-based sound on the bass-heaving growl of 'I'm Gonna Booglarise You, Baby' and train-chugging 'Click Clack'. French remembers another nightmare lock-in for the band to create the album. 'After his picture was on the cover of *Rolling Stone*, he became an insufferable egotist, and band life slowly deteriorated into a worse condition than it had been during *Trout Mask*. I left shortly after recording.'

With original Mothers bassist Roy Estrada on board (renamed Orejon), the Magic Band toured the UK in early '72, including a memorable gig that March when Beefheart treated a packed Royal Albert Hall to the remarkable show I witnessed 13 rows from the front. After Peel's tearful introduction, a ballerina then belly dancer did short turns before Rockette Morton appeared, strutting through 'Hair Pie Bake 1' in garish suit and fedora before joined by Zoot Horn Rollo, Winged Eel Fingerling, Orejon and new drummer Ed Marimba (sporting monocle and a pair of panties on his head). Finally, the Captain strode on in voluminous black cloak emblazoned with the moon and puffing clouds to lead his oddball space-warriors through a career-straddling set leaning towards *The Spotlight Kid* but packed with incandescent peaks including 'Abba Zaba', 'Steal Softy Through The Snow' and Fingerling guitar showcase 'Alice In Blunderland', along with unaccompanied 'Black Snake Moan' and lengthy sax improvisation 'Spitball Scalps The Baby'.

Vliet had been considering an album of poetry and music called *Brown Star* which morphed into *Clear Spot*. Recorded at LA's Amigo studios in late '72, songs were created around harmonica lines rather than abstract piano pumpings; more of a group effort, even if Vliet still claimed credit and publishing. The sound was done powerful justice by Warners' producer Ted Templeman (Van Morrison, Doobie Brothers), embracing a previously-unheard sensitive side on soulful single 'Too Much Time' and 'Her Eyes Are A Blue Million Miles', which he attributed to making music for women, probably inspired by wife Jan. The set also included the mindblowing 'Big Eyes Beans From Venus'; maybe the ultimate Beefheart blow-out. *Clear Spot* (released the following January in clear plastic sleeve) should have been monstrous but didn't chart. The group toured the US and Europe through spring '73 with Alex St Clair back along with Ed Marimba, Harkleroad and Estrada. I caught this stellar lineup at Oxford Polytechnic and Friars in November '75. Here I plucked up courage to approach the man, sitting in a corner of the Civic Centre after the show, sketch-pad on his lap, chatting amiably and drawing constantly. He gave me the sketch of some birds he'd been doing during our conversation and remarked, with authority, 'I've seen you before. You were sitting near the front at the Albert Hall, wearing a yellow jacket.' I had indeed been sporting a fetching mustard yellow creation that night.

In September '77, I managed to land a Beefheart interview; he liked the magazine Frame had named after his song and its previous coverage so agreed to meet one late November afternoon at the swanky Montcalm Hotel, near Marble Arch. Accompanied by photographer Erica Echenberg, we waited in the foyer until then-manager Harry Duncan appeared and went to fetch the Captain. Shortly afterwards, this familiar-looking figure with walrus moustache stepped out of the lift in casual work-clothes, rust-coloured cashmere scarf and grey trilby hat, shuffled over, extended his hand and said, 'Hi, I'm Don.'

We settled in the tea room and, for the next few hours, were entertained by Captain Beefheart; funny, fascinating and charm itself as he lived up to his image in the way a true fan could only dream of. It was best to let him chart his own wayward course, answering questions but letting whatever idea entered his head pop out and be developed as observations, stories, jokes or theories. He loved showing off new possessions like his gloves or ever-present sketch-pad. At one point, he stopped mid-sentence and let out a ferociously-powerful blues-roar, which had a profound effect on the elderly couples and businessmen sipping tea in the hushed lounge. 'Look at that little bit of freedom!' he chuckled. He put the suddenly-unleashed noise down to pent-up joy since the new Magic Band slaughtered several thousand Parisians a couple of days earlier. He said he couldn't sleep for excitement at his 'fantastic' new band and wanted to communicate his pleasure on this one-day stop before flying back to the States. 'I'm real happy now. I mean REAL happy. I played Paris and the people were dancing and everything to this far out music. It's amazing, people dancing to avant gardy music, or whatever they call it now.'

When Erica asks if she can photograph him while he talks, he says, 'Oh, I should have told you, I'm just a piece of meat...I run six miles a night. Have done for a long time. Have to, in order to keep gravity away. Got to. It's been difficult to find a running place here, but I have a trampoline kind of thing which you can jog on, but it's a lot better for you because it doesn't jerk your brain or your back. It's dangerous to run on the ground or cement.' There's the expected concern about whales, griping about record companies ('They're releasing *Strictly Personal* and *Safe As Milk* again. I have never received a penny from any of my albums....free music! Just touring makes me money'), legal wrangling preventing release of recently-recorded *Bat Chain Puller*, even Virgin's name because 'It's against womankind, it's such a pretentious name.'

There's another Beefheart Moment when he abruptly stops in the middle of a sentence, points at Harry Duncan, who's been interrupting in concerned managerial fashion, and growls, 'I wish that guy would quit thinking about me over there! He's had too much to think. He's so focused on me it's incredible!' Harry looks uncomfortable as the intense Beefheart glare bores a hole through his skull. Then he turns to me: 'You're not in a hurry to hear these are you, cos of all those things that are coming through (points to his head), I'd hate to say something and have it cut up like before you get to say it (to Harry). You go ahead and say it because you're on my case, man.' Was this the Captain's legendary ESP or just the mean side that former band-mates mentioned in later years?

I asked if he still painted. 'All the time. I'm doing an exhibition (produces flyer). I knew you'd ask me that. I didn't know you'd ask me that but I brought it along in case you asked me that.'

Do you do a lot of exhibitions?

'Yeah, I exhibit myself all the time!' Then he's off again about the group. 'I'm happier now than I've ever been since I had this group. I

222

can go into way more dimensions than I ever could before. I want to make people happy, get smiles on the faces of the people in the audience, break up all of that catatonic state that you get in when you're supposed to listen to music! None of these people use poison while they're playing. Perfect. That is to say that they are imperfect, but they're perfect.'

He pulls out his sketch-pad, showing us Count Basie's autograph and drawings he explains are songs the group could play from but, 'I write it on tape.' He draws a message to *Zigzag* readers depicting a dancing native in front of a sinister alien-looking fellow clutching a tomahawk. In the back is a clock-face. 'You know what it's saying? Black people are being thrown out of England. That's Big Ben. Big Ben there too long, har har!'

We jokingly tell Beefheart that he's a punk and he's happily supportive of the movement currently sweeping the UK. 'It's very honest. Isn't it more honest than when the Beatles sang, 'I wanna hold your hand'? Who held their hand?' He adds that an interviewer the previous night introduced him to long-time Beefheart fan John Lydon over the phone but he'd never heard of him.

Vliet took us to his room where he played five tracks from *Bat Chain Puller*, pointing out guitar lines and explaining lyrics. I feel I've passed the test when I remark beautiful instrumental 'A Carrot Is As Close As A Rabbit Gets To A Diamond' reminds me of my furry pets at home.

Never mind what's emerged since, that little time spent with Captain Beefheart remains the kind of magical experience you don't forget. Before we left, he signed my *Trout Mask* LP (sitting over there right now) and a large poster for the Paris show (sadly stolen from my house, while the Big Ben sketch got squirted by the New Jersey fire department ten years later - long story). After our meeting, Beefheart continued making music for another five years before bowing out with full throttle swan-song *Ice Cream For Crow*.

'At that point he was burnt out on the business,' Gary Lucas told me. 'He was looking to save money so we were hoping to come in under budget. He wasn't focused or really inspired to write new stuff but there are some great songs, like the famous last track 'Skeleton Makes Good'. That came about after a Zappa meeting. He said, 'Don't worry,' takes a hit off a joint, which I didn't see him do too often, and started going, 'Okay, you play this' and started scatting. The whole thing came together in about half an hour and Boom! He put a poem on it, we recorded it and it was great. When he wanted to he could come up with the stuff.'

The title track's coruscating take on John Lee Hooker's 'Boogie Chillun' stomp was lead track on an EP, promoted by surreal video shot in the Mojave with hats whisking off and rolling tumbleweed. It was Beefheart's last record. 'There was talk of another album and some demos, little sketch type things with him jamming,' said Lucas. 'I have copious notes of those songs and titles like 'An Impetuous Dream Bubbled Up'. I got an hour of him just going berserk with great improvisation and funky images. When he was on there was nobody funnier. He was like the fountain head. I never met anybody who had such an liberated id. It just bubbled up out of him. The TV was on and they were talking about the race riots and black rage that swept America in the 60s. He went, 'Black rage! What a hip name for a perfume, Gary!' That was fun to be around. I never met anybody like that.'

Tired of music biz shenanigans, Vliet found he made more money for his paintings as he exhibited around the world before going down with MS saw him spending his last years as a quiet recluse in Northern California with wife Jan. Gary summed him up beautifully when he said, 'He was a sculptor and a scoutmaster, a bully, a visionary and an intimidator. He took the techniques of the artistic world to create a new way of writing and composing, without notating it down. Who would have thought to do music like sculpture? That's an amazing concept: found sounds out of nature, taking dog whistles, windshield wiper noise, rubbing shopping bags. He was quite brilliant that way. He had an expansive vision. He's one of the greats of all time, an American master, a genius up there with Charles Ives, Mark Twain, Walt Whitman or Allen Ginsberg. He really saw a new way of looking at the world. The main thing was the playing. The playing was ecstasy.'

When we spoke in 2008, Gary hadn't had any contact with Vliet since leaving the Magic Band and French hadn't spoken to him since he asked for his long-awaited credit on '89's CD reissue of *Trout Mask*. 'We had a pleasant conversation but I finally said 'I want my name on the CD.' Don started accusing me of 'deserting him.' I told him that I left whenever I 'sensed the presence of evil'; actually, I was fired most times. He became silent and did his usual thing, left me listening to a record of One-String Sam, probably while he talked it over with Jan. I had threatened to sue. Finally returning, he said, 'I'll do it.' '

Don Van Vliet passed away in December 2010, two years after I spoke to his former bandmates, leaving a colossal footprint nobody could ever stick a toe in. I love this quote from John French, the man without whose suffering the world would have been deprived of *Trout Mask Replica* as we know it. 'I've never received a penny in royalties from any Beefheart album but I am grateful for the recognition I have received for being associated with a man who I consider both a brilliant and deranged artist with such a special flair and charming public personae, all of which appealed to me somehow. Normal people are, after all, so BORING!'

Go Ask Alice

It's late '86 and I'm sitting on Elvis Presley's old bed in the King's suite in the Las Vegas Hilton, where Alice Cooper is staying tonight. 'That's his bed and there's the TV that Elvis used to shoot up,' grins Alice, pointing at a large wooden cabinet shell, obviously fitted with a new tube. His band, complete with muscle-bound poodle-jock axe-shredder, isn't playing the famous hotel lounge Elvis played over 800 times. That era hasn't dawned yet. Instead, he's doing his guillotine panto villain routine at a gym-like arena a short tour-bus ride away. But Alice revels in the history with a tangible sense of envy; nobody ever comes close to The King when it comes to unbridled adoration, extravagant glitz or superstar excesses.

Alice had recently released his *Constrictor* album and I was interviewing him for *Creem*, having recently relocated to New York. For the next three years, I'm a roving correspondent for the magazine I'd read devoutly as a teenager, although my '69 issues are courtesy of Frame when he had a clear-out. Of course, things were rarely that simple back then and my Alice assignment would end up in LA, experiencing situations straight out of one of his songs. The self-styled original Prince of Darkness himself had cleaned up. No crates of Budweiser or bottles of scotch, which effectively derailed his 70s career, now. He's come back from the dead as a clean heritage act, slipping new lumpen metal tunes among the enormous hits - the 'something we know' a new generation craved, along with watching Alice get his head chopped off.

Of course, over 30 years later Alice is the world's 'most beloved heavy metal entertainer', its Bruce Forsyth in spider makeup, always ready with a ghoulish quip and grin as the quintessential Mr Nice Ham. The danger had gone long before but, between his '69 debut album and '75's *Welcome to My Nightmare*, Alice flaunted a genuine hold as the extreme comic book Mr Nasty who rose to power with '71's *Love It To Death* and *Killer*.

In '69, his reedy innocence didn't even sound like Alice. As one of Zappa's other Straight label 'animal crackers' Beefheart didn't want to be lumped in with, *Pretties for You* sounds like a band trying different styles to find its true vocation, including proto-prog 'Fields Of Regret', west coast rock ('Apple Bush') and wigged-out psych ('Earwigs To Eternity'), while the whimsical 'Levity Ball' was influenced by hanging out with Syd-era Floyd when they were over touring. He got closest to the *Killer* sound with the gothic chords of 'Titanic Overture' and 'Reflected', the prototype for 'Elected'. Manager Shep Gordon later said that, when the band entered Whitney Studios to record, supposed producer Zappa left his brother in charge while he went out. On his return, Zappa declared the taped rehearsal would be the finished album.

By then, Alice Cooper (the band) had already been going a few years under various names. Hailing from Detroit then moving to Phoenix, Arizona, Vincent Furnier, guitarists Glen Buxton and Michael Bruce, bassist Dennis Dunaway and drummer Neal Smith were influenced by the Beatles, Stones and Yardbirds when they released a couple of local singles, relocating to LA and renaming themselves the Nazz around '67. With Todd Rundgren already fronting a band of the same name, and needing a gimmick, Alice Cooper was adopted (legend says after a Ouija board session) and the band became more like a cross-dressing Living Theatre-inspired Barbie doll assault, attacking society using props to shock. Alice caused uproar at '69's Toronto Rock 'n' Revival Festival for throwing a live chicken into a murderous crowd with feather-flying consequences. 'I never meant it to get ripped apart like that,' he told me. Alice Cooper might have looked like another bunch of Straight Records freaks but there was a monster in the making that started emerging when the band relocated to Detroit after second album *Easy Action*. '71's punk-predicting 'I'm Eighteen' single would be the breakthrough, the live lid walloped on the increasingly-outrageous stage show when Alice got executed in the electric chair.

Even if *Pretties For You* was a fairly innocuous debut that got most attention for the cross-dressing singer with a girl's name, Alice Cooper found he'd arrived at exactly the right time. Observing how dull and dowdy rock had got, he introduced old-fashioned showbiz to take the world's arenas with his outstretched claw.

Although I gave *Pretties For You* a cursory listen in the record shop, the GTOs commanded greater investigation. In '69, girl groups still meant my beloved Shangri-Las and, with the rampant misogyny still going on despite supposed counterculture equality, it was the Joni Mitchells and Laura Nyros showing that female artists could dwarf self-satisfied males when it came to soul-baring grip and recycled classic melodies. The GTOs did it the old-fashioned way, playing on their outrageous image and status as premiere groupies on the Sunset Strip scene to entice Zappa into producing and releasing the only album of their two year existence: *Permanent Damage*.

Of course, I was too young to grasp much of what they were on about but the impossibly exotic-sounding Misses Pamela (later uber-groupie author-stateswoman Pamela Des Barres), Mercy, Cynderella (briefly betrothed to John Cale before Kevin Ayers steamed in), Christine (Zappa's babysitter and inspiration for the Flying Burritos' 'Christine's Tune', who OD'd in '72), Zappa movie star Lucy (who died of AIDS in '91), Sandra (who died of cancer that same year) and Sparky. As a document of that place and time, the album is a lively period piece. 'The Captain's Fat Theresa Shoes' comments on Beefheart's footwear, Ry Cooder, Lowell George and assorted Mothers play on tracks and there are hilarious telephone skits, inevitably bringing in Chicago's Plaster Casters. Short-arsed Sunset Savile Rodney Bingenheimer pokes his nose in (and 'I'm In Love With The Ooo-Ooo Man' is about Steppenwolf's Spinal Tap-predicting Nick St. Nicholas).

Most musically rich of the Straight threesome was *Farewell Aldebaran* by former Lovin' Spoonful singer-guitarist Jerry Yester (who has recently owned up to child porn charges) and amazing Judy Henske. Now hailed an acid-folk pioneering classic, the album flew under the radar then but thankfully lands with a spangled plop on my turntable after Peel hammers the ethereally-strange 'Three Ravens', and allows me to bask in Judy's elemental vocal on 'St Nicholas Hall', ecstatically stirring 'Rapture' and Pearls Before Swine-like 'Lullaby'. Yester sounded a bit postured but Judy was a barely-containable force of nature. The backdrops from LA's finest, including Kaleidoscope's

227

David Lindley and Ry Cooder, are exquisite baroque tapestries, glistening frames for the hauntingly evocative songs. The title track, hotwired by Bernie Krause's synth, pioneers space-rock.

In 2016, I was excited and honoured to speak to Judy Henske for Ace's reissues of her first two Elektra albums, including the classic *High Flying Bird*. Now in her 80s and blind for a decade, she's still a beautifully-vibrant spirit, prone to unleashing a force ten laugh from the same place as that glass-shattering voice as she spoke on the phone from the Pasadena house where she's lived with piano-playing husband Craig Doerge for over forty years.

The Sunset Strip folk scene had never seen anything like Judy when she roared into town in 1960. Standing over six feet tall and stomping a hole in the stage when she got carried away, Judy could belt out whorehouse blues with the elemental power of Bessie Smith or soar through her beloved murder ballads; introduced using patter sharpened while warming up hard-bitten crowds waiting for Lenny Bruce. Her two 1963 Elektra albums highlight a major talent blossoming before and out of her time, predicting folk-rock the Byrds would mint two years later. At a time when female folk singers were usually quietly demure and forty years before Amy Winehouse, Judy let fly with folk-stoked torch ballads and didn't give a shit.

Her story starts in 1936 in Chippewa Falls, Winconsin. 'My mother was a very good piano player and a very good singer,' she starts. 'She sang songs from minstrel shows, including 'Mammy's Little Coal Black Rose' and 'Lilac Blooming In The Corner By The Gate'; this very sad, terrible song about how black children are abused by white children. I was in Wisconsin so what did I know? We never had an African American person in our town. She taught me all these songs that she knew and they must have come from listening to the radio; WCCO in Minneapolis. She sang and played all these sad songs to me and I thought they were so great.'

Judy discovered she had a voice in church and got paid for using it at weddings. Flunking out of college in her last semester, she took an office job at Ohio's Oberlin College. 'They said you can't keep on like this', so I didn't. I withdrew from college and followed my boyfriend, who was at Philadelphia's Oberlin College but quit and went to India. I never thought in a million years that I would be a singer. I thought my talent was in studio art so I went out there to become an artist. I learned how to play a banjo because my boyfriend just left me his banjo. I learned to play it and knew some songs and could actually support myself. People liked it so that's what I did.'

Judy discovered murder ballads, those odes from the past concerning outlaw legends, deadly deeds and crimes against humanity, after her 'brilliant scholar and poet' uncle, who scored a scholarship at Oxford University, gave her *The Oxford Book Of English Poetry*. 'There were all these murder ballads in there. They were so wonderful; they all had a plot but they weren't set to music. It was a little short story so you could sing it. Everyone at Oberlin College was super-hip in the days when nobody was hip. There were a lot of Quakers there, who were wonderful people. I knew a person there and his people were big Quakers so I went with him and joined this co-op that he knew of. It was a perfect place for me. I met other people like myself. Not necessarily artists but a lot of people who were sort of like Don Quixote. It was perfect for me to grow in that way. It made me even more sure of one thing; that I really didn't want money. I wanted something else. And it's all come true! I have enough money, but I've never been rich. I really do think that the love of money is the root of all evil. Did you see what happened in the US; did you see who our President is? What the hell is going on here?!'

In 1960, sporting a duck-hunting jacket, sandals and carrying her banjo, Judy travelled to San Diego and New York, then pitched up on the Strip. She knew Herb Cohen was the dynamo behind the folk scene since the mid-50s, owning the Unicorn and Cosmo Alley niteries. 'Of course, when I first came to LA I didn't have a job. All I had was my banjo. I said 'Where's Herb Cohen?' They said, 'He owns these two clubs, the Unicorn and Cosmo Alley.' The first night I got to Hollywood I sat down on this little wall outside the club with my banjo. A man came up to me and said, 'Can you play that?' I said, 'Sure.' He said, 'Okay, go up there and play something.' That was Herbie. I went and sang and played and he hired me immediately. That was it, bang! He became my manager that night. Then he said, 'I'm gonna have you sing at the Unicorn. I'll give you fifteen dollars a night.' So I made 90 dollars a week and that wasn't bad then.'

Cohen advised Judy to upgrade her repertoire; 'So I started singing those black whorehouse songs because I liked them a lot and I still do. They were story songs, something happened in 'em, and they weren't so yucky like so many of those icky songs were. They really said something, plus they suited my voice.' Herb felt Judy could hold her

229

own warming up for Lenny Bruce, who he managed and was one of the most controversial figures in America for tackling taboo subjects like racism, homophobia, drugs and society's injustices. Lenny attracted a tough, jazz-loving crowd who proved a perfect trial-by-fire for Judy, who perched on a piano with her banjo singing without amplification, honing an act that included long, comic introductions to songs she belted to rise above the crowd's din.

'It was really a tough audience. That was in the days when people smoked and drank; nobody does both any more. It was very, very hard. They were very sarcastic, hard bitten and hip and mean as anybody could ever be. I was singing a couple of murder ballads but hadn't yet shaped my act into the bloody fun it became. I'd try and make 'em be quiet before I'd start singing. I had to yell because nobody was listening. Sometimes I'd just stamp on the stage really loud and everybody would sort of quiet down and then they'd start talking again! That was fine because it was good for me.' The boards-demolishing became one of her trademarks. 'I like stuff with a beat very, very much and if I didn't have drums I used to pound my foot so it sounded like a drum. I did put my foot through the stage. I used to put my foot through all kinds of things! It's the beat, that's all.'

When Cohen sent Judy to play Oklahoma City, she was spotted by former Kingston Trio warbler Dave Guard, who recruited her for his somewhat square Whiskeyhill Singers. She stuck it for two years, appearing on their self-titled 1962 debut album. After the band split, Judy was back on Hollywood's folk circuit, recording a single with jazz singer-pianist Les McCann called 'That's Enough' under the name Judy Hart. By '62, Jac Holzman had set up Elektra's LA outpost, but wasn't excited about much until he saw Judy in action. 'I still have the piece of paper that said he would give me one thousand dollars to sign with Elektra Records, and the one thousand was crossed out and two thousand was written in. That was the most money I'd ever heard of at that time. So of course I signed with Elektra. I was off and running.'

Holzman wanted to capture Judy's live magic, splashing out on an orchestra arranged by veteran LA bandleader Onzy Mathews, recording in front of an invited audience at RCA Studios. From the opening big band swing arrangement of the traditional 'Low Down Alligator', *Judy Henske* sounded like no other album released in '63 as she ripped raw emotional entrails out of Bessie Smith's 'Empty Bed Blues', presaged folk-rock's jingle-jangle on traditional blues 'I Know You Rider' and hijacked underground railroad spiritual 'Wade In The Water', first published by the Fisk Singers in 1901, recorded by the Sunset Four Jubilee Singers in '25 before later versions including Odetta and Graham Bond, who made it his signature song. As the well-received album sold slowly, Judy hit the road with the Modern Folk Quartet's Jerry Yester, who she started writing songs with as he went on to produce Tim Buckley and joined the Spoonful.

As we heard earlier, Judy hit New York's Greenwich Village running, but found time to record '64's remarkable *High Flying Bird* in LA. Minus orchestra, she was captured in a small studio with a band including legendary drummer Earl Palmer, who'd played on Little Richard's seminal recordings. Judy started the album with an uncanny blueprint for folk-rock on her jazzy version of Billy Edd Wheeler's 'High Flying Bird', later covered by Steven Stills in the Au Go Go Singers, Jefferson Airplane and Richie Havens. The song's more startling when remembered this was before the Mamas And The Papas, Dylan going electric or San Francisco's folk-birthed psychedelic liftoff as Judy steams in with all guns blazing to convey the lost love, despair and morbid contemplation of the lyrics.

'I was doing something that sounded like it had an influence in rock 'n' roll. You know the thing that's really great about rock 'n' roll is it's so much more physical than sitting around listening to a folk ballad and just nodding your head. Later on you could dance to stuff; whoever thought I could do that? It's a terrific song. Neil Young had his secretary call once to say 'Neil would like some music for 'High Flying Bird'.' I said 'If Neil would like some music for 'High Flying Bird', Neil should ask me himself and not send a secretary.' He never sang it; I think he got too scared.'

Sadly, Judy's larger-than-life impact proved too big for polite times. After leaving Elektra, she recorded a 'horrible' album for Mercury, '66's *The Death Defying Judy Henske* with Jack Nitzsche (who named her 'Queen of the Beatniks') then *Farewell Aldebaran*. After that peak, she climbed even higher when she formed a band called Rosebud with Yester, their same-named album a widescreen, multi-hued masterpiece. After falling in love with the piano player Craig Doerge, she ditched creepy Yester and retired to bring up their daughter Kate. Still composing, Judy returned in 1999 with *Loose In The World* and 2004's *She Sang California*, before her blindness set in. 'It's a drag, I tell you,' she confides with good-humoured brutal honesty. 'When I first lost my

231

eye-sight I thought 'I do not want to live', because I read all the time. But then you get to like something else and continue on. It's a drag but I'm fine now. I've gone on to whatever level it is that you go on to.'

That encounter with Judy remains one of my favourite interviews in 45 years of doing the things. It was hard not to be touched by one of the last century's finest singers and shape-shifting pioneers reacting so rapturously to learning those first two albums were being reissued, or how highly *Farewell Aldebaran* was now regarded. 'It's so wonderful and I am totally thrilled about this whole thing,' she confided, before asking with uncharacteristic gentleness, 'Isn't it nice that this is happening?'

Come Together

Disco has been an obsession of mine from before it was called that. As I just said, witnessing Andy Dunkley seduce a crowd mapped one definite life path to follow and, by the following year, I'll be spinning records piped into the common room of Aylesbury College, where I'm sent after flunking out of Aylesbury Grammar School for all manner of reasons and have to re-sit my O levels. This spinning fixation will carry on at local punk gigs then goth epicentre The Bat Cave until the late 80s acid house revolution means I finally get to play records at clubs and gigs, then as tour DJ for Primal Scream and Prodigy, and make a living out of it. Not only that, I can make records too, but that's another story too.

The techniques, ethos and role of the DJ from background music provider to spiritual messenger taking their crowd on a journey through their selection, sequencing and seamless onslaught was under way in New York City in '69 but it took that year's Stonewall riot to liberate the throng and open the gates to modern clubbing. Disco, hiphop, house music, techno and everything came later; first audiences had to be allowed to dance together. I knew nothing about all this at the time but I'm sure glad Stonewall happened, otherwise things may have taken a very different turn.

Before Stonewall, New York's huge underground (by necessity) gay population suffered similar oppression from police as African Americans did in the south. By law, disco dancefloors had to comprise at least a third females, while two men dancing together could get

232

hauled in. Humiliating raids had been going on for years, cops busting in, cracking heads, trashing the bar and making their nominal arrest quota for the night, while having a bit of fun in the process (and a backhander to avoid future trouble). Like the black ghetto riots, a concerted reaction to gay oppression was a pressure cooker waiting to explode. The catalyst arrived the night after gay icon Judy Garland's late June funeral when cops carried out one of their routine raids on the Stonewall Inn on Christopher Street (a smallish place with a jukebox and two dancefloors), thinking they'd pull in the usual drag queens and have a bit of sport roughing them up. The bullies hadn't reckoned on a lesbian called Storme DeLaverie fighting back. Buoyed by recent civil rights actions, her fellow bar patrons, then gathering crowd outside, joined in, throwing bottles, rocks and lighting fires. Like the riots in Detroit, Newark, Watts and any number of US cities, it was like decades of bullying oppression and beatings, along with seething frustration at the law's ritual humiliation of anyone seeking a same sex relationship or liaison, erupted out of the bar and onto the street. While the Stonewall riot carried on for the next few days, its implications resonated through the city and around the US, sparking the formation of the Gay Liberation Front and Pride.

The discarding of cruel, arcane old laws ignited a celebratory atmosphere, tinged with emotions from euphoria to anger, that paved the way for disco as a movement started in the gay and African-American undergrounds. For the next few years anything went, impacting directly as a creative musical surge that would be felt in coming years, including inventing the 12-inch single to accommodate new musical styles exploding and the spirit of unity on dancefloors that carries on today. As it sprouted from seeds sown by the first modern DJs in '69, disco became the soundtrack of the new party hedonism, charged with drugs, decadence and rampant sex, although the best stuff retained the emotional element and sense of melancholy of its soul music origins.

While the UK had its rock DJs, since '68 Anthony Grasso had held court as the first modern disco turntablist at the Haven on Christopher Street and Sanctuary, a converted German church in Hell's Kitchen. Forget rock 'n' roll, even if many such records fuelled the fever that broke out on Grasso's berserk dancefloors, his background as a club go-go dancer told him what the crowds (stoked on uppers, downers and acid) craved. Flying the motto to 'keep 'em juiced', Grasso was first to segue and beat mix records, spinning the Stones, Santana (mixing together the album and Woodstock versions of 'Soul Sacrifice'), James Brown, Sly and the Family Stone, Memphis Stax soul, Norman Whitfield's psychedelic soul and always closing with the Doors' 'The End'. Boosted by the power of speakers acquired from Mountain, Grasso was first to overlay records, bringing the house down when he placed the orgasmic drop in Led Zep's 'Whole Lotta Love' over percussion break in CTA's 'I'm A Man' or Rare Earth's 'Get Ready'. Grasso's crowds often didn't escape until noon the next day.

As the notoriety of Grasso's packed nights spread, other venues gave DJs such as Michael Cappello and Steve Acquisto the chance to unleash vinyl onslaughts (and special mention must be made of Pete DJ Jones, whose mixing and breakdowns on J.B. and Fatback tunes inspired Kool Herc, Grandmaster Flash and Afrika Bambaataa, the architects of hiphop). The inestimably-influential prototype for the modern club appeared when David Mancuso started his invite-only, intimate Loft parties in 1970. Unfettered after Stonewall, Mancuso could continue propagating peace, love and unity he'd experienced on New York's psychedelic scene, including acid guru Timothy Leary's multi-media freak-out events at his League of Spiritual Discovery HQ in Greenwich Village. Six weeks into the new decade, on Valentine's Day, Mancuso held the first invite-only party at his lower Broadway loft, circumventing the law as the two dollar admission went towards his rent. He called the night Love Saves The Day, meticulously creating a special atmosphere with balloons, lights, mirror-balls and best custom-built sound system yet heard in a club, along with DIY theatrical effects like cutting the lights to unleash an industrial fan and howling wind effects. There was no sign, membership, bouncers or curfew, the crowd mainly black, Puerto Rican or gay, although anyone was welcome as long as they were cool and allowed Mancuso to take them on a spiritual journey, warming up with latin and jazz, easing into soul, gradually building to a euphoric peak. At the cusp of the new decade, with Stonewall still fresh in the memory, nothing had been experienced like this before and the door to modern clubbing was flung wide open. Loft regulars went on to start their own clubs, including Larry Levan's epoch-making hedonists' cauldron Paradise Garage.

What's this got to do with '69 or even this writer? Well, being regularly poleaxed by whatever hot new biscuit Peel had landed, witnessing Dunkley do it to a crowd and the black music styles I loved

234

(that morphed into disco), all congealed into a subliminal desire to move people with music, whether mentally, spiritually or physically. This desire was consolidated when a quest for illicit refreshments in lower Manhattan sometime in the early 80s led me to traverse a dark ramp illuminated by small white lights either side - straight into the Paradise Garage. I was DJing at the Batcave at the time so my skin-tight Marilyn strides and make-up got me whisked through the door. It's a bit hazy as I wasn't aware of the club's legend then. I just remember the inferno of ecstatic dancers cavorting joyously, making a lot of noise in the direction of their high priest, the awesome Larry Levan, who played The Clash's 'Rock The Casbah'. So life's arc continued pointing upwards. It would be a few years before I hit the world DJing circuit, but the seeds were long planted.

In other news...

All's not great in the Hendrix camp. On May 3, he'd been busted at Toronto airport after being searched in full view of queuing passengers, then arrested for 'allegedly possessing narcotics'; meaning the heroin supposedly found in his flight bag. 'I'm innocent,' protests Jimi, who's out on ten grand bail but faces ten years' prison for trafficking. At the following night's gig he debuts a new song that reveals 'I was in this room full of light and a thousand mirrors.'

Tired and bored of grandstanding through his hits, Jimi has been thrust into the biggest-grossing US tour of all time, laying the six-figure template for acts like the Stones. On June 29 after a show in Denver, Colorado, relations between Jimi and Noel Redding have so deteriorated the bassist flies back to concentrate on his ill-fated *Flat Mattress*.

RECORDS

Otis Redding: *Love Man* **(Atlantic)**
Even though it's 52 years since Otis Redding and most of his band lost their lives in an icy Wisconsin lake, I still feel in mourning for the greatest soul singer the world will ever see. Nobody ever comes close to the unfettered elemental emotion, heart-breaking beauty of his ballads or mighty sob of a voice radiating from that huge heart. Otis still feels like a shape-shifting force of nature who's been with me through many tough times, including most recently. Even 'My Lovers Prayer'

showing up over the closing credits in *The Sopranos* stopped me in my tracks.

Much has been made of *Sgt. Pepper's* influencing Otis's mature new direction away from standard soul tropes, but he was always something else. Everything came from that amazing voice, bottomless soul and immense charisma. February '68's *The Dock Of The Bay* began the inevitable record company trawl through the tapes to make new albums, although it seemed patchy matching that lovely title hit with earlier tackle. The fruits of recordings he made with Steve Cropper in late '67 started with June '68's *The Immortal Otis Redding*, including the unbearably poignant 'I've Got Dreams To Remember', and other gorgeous ballads such as 'Thousand Miles Away'. *Love Man* featured more final recordings, including Otis co-compositions 'I'm A Changed Man', swaggering 'That's A Good Idea', 'Direct Me' and 'Got To Get Myself Together'. But it's always those ballads that elevate any Otis album from good to great and there are two heavenly confessionals here: 'I'll Let Nothing Separate Us', obviously another ode to wife Velma, Otis poignantly declaring NOTHING will ever get in the way of that special emotion he feels burning deep in his soul, and the heart-breaking 'Free Me'. Oh Otis.

Procol Harum: *A Salty Dog* (Regal Zonophone)

Just the waves and seagulls, Gary Brooker's haunted narrative, bosun's whistle and simmering drama of the strings are enough to conjure that day I bought home 'A Salty Dog' as a 45 and the gentle swoon that accompanied the first play. A beautifully-evocative maturing of the sound ignited by Procol's first hit, the song masterfully conjured images of the doomed galleon and skeleton crew in loincloths as Brooker's tale unfurled like a ghostly flag, its swelling climax still one of music's most heart-flooding crescendos. With organist Mathew Fisher gone, it was Procol's first to use an orchestra, subtly enhancing the emotion swelling through Brooker's brine-battered vocal. Back on land, the rest of the album straddles a gamut of weightiness, from robust progressive rock to soul ballads. 'The Devil Came From Kansas' plugs into a strain of proto-Americana, guitarist Robin Trower indulging in the bluesy shredding he'll shortly leave to pursue. Just to illustrate the circular undercurrent bubbling beneath this book, Brooker still leads a Procol, now with Pete Brown supplying lyrics.

Grateful Dead: *Aoxomoaxoa* (Warner Bros)
Try as I might, I couldn't get as hooked on the Grateful Dead as many others. Music had to hit me so hard it stuck and, like now, much did hit but didn't stick. I loved Rick Griffin's graphics and Jerry Garcia's liquid acid guitar flights on *Live/Dead* when that appeared later in the year, but there was no compulsion to rush out and investigate *Aoxomoxoa*, their third studio album said to be the pinnacle of their experimenting (helped by new 16-track technology). Garcia sings future live faves such as 'St Stephen', has a ball multi-tracking his wheezy serenades and 'Mountains of Madness' trailers acoustic roots explored on *Workingman's Dead*. It's only later in the album, when Garcia flies, that any transcendent moments glide in.

Kaleidoscope: *Incredible! Kaleidoscope* (Epic)
Yet *Kaleidoscope* struck an instant chord when I picked it up for 29 shillings in Ken Market. After psych classic *A Beacon From Mars*, and with the last track clocking in at over 11 minutes, I knew it had to be a winner and was proved happily right, even if it ran to only 29 minutes (Still, a shilling a minute isn't bad). Downhome rustic ambience and global flavours had permeated the band's San Fran ballroom sound, multi-instrumentalists David Lindley, Solomon Feldthouse and Chester Crill (joined by bassist Stuart Brotman and drummer Paul Lagos) draping songs like 'Killing Floor' and traditional 'Cuckoo' (now a raging anti-war harangue) with fiddles, mandolins and more esoteric instruments. Lindley's 'Banjo' is just that while the epic 'Seven Ate Suite' is an eastern/Greek-hued blow-out giving Solomon a chance to exercise his lungs rooftop wailing-style.

It's A Beautiful Day: *It's A Beautiful Day* (CBS)
Another corker splashed out on at the time, thanks to George Hunter's evocative design around Kent Hollister's painting based on Charles Courtney Curran's *Woman On Top Of A Mountain*, San Francisco mystique and ethereally seductive lead single 'White Bird'. I bought in big time, even if it now sounds rather twee. Apparently, 'White Bird' was inspired by founding duo David and Linda Laflamme being caged in a Seattle attic to rehearse by dodgy manager Mathew Katz. Deep Purple would nick 'Bombay Calling' for chest-beating squeaker 'Child In Time', their histrionic singer sounding like his testicles are being mangled in a bear-trap.

The Flock: *The Flock* (CBS)

After starting its pocket money-friendly The Rock Machine Turns You On campaign in '68, CBS continued releasing bargain compilations to enhance its pole role signing cutting edge contemporary American music. The cover of 1970's *Fill Your Head With Rock* featured electric violinist Jerry Goodman in curtain-haired flight while the compilation featured his band The Flock's version of the Kinks' 'Tired of Waiting'; unrepresentative of their self-titled debut album's nudging of the jazz-rock envelope further out than their Chicago label-mates Blood, Sweat and Tears and CTA. With enthusiastic liner notes by John Mayall, the album commenced with Goodman's keening 'Introduction' announcing the band's dense-textured jazz-rock charged with classical and avant jazz, climaxing with epic slow blues 'Truth'; all helmed by veteran jazz-classical producer John McClure. The Flock looked set to take off with a *Melody Maker* cover and successful appearance at the Pop Proms at the Albert Hall, but the following year's acid-inspired *Dinosaur Swamps* clipped their wings. Inevitably, all these directions were pulling the band apart when Goodman got poached for the Mahavishnu Orchestra, sealing their fate.

Junior's Eyes: *Battersea Power Station* (Regal Zonophone)

Fleetingly, quintessential second division live circuit stalwarts Junior's Eyes scored with a hefty Peel session before their single 'Mr Golden Trumpet Player' turned up in the local Oxfam shop (This was in the days before there were ten every high street; this place had serious shit at knock-down prices). Formed by Hull-hailing guitarist Mick Wayne in '68, the band were among those who played on Bowie's 'Space Oddity' and attendant album, bassist John Cambridge going on to join The Hype with Tony Visconti and introducing homeboy Mick Ronson. Somewhere in '69, Junior's Eyes found time to knock up their only album, a typical period melange of west coast guitar freak-ups, 20s pastiche, stoned humour, TV sport dullard commentator bottom-baring and solid rock, highlight that Peel session's heaving tour de force 'White Light'.

Johnny Cash: *Johnny Cash At San Quentin* (CBS)

Two things led me to Johnny Cash: his duet with Dylan on *Nashville Skyline* and this second prison-recorded album's breakthrough 45 'A Boy Named Sue' being hammered on local freak pub the Dark

Lantern's jukebox. Then came the Granada TV special created out of February's gig at the foreboding San Quentin where, like its Folsom-recorded predecessor, the man in black again won over an audience of lifers and hardened cons with his sympathetic outlaw stance, 'I Walk The Line' and specially-minted 'San Quentin' bringing the house down.

Pete Brown & His Battered Ornaments: *A Meal You Can Shake Hands With In The Dark* (Harvest)

As seen earlier, after years of jazz poetry, Pete Brown gave Cream lyrics then formed his Battered Ornaments, who release their one album on Harvest before, maybe incredibly, throwing their leader out. Their sound is untamed and raggedy dense, folk and jazz flavours creeping under Brown's florid words (including 'The Politician' with Jack Bruce). *Zigzag* describes it as 'a wild, wild record...sometimes sounding close to Cream', shot with 'knockabout gutsiness and musical surreality', cited 'much freer' than also-released *The Amazing Adventures of The Liverpool Scene*; Peel producing scouser poets Adrian Henri, Mike Evans and Mike Hart, graced with Andy Roberts' guitar glue, on titles like 'Tramcar To Frankenstein'.

Jeff Beck Group: *Beck-Ola* (EMI Columbia)

After the triumph of the previous year's *Truth*, relentless touring renders Beck's band's second LP short and patchy. The volatile guitarist's lineup juggling impacted on continuity, drummer Mickey Waller replaced by Tony Newman 'cause Beck wanted to go heavier, bassist Ronnie Wood getting sacked then recalled and ubiquitous pianist Nicky Hopkins bolstering a sound that's weighty enough when it gets going (shining on his 'Girl From Mill Valley' instrumental). The band combusts on two Elvis covers and their originals, particularly 'Spanish Boots' and 'Plynth (Water Down The Drain)' but *Beck-Ola* will be their last spluttering gasp. Of course, Rod Stewart is already planning a solo career and will land in the Faces with Woody.

White Noise: *An Electric Storm* (Island)

Although Peel played some of its shorter tracks, the only way to hear and fully appreciate the astonishing White Noise LP was by buying it (in my case after experiencing its infamous side two in the listening booth). With its groundbreaking electronic sounds and scary-sleazy female vocals, *An Electric Storm* initially hit like a UK answer to '68's

239

United States Of America LP, but eschewed socio-political comment in favour of brazen sex, ghostly hauntings and black magic rituals. Only later did we twig that Delia Derbyshire and Brian Hodgson were BBC Radiophonic Workshop technicians who'd created *Dr Who*'s startlingly futuristic theme and the voice of our beloved Daleks. Joined by US boffin David Vorhaus, at Island boss Chris Blackwell's behest, the pair took a year to construct the album at their Kaleidophon Studio in a Camden flat, working around the clock on primitive machines and laborious editing to painstakingly construct side one's complex, evocative pop blasts and the flip's pair of epic tapestries. 'Love Without Sound', 'My Game Of Loving' and 'Your Hidden Dreams' shimmered evocatively, draped or spiked with Annie Bird and Val Shaw's sexually-charged attitude and playful defiance. The intricately-conceived mischief of 'Here Come The Fleas' was a hoot, but it was 11 minute ghost story 'The Visitation' that shivered me to my teenage timbers, the sobbing spirit-girl lost in post-car crash limbo, represented by great swathes of electronic whooshes, still guaranteed to send delirious shivers. Nightmare horror-soundscape 'Black Mass: Electric Storm', knocked up in a day after Island demanded the album, ends the album with a Bosch-meets-Hammer-horror barrage that oddly presages Suicide's 'Frankie Teardrop' with its blood-curdling screams. Maybe oddly, we were convinced the resounding clang following one particularly agonised howl was the sound of a demon todger dropping off. Of all the albums in this book, White Noise's overlooked one-off miracle comes closest to evoking this time and all its beautiful, forbidden newness.

More

One of many golden memories of my too little time with Helen is lying on the same sun-baked Ibiza rocks at Punta Galera where Franco-Swiss filmmaker Barbet Shroeder shot *More*, '69's cautionary tale about the perils of heroin addiction. Little-seen before its DVD release, *More* was often dismissed as a 'second-rate hippy movie', when it was one of the first addiction statements way before heroin got stupidly romantic for a while thanks to lightweight chancers like Pete Doherty. 20 years before Ibiza's ascension to acid house party island, *More* beautifully captured the island's mysterious, breathtaking beauty before the underlying dark side crept in and took over with fatal consequences.

The soundtrack is Pink Floyd's first album after Syd's ejection. Shroeder, making his directorial debut after years producing French new wave movies, told the band he wanted to retain the film's dreamy atmosphere by presenting what the characters were listening to rather than traditional soundtrack; music on the radio, at a party or complementing the light over the sea. The Floyd's atmospheric compositions perfectly frame the island's unique golden light; maybe because they knew Ibiza and neighbouring Formentera themselves. Syd had been to the latter island with Wright and Waters in August '67. Hipgnosis photographer-designer Aubrey Powell first visited Formentera in '68 with Gilmour, returning with Barrett and eventually buying a house there. The island's strange allure infused the music Floyd envisioned when they entered Pye studios in March, some prototyped when the band toured a two-suite production (also including old songs) called The Man and The Journey.

'Cirrus Minor' starts the album with sound effects album birdsong before Rick Wright's Hammond-Farfisa coda that started life as 'The Massed Gadgets Of Hercules' on a '68 Peel session and will soon climax 'Sisyphus' on Umma Gumma. *More* is Wright's album more than anyone else's, pursuing his original jazz impulse to create innovative sounds in the way that distinguished the early Floyd. 'The Nile Song' is often numbered as the Floyd go metal but rescued from numbskull thrash by relentless upwards chord modulations and raging drama (revisited on 'Ibiza Bar'). The rest of the album is predominantly pastoral, including the gorgeous pair of 'Green Is The Colour' and 'Cymbaline', even experimental (the dubbed-out drums, tape effects and avant piano splashing 'Up The Kyber', and Wright extrapolating on 'Quicksilver').

Actually experiencing this magical place and seeing the film cast a different hue over the album I'd played to death in my teenage bedroom, my afore-mentioned life's arc approaching a minor peak when I spent time on Ibiza DJing at the colossal Manumission club in '98. It reached its absolute summit when I returned with Helen in 2014 while she worked on her definitive book about the island, *Shadows Across The Moon*. We never felt more in love as we watched a spectacular sunset on Punta Galera, a rare green halo surrounding the white sun before it vanished below the shimmering sky-line. Almost in tears, Helen told me this was special. I don't think I appreciated how much until writing about it now. Out of countless special moments, that was our most magical one.

ENDGAME/EPILOGUE

Around 50 years on from the action just described, I was faced with writing the most difficult words of my life to go on the cover of 'Windmill', the very special record that Pete Bingham of Sendelica (one of the few bands to carry the spirit of '69 in the modern world) had organised in tribute to Helen. These words just flowed. This is where life ended up taking me to the present day and it seems like a good way to end both volumes of this book. Thank you for listening.

On the night of Sunday June 3, 2018, I lost my beloved soul mate Helen Donlon after an illness she preferred not to know about. We had spent our last weekend in silence, apart from the sounds from annual Thaxted morris festival cavorting outside and her astonishingly-intuitive and much-loved dog Jack snoring on guard at the end of the bed.

Helen hadn't been well for some time, the little upstairs bedroom of our medieval cottage our loving cocoon where we watched her favourite DVDs, from David Lynch and Paul Thomas Anderson's *Boogie Nights* to lightweight 70s dramas. That Friday afternoon had taken a different turn from usual when she asked me to sit with her and just hold her hand. Not watch or listen to anything, or even talk. 'Please just stay here,' she asked. So I did, for the next 56 hours. We mainly sat in silence or she would talk a little, maybe recalling a brilliant memory that just flashed up. Sometimes I told her stories through a little cuddly rabbit, named Paddy McGoohan after one of her favourite actors; off the top of my head, flying by the seat of my own inner turmoil knowing something was going to change everything soon.

By the Sunday afternoon, Helen agreed we would have to call the medical attention she always denied (reinforced when the first paramedic arrived and immediately misdiagnosed her condition as 'non-emergency'). While we waited for the ambulance she knew had to come one day, I got her overnight bag and Helen herself ready for whatever lay ahead. 'I think I'll have a little sleep now,' she whispered as we waited. I went downstairs to meet the predictably-late medical team. Finally they arrived to take her, but when I went back upstairs she had gone; in her own way, on her own terms, just like everything else she'd done in her amazing life. Ironically, within minutes there were six different ambulances blocking the tiny street but it was too late now.

The last time I gazed on her lovely face, she was smiling, maybe having reached the peace she craved, definitely now out of that pain.

I'd already started planning some recording with Pete Bingham and Sendelica, loosely based on Tim Buckley's 'Driftin'. On hearing the unimaginable news, Pete went off and quietly transformed it into a poignant eulogy with this tragic new dimension to deal with, bringing in Sendelica bassist Glenda Pescado and sax titan Lee Relfe to enhance its gorgeous swirl. When Wonder, the marvellous American singer who coupled with me in Secret Knowledge 25 years earlier, heard the piece she called it 'Windmill', after the beautiful place where Helen was laid to rest one sunny day in late June I barely remember. 'The windmill looks so big and strong and beautiful,' she explains. 'In a silent way it watches over her, like you did for those 56 hours. And it never stops, always protecting.'

Wonder flew all the way from Cleveland to sing the song at the remote but perfect Mwnci Studios near Cardigan. Her heart-wrenching performance of words she wrote on the spot while facing the photo of Helen reproduced here (wearing her favourite purple velvet scarf) brought the room to tears.

It didn't stop there. My old friend Alex Paterson had already said he wanted to do a remix and, with Paul Conboy, his co-pilot in Orb spinoff Chocolate Hills, produced two time-stopping versions, using a recording of Helen doing the Breaking Convention speech on her beloved Ibiza that marked her last major appearance in public (How she worked and psyched herself up to achieve that, entrancing the crowd at the world's foremost psychedelic conference).

A rare heavenly synchronicity seems to have been working since Helen passed to produce this record. I know she would love the tribute that some friends she knew and some she never met have come up with. I thank them all deeply, and speak for her friends and family too.

When Helen smiled, she lit up the room. Now this beautiful record has arrived, it lights up the skies. As Nick Cave sang in 'Skeleton Tree', his own coda of personal grief, 'And it's alright now.'

ACKNOWLEDGEMENTS

Two figures who helped define and make my 1969 special were immediately among the most supportive and compassionate after Helen's death and on this book: Robin Pike, my former teacher who organised those formative coach trips to my first gigs and came up with the idea to start Friars Aylesbury, the local club where I saw Mott The Hoople and many more, and Pete Frame, founder of *Zigzag*, my main writing influence then mentor who changed my life when he gave me the mag in 1977 (although I have to apologise for phoning Pete and partner Steph during that short period after Helen passed when I lost it completely and seriously believed Run DMC had moved into our cottage). I was over the moon when Pete came up with his fitting Introduction.

Marianne Faithfull became a close friend and confidante as she worked on her late-period masterpiece *Negative Capability*, the astonishing record that ended up soundtracking the seismic events going on in my own life. When I started this book, I was documenting her album's creation for *MOJO*, while trying to look after Helen in top secret. I still had no idea how events would turn but, as Marianne's album blossomed into her masterpiece, Helen was fading upstairs. When she passed, Marianne was in touch every day with love and support. The daily phone calls continued for months and became my lifeline, even as she battled problems of her own she's now dealing with. Thank you Marianne, I love you in a very different way now.

I have to thank my parents for buying me a record player for Christmas '68 and putting up with my rampant rock 'n' roll impulses and teenage tantrums. Sadly, my dad was taken away in 1993 but my mum's still here; radiant at 93 and in love with Jack. My beautiful sister Julia and her family; my brother Adrian (who unfortunately had to share this bedroom all through my teenage years), his wife Lisa, their daughter Alice and son Tom. My son Daniel Lee, who got himself together while this book took shape thanks to my dear friend Wonder Schneider in Cleveland, Ohio (herself another recent tower of strength and one of the family). My cousins Anthony and Gerald, who lost his own partner a few years ago and gave me valuable advice.

I have to thank my extended family in The Clash. Nick Headon has been a constant source of support, humour and help, even through a recent health issue I've had to deal with, and it was great to meet him and Melissa recently. Thanks also to Robin Banks and Johnny Green for regular cheering up and horned animal impressions.

My thanks also go to Christina, Christie, Hilary, Andrew and the Donlon family, Andy Griffin for saving my life; Kate Thomas for helping me leave the cottage and her continuing support, my oldest friends Rick and Judy Pearce (We've started a monthly record listening event in Aylesbury called Vinyl On Wednesdays!), MC Dynamax (who rapped me through the night before Helen's funeral), Victor Bockris, Martin Rev, Pete Bingham, Glen Pescado and Sendelica (for Helen's 'Windmill' tribute and more), Alex Paterson for love and the beautiful 'Windmill' remix with Paul Conboy, Jay Burnett, Irvine Welsh, Rupert & Sally Williams, Alyson Weston, Karen and Tony Chmelik, Cecilia Miraboli (who gave Jack to Helen), Jenny Fabian, Carl Stickley, Cucho Penaloza, Colin Keinch, Dave Strong, Bernie Thomas, Helen at *Gifted*, Anne & Michael of Fishmarket Street, Sarah Lowe & Jim Sclavunos, Abbey & Joe, Morgan Fisher, Kif Redworth, Sue & David Stopps, Hayley O'Keeffe & Peter Finch, David Barraclough, Chris Charlesworth, Push and Neil at *Electronic Sound,* Jamie Atkins, Paul Lester & all at *Record Collector*, Ian Fortnam at *Classic Rock*, Jo Kendall at *Prog*, Eugene Butcher at *Vive le Rock*, Jenny Bulley at *MOJO*; Jon Mills at *Shindig!*, Andy Crispin and Tom Saunders at Silverback for their patience, Andy Morten for the great book cover, Teddie Dahlin at New Haven for making it happen and Sarah Healey for her kind editing.

Regarding credits, the memories are all mine, so are the quotes, unless stated in the text, including Keith Richards, Marianne Faithfull, Captain Beefheart, John 'Drumbo' French, Ian Hunter, Overend Watts, Mick Ralphs, Buffin, George Clinton, Bootsy Collins, Nico, Dave Mason, Izzy Young, Pete Brown, Alan Vega, Martin Rev, Irmin Schmidt, Simeon Coxe, Ed Sanders, Chip Monck, Rob Tyner, Tim Rose, Ray Manzarek, Robbie Krieger, Bruce Botnick, Bonnie Dobson, Judy Henske, Gary Lucas, Michael Horovitz, John Sinclair, Mark Andes, Bobby Gillespie, Michael Chapman, Pete Frame, Topper Headon, Johnny Green and Robin Pike. Thanks to Johnnie Johnstone for Tom Rapp's last interview.

For these last 50 years, from original mixed-up kid to grown-up 65-year-old, I've often turned to Ian Hunter in some way or other. He was life-affirming as ever in a recent interview with *The Guardian*; 'If you're lucky enough to have a passion – most people aren't – grab it. And that's what you do for the rest of your life. It might take a while and it might not be easy. But grab it and you'll be happy. Fuck the money. That'll come or it won't. But you'll be doing what you want to do and that's what life is supposed to be.'

Hit the nail on the head again there, Ian - for myself and for Helen, who lived that way to the end, as I do now. This book would not exist without her. RIP darling and thank you; we did it, baby.

See you in part two!

Kris Needs, Aylesbury, August 2019

SOURCES & BIBLIOGRAPHY

Outside my memories and interviews, background narrative was informed by my copies of *Zigzag* and *Rolling Stone*, original Detroit *Creem* broadsheets from 1969-70 that Pete Frame kindly gave me, along with *NME*, *Melody Maker*, *International Times*, *Jimpress* and *Gandalf's Garden*. Some of this stuff has appeared in features I've written for *Zigzag*, *Shindig!*, *Record Collector*, *Mojo*, *Classic Rock*, *Electronic Sound*, *Vive Le Rock* or the odd liner note.

Online it was down to Rock's Back Pages.com and the amazing Friars Aylesbury website.

The following books were consulted, quoted as stated or read for inspiration or memory jogging.

Bockris, Victor - Keith Richards: The Biography (Da Capo, 2003)

Bockris, Victor - Transformer: The Complete Lou Reed Story (Harper, 2014)

Bradley, Doug & Werner, Craig - We Gotta Get Out of This Place: The Soundtrack of the Vietnam War (University of Massachusetts Press, 2015)

Brewster, Bill & Broughton, Frank - Last Night A DJ Saved My Life: The History of the Disc Jockey (Headline, 1999)

Burns, Peter - Curtis Mayfield: People Never Give Up (MPG, 2003)

Chapman, Rob - Psychedelia and Other Colours (Faber & Faber, 2015)

Cosgrove, Stuart - Detroit 67: The Year That Changed Soul (Polygon, 2016)

Cosgrove, Stuart - Memphis 68: The Tragedy of Southern Soul (Polygon, 2017)

Cosgrove, Stuart - Harlem 69: The Future of Soul (Polygon, 2018)

Cross, Charles R. - Room Full of Mirrors: A Biography of Jimi Hendrix (Sceptre, 2005)

Davis, Miles & Troupe, Quincy - Miles: The Autobiography (Simon & Schuster, 1989)

Doggett, Peter - There's A Riot Going On: Revolutionaries, Rock Stars and the Rise and Fall of 60s Counterculture (Canongate, 2008)

Donlon, Helen - Shadows Across The Moon: Outlaws, Freaks, Shamans and the Making of Ibiza Clubland (Jawbone, 2017)

Fabian, Jenny & Byrne, Johnny - Groupie (New English Library, 1969)

Fahey, John - Charley Patton (Studio Vista, 1970)

Faithfull, Marianne w/ Dalton, David - Faithfull (Little Brown, 1994)

Ferrari, Luca - Out of Nowhere: The Uniquely Elusive Jazz of Mike Taylor (Gonzo, 2015)

Fletcher, Tony - All Hopped Up and Ready To Go (Omnibus Press, 2009)

Frame, Pete - The Road To Rock: A Zigzag Book of Interviews (Charisma, 1974)

Frame, Pete - The Restless Generation: How Rock Music Changed the Face of 1950s Britain (Rogan House, 2007)

Geldeart, Gary & Rodham, Steve - From The Benjamin Franklin Studios: A Complete Guide to the Available Recordings of Jimi Hendrix & Complete Bootleg Discography (Jimpress, 1998)

Geerken, Hartmut & Trent, Chris - Omniverse Sun Ra (Art Yard, 2015)

Goldstein, Richard - The Poetry of Rock (Bantam, 1969)

Guerrieri, Claudio - The John Fahey Handbook Vol 1 (Self-published, 2013)

Guralnik, Peter - Sweet Soul Music: Rhythm & Blues and the Southern Dream of Freedom (Penguin, 1986)

Havers, Richard - Rolling Stones On Air in the 60s (Virgin, 2017)

Heller, Michael J. - Loft Jazz: Improvising New York in the 1970s (University of California Press, 2017)

Houghton, Mick - Becoming Elektra: the True Story of Jac Holzman's Visionary Record Label (Jawbone, 2016)

James, Darius - That's Blaxploitation! Roots of the Baadasssss 'Tude (St. Martin's Press, 1995)

Kahn, Ashley - The House That Trane Built: The Story of Impulse Records (W.W. Norton, 2006)

Kramer, Wayne - The Hard Stuff: Dope, Crime, The MC5 & My Life of Impossibilities (Faber & Faber, 2018)

Lawrence, Tim - Love Saves The Day: A History of American Dance Music Culture, 1970-1979 (Duke University Press, 2003)

Lawrence, Tim - Hold On To Your Dreams: Arthur Russell and the Downtown Music Scene, 1973-1992 (Duke University Press, 2009)

Margotin, Philippe & Guesdon, Michel - The Rolling Stones: All The Songs (Black Dog & Leventhal, 2016)

Mellie, Roger - Roger's Profanisaurus: The Magna Farta (Dennis, 2007)

Liebler, M.L. - Heaven Was Detroit: From Jazz To Hiphop and Beyond (Wayne State University Press, 2016)

Needs, Kris - Dream Baby Dream: Suicide; A New York Story (Omnibus Press, 2015)

Needs, Kris - George Clinton & The Cosmic Odyssey of the P-Funk Empire (Omnibus Press, 2014)

Needs, Kris - Keith Richards: Before They Make Me Run (Plexus, 2004)

Richards, Keith - Life (Weidenfeld & Nicolson, 2010)

Riley, James - The Bad Trip: Dark Omens, New Worlds and the End of the Sixties (Icon, 2019)

Scotto, Robert - Moondog: The Viking of Sixth Avenue (Process, 2007)

Selvin, Joel - Altamont: The Rolling Stones, the Hell's Angels and the Inside Story of Rock's Darkest Day (HarperCollins, 2016)

Stubbs, David - Future Days: Krautrock and the Building of Modern Germany (Faber & Faber, 2014)

Sullivan, Denise - Keep On Pushing: Black Power Music From Blues to Hiphop (Lawrence Hill, 2011)

Szwed, John F. - Space is the Place: The Lives and Times of Sun Ra (Da Capo, 1998)

Thomas, Pat - Listen Whitey! The Sights and Sounds of Black Power 1965-1975 (Fantagraphics Books, 2012)

Trynka, Paul - Sympathy for the Devil: The Birth of the Rolling Stones and the Death of Brian Jones (Bantam Press, 2014)

Valkhoff, Ben - One Last Experience: The Jimi Hendrix Experience; Live At The Royal Albert Hall February 1969 (Vormgeving: Ben Valkhoff, 2018)

Van Peebles, Melvin - Sweet Sweetback's Baadasssss Song (Payback, 1996)

Vincent, Rickey - Party Music: The Inside Story of the Black Panthers' Band and How Black Power Transformed Soul Music (Lawrence Hill, 2013)

Weiss, Jason - Always In Trouble: An Oral History of ESP-Disk; The Most Outrageous Record label in America (Wesleyan University Press, 2012)

Werner, Craig - A Change is Gonna Come: Music, Race and the Soul of America (Canongate, 2002)

Werner, Craig - Higher Ground: Stevie Wonder, Curtis Mayfield, Aretha Franklin and the Rise and Fall of American Soul (Crown, 2004)

Wilmer, Valerie - As Serious As Your Life: The Story of the New Jazz (Pluto, 1977)

Young, Rob & Schmidt, Irmin - All Gates Open: The Story of Can (Faber & Faber, 2018)

Youngquist, Paul - A Pure Solar World: Sun Ra and the Birth of Afrofuturism (University of Texas Press, 2016)

CPSIA information can be obtained
at www.ICGtesting.com
Printed in the USA
LVHW021227071019
633402LV00002B/360/P